The
Elephant is
Running

PROCESS AND OPEN AND RELATIONAL
THEOLOGIES AND RELIGIOUS PLURALISM

The Elephant is Running

PROCESS AND OPEN AND RELATIONAL

THEOLOGIES AND RELIGIOUS PLURALISM

Bruce G. Epperly

First Edition: May 2022
Print ISBN 978-1-948609-63-0
Ebook ISBN 978-1-948609-64-7

Printed in the United States of America

Library of Congress Cataloguing-in-Publication Data

The Elephant is Running: Process and Open and Relational Theologies and Religious Pluralism / Bruce G. Epperly

With gratitude to teachers who taught
me to join heart and mind in scholarship:
Marie Fox, John Cobb, David Griffin,
Richard Keady, and Bernard Loomer.

CONTENTS

CHAPTER ONE
The Elephant is Running. 1

CHAPTER TWO
The Spirit of Process and Open
and Relational Theologies. 13

CHAPTER THREE
Is There an Essence to Christianity? 21

CHAPTER FOUR
Judaism. 41

CHAPTER FIVE
Zoroastrianism/Zarathushtrian Religion. . 57

CHAPTER SIX
Islam. 69

CHAPTER SEVEN
Bahai. 83

CHAPTER EIGHT
Hinduism 97

CHAPTER NINE
Buddhism 111

CHAPTER TEN
Jainism 125

CHAPTER ELEVEN
The Sikhs 135

CHAPTER TWELVE
Confucianism/Ruism 147

CHAPTER THIRTEEN
Daoism 161

CHAPTER FOURTEEN
Shinto 173

CHAPTER FIFTEEN
Earth-Based and Pagan Spirituality 181

CHAPTER SIXTEEN
Native and First American 193

CHAPTER SEVENTEEN
Yoruba and Its Spiritual Children. 207

CHAPTER EIGHTEEN
The New Age and
New Spiritual Movements. 221

CHAPTER NINETEEN
Spiritualities in the Making 237

CHAPTER ONE

The Elephant is Running

For over twenty-five hundred years, South Asians have shared a parable about the quest for spiritual truth. According to the story, a group of sight-impaired persons hear that a curious animal, one they have never encountered before, has been brought to town. None of them are aware of its shape and form. Though they cannot see this strange animal, rumored to be an elephant, they want to feel it. Led to the elephant, each begins to touch this mysterious beast and reports their impression of the kind of creature it is. The first person, who caresses the trunk, asserts, "It must be a snake." One of his companions, whose hand reached its ear, describes the beast as being like a like a fan. Another companion, who took measure of its leg, announces that the creature is a pillar, resembling a tree trunk. A fourth investigator, pushing against the elephant's side, exclaims, "It's a strong wall" while his neighbor, who felt its tail, determines that it is a rope. The sixth explorer ran his hands up and down the elephant's tusks, stating that the amazing creature is sturdy and smooth, and possibly a spear.

Each investigator imagines that the part of the elephant they touch is descriptive of the whole creature. Each of the sight-impaired persons is, to some extent, correct in their description, but none of them fully understands the reality and complexity of the creature that has captured their attention. Perhaps deep down, each of them knows that there is more to the elephant than they can sense tactilely.

Historically, the parable has been employed to describe the quest for truth along with the nature and limitations of religious experience and our descriptions of the Holy. The parable affirms the complexities of the spiritual adventure and advises spiritual pilgrims and theologians to be humble in expressing their faith. The elephant is always more than we can imagine. The Divine always defies complete definition. All perspectives are finite, and although they reflect something of the Divine, none of them are final. The wise seeker can never assume that they can experience the fullness of the Divine or that their neighbors are entirely wrong in their descriptions.

Today, we might update the parable to describe persons who are blindfolded rather than sight-impaired, not only to avoid any tincture of ableism but also more aptly to describe the fact that everyone's spiritual vision is limited by choice, experience, and culture. We are like the people described in Plato's cave, who behold the shadows on the cave's wall, and assume shadows to be the full truth until we encounter the brightness of the sun. The truths we have received from others, including the religions of our childhood, both inspire and limit our perception of the world. We have also chosen to accept, and witness to, certain truths, often unaware of their limitations, and have, at times, seen our faith tradition as the only true or the most direct path to salvation or human wholeness. We have mistaken the part for the whole and neglected to admit that the elephant, and the Divine Reality, might be more complex and multi-faceted than we have thus far experienced.[1]

The parable of the elephant and sight-impaired, or blindfolded, persons has at least one other problem, beyond privileging ableism in the quest for truth, that I suspect was pointed out early on by perceptive inquirers. A living elephant never stands still nor is it silent. A living elephant is always on the move, walking, waving its ears and tail, breathing, and opening and closing its eyes. A living elephant also communicates through short cries and low frequency "rumbling" that can be heard miles away. Moreover, if we are open to new data, our experience of the elephant is always changing and in process. We may start our quest for knowledge at the tail and end at the tusk. We may hold on for dear life on the elephant's trunk once it begins to run, but if we are to make the journey, we must find a way to climb up

---

1. I am appreciative of John Thatamanil's updating of the elephant imagery in *Circling the Elephant: A Comparative Theology of Religious Diversity* (New York: Fordham University Press, 2020). Both of us embraced the elephant imagery, independent of one another, as a way of responding to academic and lay theologies of religious pluralism.

on its back, risking life and limb if the elephant chooses to charge. Even with the security of the saddle, the elephant jostles us up and down and right and left. And when the elephant starts running, its amazing complexity emerges. If we interact with this elephant over time, the elephant itself will change. It has changing moods and learns new things and may communicate these to us. It adapts to changes in its environment. It delights in the birth of its babies and mourns the death of its mate. It may continue to grow in height and weight. The elephant may become more wizened as he or she ages. The elephant may grow old and no longer be able to carry us toward our destination. Eventually, like all creatures, it will die and be mourned at the elephant graveyard. The elephant is running! Living! Growing! Communicating! And sadly, dying, perhaps to become a new elephant or different creature in its next incarnation! A living elephant is always in process and open to new possibilities of manifestation and experience and so, I believe, is the Living Divinity and our spiritual traditions!

The contrast between the living, running elephant of faith and our limited, yet growing apprehension of the divine nature is an invitation to experiential and religious humility. It is also an invitation to holy adventure. Our journey with the Holy is never-ending. New vistas, perspectives, and experiences are always emerging for the intrepid and curious pilgrim. Openness to new ideas is the only appropriate spiritual response. Recognizing how much we don't know about the Divine and the universe around us is the beginning of wisdom as well as a catalyst to adventure and humility.

The parable of the elephant and sight-impaired, or blindfolded, persons insight-fully describes the global spiritual adventure, played out in the lives of persons, faith traditions, and cultures over the last several decades. Today the elephant is racing, and faith traditions are morphing, engaging in new adventures in an interactive, interdependent world. Only dead religions stand still, limiting truth to centuries old teachings. As the philosopher Alfred North Whitehead notes, the pure conservative, consulting only the past and living in denial of new possibilities, goes against the nature of a living and evolving universe. I would add that the pure conservative, embracing tradition to the exclusion of novelty, is also going against the spiritual and moral arc of the universe, inspired by God.

Looking back on my own spiritual journey, I recall certain definitive moments in which the microcosm of my personal journey paralleled the macrocosm of our cultural and religious journeys. As a pre-teen, I was an avid baseball player, a star pitcher and hitter, who dreamed of the major leagues. Yet like most children, and frankly, their parents in the 1950s, my religious and cultural experience was parochial, to say the least. One afternoon, after Little League practice, my friend Richard and I were walking home, and I invited him to go into the Baptist church to get a ride home with my pastor-father. Richard had a look of embarrassment on his face. "I don't think I can go in," he explained, "I think it's a sin for me to go into a Protestant church." At ten, neither of us knew much about sin, but Richard grew up being told it was wrong for a Roman Catholic to go into a Protestant church building! Conversely, I grew up with virtually no knowledge of Catholicism!

Since Vatican II, things have changed radically. Protestant and Catholic priests co-officiate at weddings and funerals, share common lectionary readings and commentaries, and engage in joint ecumenical worship services. As testimony to the growing partnership between Protestants and Roman Catholics, I spent nearly twenty years at Georgetown University as its Protestant University Chaplain as well as a professor of Theology, often worshipping with Catholics, Jews, Muslims, Buddhists, and Hindus in university-sponsored events.

Today, we hear about inter-spiritual or hybrid religious commitments reflecting persons' participation in the rituals and practices of more than one religious tradition. Although they are careful in sharing their spiritual practices with their congregants, many of my ministerial colleagues, both Protestant and Catholic, join Christian faith and worship with Hindu or Zen meditation, yoga, First American prayer circles, pagan and earth-based rituals, and Asian healing practices such as reiki, Tai Chi, and Qigong. More intrepid pastors, often pastoring more inclusive congregations, share quotes from other faith traditions in their sermons or adult education classes. Some even encourage yoga classes or Reiki healing touch groups at their churches. You will meet some of these inter-spiritual pilgrims, expanding and redefining their spirituality and religious traditions in reading this book.

Although I am deeply embedded in the way of Jesus, my spiritual journey has been profoundly inter-spiritual. I learned Transcendental Meditation as a first-year college student in 1970, and within a week of my TM initiation, I began attending a progressive Baptist church at the edge of the campus. I discovered that you could be a Hindu Christian, or a Christian existentially shaped by Buddhism and the great wisdom traditions, at Claremont Graduate School, where I studied with John

Cobb, David Griffin, and Masao Abe, and learned alongside my roommate theologian and spiritual leader Jay McDaniel, whom you will meet later in this book. In the mid-1980s, I learned Reiki healing touch, grounded in the thought of Japanese Buddhist teacher Mikao Usui and became a Reiki Master/Teacher a few years later.[2] My daily spiritual practices are deeply inter-spiritual, including Centering Prayer and Transcendental Meditation, Reiki healing touch, affirmations I learned from my evangelical mother and new age sources, and breath prayers from Christian and Buddhist sources. I have taught Reiki healing touch at hospitals and congregations, including South Congregational Church, United Church of Christ, on Cape Cod where I pastored for eight years. Upon retiring, I left the church two reiki tables in hopes that the congregation's Reiki ministry would continue beyond my leadership. Although I was raised in evangelical Christianity and still have a lot of Baptist in me, especially when I sing the old hymns and get excited while preaching, I would not be a Christian today without my college encounter with Hindu-based Transcendental Meditation.

At the touch of a screen, you have access to thousands of religious possibilities. Many of our friends have do-it-yourself spiritualities, what Diana Butler Bass describes as a *bricolage*, taking what they perceive to be most helpful from a variety of religious traditions, including some apparently contrasting perspectives. I have a friend who reads daily devotions from evangelical televangelist Joyce Meyer as well as meditations from Tibetan Buddhist Dalai Lama. She goes to a United Methodist church, is a regular participant in a women's drumming circle, and attends chair yoga classes. She sees no contradiction in her own creative synthesis of what the "doctrine police" might consider opposing and contradictory religious worlds. In the same spirit, one morning, I wrote a biblically based devotional for my congregation and, also, read a few passages from Jerry Jampolsky's *Love is Letting Go of Fear*, influenced by *A Course in Miracles*, an inspirational text prized by self-described new agers. To be honest, this type of spiritual integration is the rule rather than the exception in my daily life. These days I am also re-reading the *Tao Te Ching*, a Daoist text, and plan to read a poem by the Muslim mystic Rumi at an upcoming Christian worship service celebrating the Summer Solstice. My creative synthesis of practices from a variety of religious traditions is routine in my daily walk as a follower of Jesus.

---

2. For more on reiki healing touch see Bruce Epperly and Katherine Epperly, *Reiki Healing Touch and the Way of Jesus* (Kelowna, BC: Northstone Press, 2005) and Bruce Epperly, *The Energy of Love: Reiki and Christian Healing* (Gonzales, FL: Energion Publications, 2017

In describing the evolution of religious experience, Alfred North Whitehead once titled a text *Religion in the Making*. These days, it is more accurate to say, "religions in the making" as even the conservative religious movements are evolving, albeit often in reaction and opposition to religious and racial pluralism. Whitehead also noted that advanced organisms initiate novelty to match the novelties of their environments. Organisms grow when they recognize diversity, embrace the truths that are helpful and then create new theologies and practices.

While many people respond to pluralism either through denying the truths of other traditions or asserting that all religions are inherently the same or entirely culturally based, I take another path in this book. I believe that persons can affirm their home tradition and embrace creatively the contrasting insights of other faiths. In my case, I remain a committed Christian, but my Christianity involves a creative synthesis of the insights of Hinduism, Buddhism, First American and Celtic traditions, as well as the insights of New Spiritual movements. My faith is also influenced by cosmology, physics, medical research, and literature. In contrast to those who divide the world in terms of truth and falsehood, saved and unsaved, and orthodoxy and heresy, I believe that wherever truth is found, God is its source, whether in a science laboratory, writer's desk, Hindu ashram, Buddhist medita-tion hall, or First American sweat lodge. Persons of faith are called to embark on spiritual vision quests, using the lenses of their home faith to guide their journey while learning from the many religious panoramas they encounter. In the process, they will adjust to new realities as the doors of perception are cleansed and open to larger vistas.

A Theological Vision Quest

The itinerary of this book's vision quest is inspired by Jacob's exclamation, "God was in this place, and I did not know it" and the dream of "God is in this place and now I know it." My goal as a Christian theologian and spiritual seeker is to explore the contours of the great wisdom traditions in dialogue with the spiritual wisdom of Christianity, describing their heights and aspirations rather than their failures. The spirit of this text is more akin to mysticism and poetry than analysis and doctrine. I am a theologian and philosopher of religion, but I believe that reflection on concrete experience is essential to understanding our own and other peoples' faith. While it is helpful to read more analytic and exhaustive discussions of the world's wisdom traditions, my approach will be that of a pilgrim, a follower of a living faith encountering pilgrims from other living faiths, learning, sharing, and challenging both other faiths and my own. In my description of other traditions, I will focus on them at their best, and share what I perceive to be most definitive theologically and spiritually. Although I recognize the limitations of my descriptions of other wisdom traditions, I will relate my perceptions of the intersections of these traditions with the insights of progressive, open and relational, and process-relational forms of Christianity. I will explore the living and changing contours of each faith tradition, knowing that every religion is multi-faceted despite common affirmations and practices.

Religions, like the elephant, are alive and running, and can be described in many ways depending on the experience, insight, and lenses of the practitioners. Others, including practitioners of the faith traditions we explore, might articulate their spirituality and world view in different ways, and with different foci, than I have done. My own analyses are written with humility, recognizing the limitations of my perspective and the reality that no religious tradition can be encompassed in a few short affirmations.

I write as a Christian, influenced by mysticism, process and openness theologies, social gospel, Celtic spirituality, and the evangelical faith of my youth. My unique journey shapes both what I see and how I see it. Recognizing my limitations and the necessity of constant growth, I enter this dialogue with the "beginner's mind" of Buddhism and the "childlike faith" of Christianity, respectively, not knowing all the answers but growing in wisdom and stature, humbly embracing the truth wherever it emerges.

I also write as a pastor-theologian, who has been called upon by congregants and friends to share my wisdom regarding how they can best respond to persons of other faiths and the quest for truth. I have performed over 200 interfaith weddings, often co-officiating with a rabbi, and occasionally joining Christian, Hindu, and Buddhist wisdom in a ceremony. As I noted earlier, my interpretation of each tradition reflects my own sense of intersections where Christians and members of other wisdom traditions can meet in dialogue, either in congruence or contrast, recognizing that contrasting views can lead to new insights when shared with humility and grace. I recognize the multiplicity within other faith traditions just as I affirm the multiplicity of Christian faith perspectives.

In today's pluralistic age, Christians must endeavor to learn from their encounters with other religious traditions. Living religions grow in dialogue, embrace, and critique. I believe that when appropriate and welcomed, Christians can share their gifts humbly with other traditions, not to convert but to support and edify. Others can learn from us just as I have learned, and continue to learn, from my encounters with Buddhist, First American, Hindu, Jewish, and other spiritualities. Our sharing must be a path to initiating dialogue and growing together, not for the sake of evangelization or conversion. We can share our gifts only when we have earned the right to dialogue and when our gifts are welcomed by others. We can share our own spiritual feast without assuming that others will have the same culinary spirituality. I also believe that Christians can faithfully learn from other faiths without abandoning the centrality of Jesus in their spiritual and ethical lives.

I come to this text with a perspective that both enhances and limits my vision. Others might look through other lenses and see different landscapes. Process and open and relational theologies shape the geography of my theological and spiritual approach to religious truth and diversity. Process and open and relational theologies and Christian mysticism are open-ended in their recognition that God is more than we can imagine. Both see the presence of God as both universal and intimate, touching everyone but possessed by no one.[3]

In the spirit of dynamic and open-ended dialogue described earlier, each chapter will conclude with a reflection on what Christians can learn from other wisdom traditions, as well as ways Christianity might humbly augment the perspectives and practices of other faiths. I speak with recognition of the insights and limitations of the lenses through which I understand Christianity in its concreteness, and not from the abstract perspective of some imagined Christian orthodoxy!

I will also describe a contemporary version of a spiritual practice, emerging from my reflections on each tradition, that I believe can edify Christian, or

---

3. Process theology emerges from the philosophies of Alfred North Whitehead and Charles Hartshorne, focusing on issues such as divine and human creativity, interdependence, and companionship. God's work in the world is global and inspirational. God shapes but does not control in God's symbiotic relationship to the world. The future is open for God and for us. God knows everything (omniscience) as it occurs but not in advance. While process theology comes from the liberal tradition in Christianity, open and relational theology emerged from the evangelical tradition of Christianity, focusing on the nature of love as creating a world of free creatures, who can choose for or against God's vision. In both process and open and relational theology, the future is open and undetermined. God can change God's approach to change, depending on what goes on in the world. Open and relational theology, while closely related to process theology, leaves open the possibility that God can in rare moments act unilaterally and directly rather than persuasively. For more on process theology, see Bruce Epperly, *Process Theology: A Guide for the Perplexed* (London: T&T Clark, 2011). For more on open and relational theology, see Richard Rice, *The Future of Open Theism* (Downers Grove, IL: Inter Varsity Press, 2020) and Thomas Jay Oord, *Process and Relational Theology* (Grasmere, ID: Sacra Sage Press, 2021).

non-Christian, experience. These practices are a creative synthesis of other traditions' wisdom and progressive and open relational Christian experience.

The goal of these exercises, updated to respond to challenges and busyness of 21st century life, is to embrace a wide variety of spiritual practices with respect and honor. Religions are always in the making and appropriating wisdom from one another and the technologies and cultures with which they interact. The Transcendental Meditation I learned in 1970 was a creative transformation of certain types of Hindu meditation in response to Western culture just as the contemporary practice of Lectio Divina, taught in Benedictine monasteries, is a short form of hours long "cloister walks" of monastics. Growth occurs by embrace and transformation. While, in certain cases, the process of transformation can be seen as consumerist appropriation, it is also an affirmation of global wisdom as well as the reality that religious practices usually have several sources and that there is a common religious journey, revealed in the diversity that often divides us. The practices I describe are hybrid practices, emerging out of my own experience of other religious traditions and tailored to the twenty-first century and to emerging points of common ground among the religions. I share them with appreciation, and as a witness to how I have entered the spiritual worlds of my religious companions. No religion is complete, nor is any religion an island, isolated from its neighbors. The universality of revelation and the specific gifts of each tradition bid us to embrace others' practices and entertain their worldviews, even when they are different from our own. We can grow from the give and take of creative conversation and wisdom seeking. I have spiritually "road tested" each of the spiritual practices I provide in this text.

Throughout the text, I have dialogued with practitioners of the various spiritual traditions and those who synthesize their Christian faith with the wisdom of other spiritual traditions. The dialogue partners that I have chosen exemplify progressive and open-spirited seekers from each faith, knowing that fruitful conversation is about mutual learning and sharing, and the willingness to be changed in the encounter.

Now more than ever, we need the willingness to learn from each other in the quest for common ground. The survival of the planet is in the balance. The fate of our democracy and its pluralistic spirit is at stake. The healing of the world needs us to nurture expansive, humble, and loving spirits for the planetary journey ahead.

A Note on the Origins of this Text

This text emerged from two seminars, occurring almost a decade apart. In Fall 2012, I taught a seminar on "Process Theology and the World's Religions" to seminarians and graduate students at the Claremont School of Theology. In the Spring of 2021, I convened a seminar on "Christianity and the World's Religions," attended by several laypeople from Cape Cod and across the nation, including a pastor from Colorado, sponsored by South Congregational Church, United Church of Christ, Centerville, Massachusetts where I served as pastor. Inspired by the beaches of Cape Cod and my companions in the seminar, my thoughts ranged high and low, in wider and wider circles of wisdom. During heart of the COVID season, we met on Zoom rather than in person. This approach had its limitations, but also invited participation from persons across the country. The questions and comments from seminar participants have shaped and enriched this text.

I am deeply grateful to those who have inspired me to become a global Christian: my teachers Marie Fox, Richard Keady, and Shunso Terakawa at San Jose State University; John Cobb, David Griffin, Masao Abe, Bernard Loomer, John Hutchison, Jack Verheyden, and Aurobindo Basu, at Claremont Graduate School; pastors John Akers and George "Shorty" Collins who identified a spiritual seeker and future pastor-professor in a long-haired hippie kid; and my friend and graduate school companion Jay McDaniel. Each of these theological and spiritual companions revealed what I perceive to be the deepest truth of the religious journey, so essential in this time of pluralism: wherever truth and beauty are present, God is its source. I am also grateful to South Congregational Church, United Church of Christ, Centerville, Massachusetts, which during my eight-year pastorate supported my vocation as a pastor-teacher-writer. I thank Thomas Jay Oord and Alexa Oord for inviting me to publish this book with SacraSage and Carole Green-Weishaupt for her editorial acumen. I thank my teachers, colleagues, and students as we embark on a holy adventure with the living, breathing "elephant of the Spirit" as our companion. I honor my dear friend and colleague Rabbi Harold Saul White, who taught me the deeper meaning of Jewish spirituality and with whom I celebrated over 200 interfaith weddings. May his memory be a blessing.

I dedicate this text to my grandchildren James and Jack with the prayer that they may live in a world of religious and ethnic understanding, where the diversities of experience, be they religious, sexual, or cultural, add to the dynamic tapestry of their lives and those of their companions. The South African word Ubuntu inspires this endeavor, "I am because of you, you are because of me, we are because of one another."

CHAPTER TWO

The Spirit of Process and Open and Relational Theologies

In speaking of the dynamic interdependence of reality, philosopher Alfred North Whitehead, the parent of process-relational thought, asserted that the pure conservative goes against the nature of the universe. The Creative Wisdom that guides the universe is patient and yet evolutionary. The aim of the universe, according to Whitehead, is toward the production of beauty, and the production of beauty requires the evocation of new possibilities and greater complexities of experience. God is alive, moving through the universe and our lives, bringing forth novel possibilities in response to the ongoing evolution of the universe. The elephant is running, and its aim is beauty and wholeness for all creation!

Just as there may be no clear essence to Christianity or any other wisdom tradition, process and open and relational theologies are not themselves homogenous in nature. Like the sight-impaired or blindfolded persons trying to discern the nature of a moving elephant, process and open and relational theologians focus on different aspects of God's nature and human creativity.[4] Built into these theologies is the common affirmation that no one theological position is complete or final,

---

4. I will often abbreviate "open and relational theology" with "openness" or "open" theology throughout this book. At times, the term "process-relational" will be used to encompass both movements, despite the different nuances of the various theologians in these movements.

and that we must always seek guidance and illumination from the contrasting perspectives of our peers in process and openness theology and the wider world of theological and religious experience. Process and openness theologies are always in process. Process and openness theologians see the nature of God and the world through varied lenses and are willing to grow theologically and spiritually in relationship to science, other Christian viewpoints, and encounter with other wisdom traditions. The quest for truth and beauty evokes a variety of honest and inspiring responses.

As I noted earlier, the experiential lenses that shape my vision of theology involve a creative synthesis of perspectives: global spirituality, mysticism, healing and wholeness, prophetic politics, the teachings of Jesus, Celtic spirituality, my evangelical and Bible-oriented roots, and the progressive movements in Christianity, all of which are still spiritually important to me. My lenses also include race, gender, sexual identity, ethnicity, economic status, national origin, age, and my religious roots as a Christian. Rightly understood, our lenses and our social and spiritual locations do not limit but invite us to dialogue and companionship with persons who see the world through different experiential and theological lenses. Good theology is, like the living, breathing elephant, always on the move, evolving and growing, through its openness to the insights and experiences of others. As my theological mentor John Cobb asserts, Christ is the way that excludes no authentic spiritual way. Wherever we experience creative transformation, spiritual growth, healing, and justice-seeking, Christ is the inspirer and motivator. In a similar fashion, theologian Thomas Jay Oord reports a comment on open and relational theology by a layperson: "If God is present to everyone and reveals in an uncontrolling way, we should expect a variety of religions and diverse views of God."[5] God is always doing a new thing and the "most moved mover," to invoke the language of Charles Hartshorne and Clark Pinnock, challenges us like the Living Elephant to be on the move theologically, ethically, and spiritually.

As a pastor, professor, spiritual guide, and healing companion for over forty years, bringing together pulpit and classroom, and study and hospital room, my theological approach is profoundly experiential and practical, and this shapes my approach to religious and cultural pluralism. With Hebrew Bible scholar Terrence Fretheim, I believe the question "What kind of God do you believe in?" is as

---

5. Thomas Jay Oord, *Open and Relational Theology,* 142.

important as the query "Do you believe in God?" Our images of God shape our character and behavior. Our sense of God's relationship to the world and history opens or closes certain political, environmental, economic, and experiential doors. From my perspective, "orthodoxy" does not primarily refer to unchanging rules or doctrinal viewpoints, but lively relationships guided by our evolving theological understandings and ethical values. Authentic orthodoxy inspires us to "doxological" living. To live by "right praise," that is, our orientation of gratitude, wonder, amazement, glory, leads to "orthopraxis," inspiring right action or behavior, prophetic healing, or creative companionship in healing the world.

My goal as a process and openness theologian is to embody in my daily life and political involvements, the heartbeat of process and openness theology, letting its visions broadly and poetically shape my experience of the world and way of life. I am more interested in the "spirit" of process and openness theology than the scholastic "letter" of the process-relational and openness traditions. Accordingly, my enumeration of the spirit of process and openness theology is intended to be inspirational, transformational, dialogical, poetic, and spiritual. My descriptions are open-ended and subject to creative transformation as I encounter new insights from other faith traditions, science, cosmology, astrophysics, literature, politics, and economics, as well as other Christian theologians.

The spirit of process and openness theology involves a flexible and evolving group of affirmations that shape how we experience the world, ourselves, and God's presence in our lives.

- *The universe is a dynamic process of creative advance.* The elephant is running. Galaxies are evolving. Children are growing. New spiritualities are emerging. The scope of compassion and empathy is widening. While there are stops and starts in the physical and moral evolution of the universe and our lives, the process of change is constant. Still, through all the changes, process and openness theologians affirm both "Great is God's faithfulness" and "morning by morning new mercies I see." In a dynamic, relational, and open-ended universe, moved by our evolving history of joy and sorrow, God grows and learns along with us.

- *We are joined in an intricate fabric of relatedness.* The whole universe conspires to create each moment of experience. We are connected. We are all in the same storm, despite our different cultural, economic, and spiritual boats. Try as we may, rugged individualism and nation-first approaches to life are metaphysically impossible. The COVID virus has tragically revealed the illusion of separate nations and individuals, not to mention isolated churches and faith traditions. In the spirit of Martin Luther King's "Letter from the Birmingham Jail," process and openness theology affirms, "I can never be what I ought to be until you are what you ought to be, and you can never be what you ought to be until I am what I ought to be... This is the inter-related structure of reality."[6] Moreover, God is ultimately relational. The "amipotent" God, to use Thomas Jay Oord's imagery, is known by intimate and uncontrolling love, not distant and all-controlling power.

- *Experience is universal.* Life and energy course through all creation. Experiences vary, but there is a divine spark in all things. The heavens declare the glory of God. Snow and rain reflect divine energy. Humpbacked whales praise their creator. Bees search for pollen, and flowers lure bees to feast and spread new life. The universe is alive: though levels of experience vary markedly, there is some scintilla of experience in every being. The heavens declare the glory of God, but so do right whales, pangolins, gusty winds, and cypress trees. In a "pan-experiential" world, every creature is touched by God's love and reveals, to a greater or lesser extent, divine wisdom and creativity.

- *Value is universal.* Psalm 148 presents a universe of praise, from natural phenomena to national leaders. If a creature praises God, it must also have value to God and, hopefully, ourselves and our political and economic institutions. Value pervades the universe and calls us to amazement, respect, and ethical consideration. Conflict as well as cooperation is inevitable. Life is, as Whitehead notes, robbery. Destruction is necessary for survival even among non-violent religious tradition like Jainism. Yet, in a world of praise, we are challenged to maximize gratitude and minimize destruction. Reverence for life is the most appropriate virtue in a world of praise. Every healthy religious path and those who follow them is loved

---

6. Martin Luther King, *A Knock at Midnight* (New York: Warner Books, 1978), 201.

by God. The Infinite is the Intimate. Valuing all things, God's eye is on the sparrow and God is also watching me.

- *Revelation is Universal.* God's witness is dynamically present in all persons and all things. All things are words of God. The universe is full of God's glory. Cleave the wood and God is there. Every newborn reveals the face of God. We can learn from every encounter. We can grow by listening and loving and by cultivating an "impassioned embrace of reality," as author and environmentalist Barry Lopez proclaims. The light of God illumines all people (John 1:9) and is reflected in every creature. (Acts 17:28) Truth is found in every authentic religious quest, despite their differing cosmologies, practices, doctrines, and views of human wholeness or salvation.

- *God is the source of diversity in spirituality and religion.* The Poet of the Universe delights in diversity. Divine artistry can be found in the non-human world of flora and fauna, in sea creatures and rock formations, in scudding clouds, colors and shapes, and diverse humankind. Within the diversity of creation, God also touches persons and communities—spiritual movement leaders and their followers—in diverse ways reflective of their unique and evolving culture and history. Diversity in religions is not a fall from grace but a reflection of divine intimacy and an opportunity for adventures in partnership with God and our neighbors. A loving God desires that all be healed and saved and provides each culture and person with pathways to wholeness.

- *Revelation is universal and finite, and imperfect and subject to growth.* We see in a mirror dimly. Revelation requires a receiver and every receiver, every community, has a perspective and history that shapes the nature of revelation. God is the source of the many wisdom traditions related to each historical, cultural, and environmental context. Each tradition is gifted but limited. If you think you know it, it isn't God, as Augustine averred. Like the sight-impaired or blindfolded persons, we need to embrace different parts of the moving elephant and hear the message of other pilgrims along the spiritual journey.

- *The Universe reflects a movement toward beauty, wholeness, creativity, and justice.* There is, as Theodore Parker asserts, an arc in the universe that tends toward justice. Chaos exists, accidents exist, and freedom and creativity exist. Yet within the random and volitional elements of life, there is a movement toward beauty and justice, healing and wholeness, and complexity and wise creativity, that inspires our own prophetic and ethical quests. A spiritually and morally evolving universe, and its creator, challenge spiritual traditions to honor justice, inclusiveness, and diversity as avenues of grace and challenges to love. Love makes the world go round and divine love inspires the quest for wholeness in human life, calling us to be creative companions in healing the world.

- *The future is open, and we have a role in shaping what is to come.* There is no absolute terminus point to cosmic evolution. The future is not fully determined by God, our genes, our past histories, or cause and effect. The ongoing history of humankind and the planet is the open-ended unfolding of the interplay of personal and institutional decisions, past actions, planetary evolution, randomness and accident, and Divine Wisdom. Even God learns new things in the ongoing processes of history. The open-endedness of life applies to the future of religions as well as the planet. Our religions are always in process, in the making, cross-fertilizing each other, and growing in relationship to their environments.

- *As God's companions in shaping the world, our vocation is to be God's agents in healing the Earth.* God wants us to use our freedom to be creative co-creators! While our power and intentionality are limited, faith as small as a mustard seed can change the world. Five loaves and two fish can feed a multitude. A mustard seed can grow into a sheltering bush. Finite and fallible as we are, we are part of a process in which the world is saved one act at time. Healthy faith always joins in the divine quest to heal the world.

- *God is the ultimate example of love, relationship, and wisdom.* God is the fellow sufferer who understands and the joyful companion who celebrates, experiencing and shaping each moment of life. God's relationship to the world is that of loving call and response. God calls and we respond, and then God calls again. We make a difference to God. Our lives contribute to God's experience. Our actions add to or subtract from God's impact on the world. Healthy and vital spirituality expands our empathy and willingness to go from self-interest to world loyalty. For Christians, in all their diversity, becoming Christlike opens, rather than closes, our hearts toward others, expanding rather than contracting our empathy and willingness to listen and learn from the "holy other."

- *God is the dynamic energy inspiring the moral and spiritual arcs of the universe.* God's aim at beauty and wholeness, and complexity and creativity, embraces all creation and inspires emerging relationships among the world's wisdom traditions. God desires that all be healed and saved. Reflecting divine creative and emerging wisdom, religions are always in the making, evolving in relationship to culture, technology, science, exploration, and contacts with one another, seeking wholeness in unique and changing ways. This includes politics and economics, as well as spiritual practices.

While there are many other avenues of process and openness theology beyond what I have described, I believe that these affirmations will help us set our spiritual, practical, and intellectual GPS so that we might compassionately encounter the Holy Other, whether agnostic, atheist, or from the various wisdom traditions, embracing our common humanity and quest to heal the Earth.

CHAPTER THREE

Is There an Essence to Christianity?

Whenever I'm asked to introduce myself or am introduced at a speaking engagement, meeting, or to a group of new friends, I always struggle to find the right words. I realize that no words can express the fullness of my current experience or life history. With only a finite time for introductions, I need to decide which self, or which aspect of myself, to share. What professional positions will be emphasized? What books will be mentioned? Will my family life—marriage, child, grandchildren, or where I live—be included in the introduction or will the focus be on my professional and publication history?

What is definitive in one context, for example, being an author, professor, or pastor, is unimportant in another context where I might be meeting a fellow grandparent at the park, be chatting with a stranger at the market, or when I pick up my grandchildren at the bus stop after school. When an editor asks me to send a photo for a book cover or publicity release, I initially look for a photo that is flattering, but the photo I choose might be a decade old or taken in a setting that is no longer part of my daily life.

When I think of my parents, brother, or best friend, all now deceased, which memories are most definitive of my relationship with them? Which images do I remember? The same holds true of faith traditions. Just as I am no longer the child I was when I was growing up in a small-town California Baptist church and will be a different person two decades from now, if I am still living, faith traditions grow, expand, decline, reinvent themselves, and behave differently in different environments. They grow through new insights and new relationships with culture and other religious traditions. We can only legitimately speak of "Christianities" and not one Christianity. In light of recent New Testament and first century scholarship, which portrait of Jesus will we identify as the historical Jesus, knowing that the Jesus of history can never be separated from the Christ of faith, and that the life of Jesus can never be separated from his resurrection and post-resurrection experiences or the mystical experiences of his first followers?

Christianity today is vastly different from the simple pilgrim faith of the first century. Christianity in a South American or Zambian Pentecostal church looks quite different from the Christian spirit of the historic Congregational Church I pastored for eight years on Cape Cod, Massachusetts, or the congregation where I currently worship, Westmoreland Congregational United Church of Christ in Bethesda, Maryland. Christians protesting attacks on their faith at an America First Rally or Trump demonstration have vastly different views of scriptural authority, Jesus, politics, salvation, and church-state relations than progressive Christians marching with Black Lives Matter and climate change protests or getting out the vote for progressive candidates after worship at Ebenezer Baptist Church, the spiritual home of Martin Luther King. In fact, many Christians like me have more in common with a First American shaman, Yoruba spiritual guide, new age healer, and Buddhist monk than with self-professed orthodox, America first Christians.

The task of describing a faith tradition is almost as daunting as describing your own life history or deepest reality. Just as each of us has an identity that is subject to change and more than meets the eye, so does every faith tradition. You cannot fully describe the experience of loving your life companion or grandchild. You can never fully describe your relationship with God or God's presence in your life. Mystics and persons who have near-death experiences are often speechless when asked to define these life transforming experiences. No formula can fully describe your sacrifices for a critically ill loved one or response to God's call in your life. No shibboleth can completely convey the heart of Christianity or any other religious tradition. There are constants to my life and there are constants to religious traditions, and yet the constants are constantly changing in meaning and significance in the historical trajectories of religious traditions.

While we must use words and invoke doctrines and rituals, and need to take seriously our historical roots, we must always remember that there is a qualitative difference, as Zen Buddhists aver, between the moon and the finger that points toward it! The elephant is multifaceted, moving, and evolving, and beneath its grand exterior, the inner workings, heart, lungs, mind, and nervous system are hidden! Twenty-first century North American conservative Christianity, with its whiteness, affluence, nation-first agenda, marriage to capitalism, and fixation on political power, is a far cry from the persecuted church of Rome's catacombs. With nuances, the same also applies to progressive Christianity and the progressive suburban United Church of Christ congregation where I attend.

When I asked a group of Facebook friends what they thought were the Christian "essentials" or "necessaries," their descriptions varied widely from one another. The same diversity occurred when I posed the question of Christianity's "essence" to my Zoom seminar. According to my conversation partners on Facebook and Zoom, the essence of Christianity is related to one or many of the following:

- The Petrine Confession ("You are the Christ, the Messiah, the Son of the Living God")
- Following the way of Jesus as shown in the Gospels
- Healing the world and our society
- The Ecumenical Creeds (Apostles, Nicene, Athanasian)
- The sacraments of the church (whether two or seven)
- Living a Christian lifestyle
- Loving one another
- The Biblical witness
- The encounter with Jesus as our deepest reality
- The realm of God and our quest to do God's will on earth as it is in heaven
- Living the way of Jesus

These responses are far from exhaustive. One respondent stated, "If you think the essence of Christianity is _____, you must be lying." Another said, in the spirit of my earlier comments about dynamism and diversity, "the essence of Christianity seems to be whatever you say it is." A third, after remarking on the American joining of religion and politics asserted, that "it seems that those who say they are the most orthodox are farthest from the spirit of Jesus."

A Virtue in Vagueness.

While we need to look for some flexible vision of Christian essentials, we need also to remember that there is, as a sermon I heard in the early 1980s asserted, "a virtue in vagueness." Faith is poetic, ambient, and experiential. Too much clarity excludes alternative possibilities and experiences of God. Moreover, the ecumenical creeds (Nicene and Apostles) have been anything but "ecumenical." They have promoted uniformity rather than diversity and often have been employed to exclude and excommunicate rather than welcome. Tragically, creeds have led to violence when they are too closely joined with political power, whether in Rome, the Spanish Inquisition, or today's United States.

It was synchronous that during the time I was teaching the seminar on "Christianity and World Religions," I was also teaching a seminar sponsored by our church on the non-canonical or "Gnostic" Gospel of Thomas. The Gospel of Thomas speaks of Jesus' "hidden teachings." In contrast to the four canonized gospels, Thomas and other "Gnostic gospels," give little attention to the events of Jesus' birth, ministry, interpersonal encounters, death, crucifixion, and resurrection. Thomas gives no attention to the cross as a sacrifice on our behalf but sees salvation in terms of self-awareness of the Christ within. For Thomas, every stone or person reflects God's inner presence. Jesus has given us living waters to drink that satisfy every spiritual thirst. These waters become our essential nature and do not require divine sacrifice to bring about personal transformation. While the Gospel of Thomas was excluded from the authorized canon, those who wrote this ancient text considered themselves to be faithful followers of Jesus, piously sharing their image of the Jesus who had changed their lives. They were writing and worshipping as committed Christians, not as the heretics some of their contemporaries made them out to be. Four centuries later, the Celtic Christian Pelagius, labeled as a heretic by Augustine, could claim to be just as devout as the North African bishop who wished to excommunicate him, just more concerned with the role of human agency in our spiritual growth and the essential holiness of human life, not to mention the positive role of women in the church, rather than focusing on original sin.

There is wisdom in Jesus' question, "Who do people say that I am?" and the various answers Jesus receives. While Peter's response "you are the Christ, the Messiah," is the "approved" answer to those who claim their doctrinal orthodoxy, the question itself points to the fact that many visions of Jesus and Christianity are possible, based on our experience of God, Jesus, culture, history, and values. Peter's answer inspires questions asked in a variety of ways throughout Christian history, such as "What do you mean by Christ? Who is Jesus the Christ and what is unique about him?" This is not a matter of superficially picking and choosing among the options in the "spiritual smorgasbord" or "cafeteria Christianity;" it is a recognition that Jesus is always more than words can say, and that Jesus addresses each one of us through the interplay of tradition and intimacy. A living Jesus addresses us in ways unique to our time and place. As my Lancaster Theological Seminary colleague, Lee Barrett avers, there is not just one Jesus, there are "Jesai." The light of Christ is prismatic rather than monolithic.

The quest to understand Jesus, and the essence of Christianity, also reflects the contrast of *kataphatic* and *apophatic* ways of understanding God: we must use language, symbol, and ritual to describe the heart of our faith, but the heart of our faith is always more than we can articulate, thus rendering us both devoted and humble in relation to the faith we affirm.

It's How You Play the Game. For many years, I coached baseball and basketball for elementary school children, including my son and his friends. While I can't say I was a great strategic or technical coach, I sought to teach my players a handful of truths related to positive attitudes in sport and life along with basic athletic skills: everyone makes a difference, you can improve your playing skills through practice, playing the game is intended to be fun, and we need to follow the rules, but we don't need to let the rules get in the way of joy and skill in playing the game. In a similar fashion, the essence of Christianity can be compared to playing a game, whether chess, checkers, mahjong, baseball, or water polo. We need the boundaries that rules provide as a way of identifying what game we are playing and how best to excel at it. Baseball differs from basketball. Soccer, tennis, and golf all use balls, but quite differently. Though similar in many ways to tennis, pickle ball is played on a smaller court. It also has elements of ping-pong and badminton. Ice hockey differs from lacrosse or field hockey. All are legitimate games, involving different skills and attractive to different persons.

Within each game, there are vast differences in skill and style. The USGA rules of golf create a common language and community of golfers. Yet there is a vast difference between the playing skills, style, and shot execution of Rory McIlroy, Tiger Woods, Annika Sorenstam, Jack Nicklaus, Arnold Palmer, Michelle Wie, Nancy Lopez, and me. I enjoy playing basketball with my grandchildren, but LeBron James, Larry Bird, Michael Jordan, Jayson Tatum, Cheryl Miller, Sue Bird, and Diana Taurasi created a style of play that James Naismith couldn't have imagined when he invented the game "Basket Ball" in late nineteenth century Springfield, Massachusetts.

Games evolve over time. When I was a boy playing baseball in King City, California, there was no such thing as a "designated hitter." Nor were there "three-point shots" in basketball. The rules of college and professional football differ slightly, and both have adapted their rules to prevent head trauma and other injuries. Even professional skateboarding, which has no rules per se, requires, as one skate aficionado noted, "only you, the board, and concrete."

During 2020-2022, the world faced an unprecedented pandemic. We discovered, at least the most forward thinking of us, that science is reliable, and the scientific adventure reveals divine wisdom. Yet our understanding and response to COVID-19 and its variants has evolved since January 2020. To the superficial thinker as well as the dishonest demagogue wanting to politicize the scientific method, changing positions represents science's inability to give us any important truths or be a guidepost for our behaviors. The constant updating of scientific understanding reflects the scientist's commitment to seeking the truth and the recognition that our understanding of disease and its treatment and prevention, the universe, our bodies, and the planet is always expanding. New experiences and data require new understandings and evolving descriptions, whether in science, medicine, theology, or church on Zoom.

People of faith would do well to embrace a scientific approach to truth rather than accepting past experiences and doctrines as normative. A dynamic faith is an evolving faith, subject to creative transformation in relationship to a living God and living cultures. People of faith benefit when they honor those who colored outside the established lines and transformed their faith traditions by their innovative theology and unique encounters with God. There is always greater light to be shed on science, sports, scripture, and religious experience.

The elephant we call Christianity is also on the move! The dynamic nature of religious communities suggests that a better word for the "non-negotiables" of faith involves the quest to experience and embody, as Marcus Borg suggests, the "heart" of Christianity rather than its "essence." The "heart" is traditionally understood as the seat of the spirit, always beating, circulating blood throughout the body, changing its rate of beating to respond to external stimuli or internal experiences. In contrast, the word "essence" suggests something abstract and unchanging, a primordial ideal or pattern, a Platonic form that judges our ephemeral everyday experiences of faith as inferior and inadequate. While there may be "eternals" in Christianity, these "eternal verities" come alive and are meaningful only in lived historical, relational experience. The Word was, and still is, made flesh in the maelstrom of human and earthly experience, living, growing, aspiring, healing, and challenging. Our faith is made flesh in the creative synthesis of historical experience, revelatory of God's vision, yet struggling to embody the ever-flowing waters of justice and mercy in the challenges of persons and nations. Christianity was, is, and will always be in process.

A Beating Heart for Christianity.

The nature of faith has often been described as "believing, behaving, and belonging." Conservative Christian leaders assert that the order of these aspects is key: one must first believe, then behave as a member of the group before belonging. Other theologians and spiritual leaders suggest that although the order of experience may vary in persons and traditions, this trilogy provides some guidance in the quest for the heart of Christianity. The path of belief involves our vision of God, Jesus, human life, and the world, often identified as theology. The path of behavior focuses on Christian lifestyle, the way of Jesus, embodied in our personal, community, political lives, and ethics. The way of belonging involves the pathway of love, of finding meaningful relationships within a community that professes to follow Jesus. All the members of this faithful trinity are interdependent. In fact, each of the three dynamically influences the others. Our theology shapes our ethics and relationships. Conversely, our sense of community and ethical reflection transforms our theology. Community requires the interplay of flexible ethical foundations and a sense of theological purpose. Ethics requires the polestar of the spiritual and moral arcs of history and is lived out in relationship. The interactions of these three aspects of faith communities, dynamic and interdependent, might be described as Christian yogas, or ways individuals encounter the Holy, each of which is a pathway toward experiencing the heartbeat of Jesus, depending on age, personality, and culture. This faithful trinity gives concreteness, dynamism, and relativity to all our expressions of faith. Still, it is important to give some structure to the faith we affirm, the essence or the heart of Christianity.

With all humility, we can look for the heart of Christianity, the foundation for dialogue with other faiths, and the source of our own identity as followers of Jesus in terms of certain flexible and dynamic affirmations. My spiritual and theological "heart" is based on the interplay of process and open and relational theology, mysticism, scripture study, science, the dynamic and varied history of Christianity, constantly unfolding and being re-imagined, and participation in Christian community. My quest for the heart of Christianity resembles the Wesley Quadrilateral: the dynamic interplay of scripture, experience, reason, and tradition. I would add to this quadrilateral, minimally, fifth, sixth, and seventh factors, related to the first four: the advances and retreats of the cultural adventure (including literature, science, politics, and psychology), the impact our planetary environment (our identity as companions with the non-human world), and the evolution of our faith in dialogue with those who have previously been marginalized, neglected, or silenced in the formation of Christian institutions, rituals, spiritual practices, and theologies (women, persons of color, indigenous peoples, the disability community). I suspect these dynamics of faith apply to the ongoing history of religious traditions beyond Christianity.

The Heartbeat of Faith.

Regardless of religious tradition, theology is ultimately concrete in nature. Theological reflection joins: 1) *Vision,* the lenses through which we view the world, grounded in our perception of God's nature and relationship to the world; 2) *Promise,* the invitation to experience the Christian vision of reality; and 3) *Practice,* spiritual practices that enable us to experience God's presence in our lives and in the world. Some form of vision, promise, and practice shapes every religious tradition. With humility, I suggest the following flexible affirmations, subject to change and expansion, as the heartbeat of Christianity. These affirmations will guide my dialogue with the world's wisdom traditions.

- *God is love, and God's love is the motive force of all creation, including human history.* While Christians may differ in their understandings of the relationship of God and the world, and issues related to the scope and impact of divine power and knowledge, deep down Christian faith has affirmed that "God is love" and "God so loved the world that God gave God's only son." Love is the energy that brought forth the universe, guided the evolution of galaxies and planets, inspired the prophets and sages, and is manifest most fully in the life and teachings of Jesus of Nazareth. God is just and there are consequences to our actions, but above all, God is graceful and loving. We know God only through loving one another and embracing the least of these. "Amazing grace, how sweet the sound, that saved a wretch like me. I once was lost and now am found, was blind but now I see."

- *God, the origin of the moral and spiritual arc, is active in nature and history.* Creation and the unfolding of history reflect divine wisdom and purpose. Evolution and history are meaningful and exhibit God's purposes and direction. While there may be free play and chaos in the universe due to accidents and human choice, God's vision of wholeness is embedded in every event and the far horizons of history. The world emerges from divine creativity, whether the world's creation is out of chaos, nothingness, or is an everlasting and ongoing reflection of divine activity without beginning or end.

- *History is the theater of divine call and human response.* Embracing its Jewish roots, Christian faith sees history as a dynamic call and response. In the spirit of the prophets, Christian faith affirms that God is constantly inspiring humankind to seek justice and love mercy. In the teachings of the prophets, and later through the ministry of Jesus, God challenges persons and nations to liberate the oppressed, heal the sick, release captives, care for vulnerable; and let justice roll down like waters and righteousness like an ever-flowing stream. Although history has a moral and spiritual arc, God does not fully control the historical process. God responds with challenge and inspiration and is constantly calling us to embody God's vision of Shalom in history, based on individual and institutional choices. God's vision judges and inspires, calling persons and nations to account.

- *God is Speaking and Still Speaking.* God communicates to humankind in dreams, synchronous encounters, prophesies, visions, inspirations, and mystical experiences. The First and New Testaments (Old and New Testaments) emerge out of the divine human encounter. The unique status of the Hebraic and Christian scriptures is testimony to God's ongoing revelation in history. Although Christians have varied views about the authority of scripture and its fallibility/infallibility, the scriptures reflect the impact of the divine-human encounter on persons and communities. While scriptures have a unique place as inspiration for Jewish and Christian experience, God continues to communicate with humans beyond scripture in ways that transform our lives and communities. We are part of God's ongoing revelation. Our encounters, and spiritual transformation through encountering other religions, may also reflect God's dynamic revelation in history.

- *Authentic Christian faith affirms its Jewish roots.* A bumper sticker reads, "My savior is a Jewish carpenter." Jesus the Messiah could only have been born in the Hebraic tradition. While the relationship between Christianity and Judaism has been complicated and at times tragic, Christianity depends on Judaism for its theological and spiritual foundations. Jesus is Jewish and saw himself as part of the prophetic tradition, presenting God's vision of Shalom as the inspiration of and judgment on persons and institutions. Judaism roots Christianity in the earth, economics, justice seeking, and in hope for healing of persons and the planet. To be faithful to the way of Jesus, Christians must embrace their Jewish roots, beginning with the affirmation of the prophetic concern for social justice as a balance to Paul's concept of unmerited grace. God is full of grace, but grace calls us to action to change the world. Anti-Judaism is contrary to the heart of Christianity.

- *The Word is made flesh in Jesus of Nazareth.* The Word and Wisdom of God, the creative intelligence and love, that give birth to the universe appear in Jesus of Nazareth. While there are many understandings of the incarnation, ranging from virgin birth to Jesus' ethical and spiritual embodiment of God's vision, making him the glory of God as a fully alive human, incarnation means that God is present in our cells and our souls. Jesus is transparent to God's vision, growing in wisdom and stature. For followers of Jesus, God is known most fully in the life of the Galilean healer and prophet. The unique status of Jesus does not nullify God's presence and inspiration in other religious teachers, spiritual leaders, and wisdom traditions.

- *Divine wisdom is embodied in the physical world.* God is the reality in whom we live and move and have our being, as the Apostle Paul proclaims to the Athenians, using the wisdom of one of their poets. (Acts 17:28) The word is made flesh and dwells in all creation. Cells and souls alike reflect divine wisdom and creativity.

- *Incarnation is global as well as local.* The whole earth, as the angels proclaim to Isaiah, is full of God's glory. Cleave the wood and Christ is there, as the Gospel of Thomas asserts. Divine wisdom is embedded, albeit hidden, within every occasion of experience, from the simplest to the most complex. God's incarnation in the life of Jesus of Nazareth is continuous with God's presence in the wider world. Fully present in Christ, divine incarnation gives life to all creation, albeit partially and evolving.

- *God in Christ seeks the healing of all creation and every creature.* God in Christ has a bias toward the healing of persons and communities. Jesus' mission statements (John 10:10; Luke 4:18-19) involve bringing abundant life to all creation. God intends that the moral and spiritual arcs define God's quest for Shalom, personally and globally. Whatever stands in the way of God's vision of Shalom must be prayerfully, compassionately, and vigorously challenged. The Spirit of God inspires Jesus to be an agent of liberation and healing in our personal and institutional lives. Though some Christians speak of divine judgement, the God of Jesus is the celestial surgeon who disciplines only to heal and save.

- *Jesus calls us to Christ-like living.* Christianity is an ethical religion. Jesus told his followers that they are the light of the world. Our lives can contribute to God's mission. We can do greater things than we imagine by following Christ's way, by letting Christ's Spirit challenge and energize us. Our constant questions involve, "What would Jesus do in this situation? How can I be Christ's healing partner? How can I do something beautiful for God?" Our affirmation that "God is love" challenges us to be loving in our personal and political lives.

- *Christian ethical aspiration is grounded in acts of love and hospitality.* Christ-like living is embodied by acts of lovingkindness. In the spirit of Jesus' prophetic roots in the Hebraic tradition, Jesus proclaims that the great commandment involves loving God and your neighbor as yourself. Our lives are our gifts to God. Our ethical behavior contributes to or detracts from God's vision of Shalom, "on earth as it is in heaven." The personal is the political, and the political is personal. Accordingly, nations as well as persons are judged by their treatment of the least of these. The way of Jesus is ethical and transformational. Jesus' ministry calls us to be "little Christs" to one another.

- *Based on God's creative wisdom, both non-human creation and human history are meaningful.* The cosmic and individual reflect divine purpose. The universe and human history have their origins in God's loving creativity. What happens in the human and non-human worlds matters to God and to us, shaping our destiny and the destiny of the planet and contributing to God's own joy or sorrow. In the spirit of Whitehead, Christians can affirm that God is the fellow sufferer who understands; God is also the intimate companion who celebrates. Authentic living embraces our embodiment and the earth in its fullness.

- *Salvation embraces mind, body, and spirit, as God seeks to heal our lives in the here and now.* Salvation is lived out in the Holy Here and Now. Now is the day of salvation. Now is the time to embody God's vision. God's goal is to save cells, souls, and societies. Our goal is to live fully today, trusting our everlasting destiny to God's unconquerable grace and all-embracing love.

- *Survival after death is the gift of divine love and embraces personality and community.* The realm of God is God's gift beyond the grave. God's love "on earth as it is in heaven" resurrects humankind to lived community beyond the grave. Every tear is dried, every pain healed, every evil transformed into beauty. We cannot, as a theologian once stated, discern "the furniture of heaven or the flames of hell." We can trust that our earthly lives matter and live on in God's memory and in our future adventures as persons in divine community, rejoicing in one another and God's amazing grace.

My list of the heart of Christianity is not exhaustive, and others would focus on other aspects of faith as essential. Moreover, the beating heart of Christianity I report is quite different in focus than that of biblical literalists, proponents of what they believe to be "orthodoxy," or of the Christians shaped by American capitalism and nation-first. My faith is processive, open, and relational, progressive, and open to constant change in relationship to the evolving world. As important as they are in the evolution and practices of Christian faith, I have not included the institutional church, sacraments, eschatology and apocalyptic (the completion of history through divine activity), and the Trinity, although I affirm versions of all of these, in varying degrees, in my personal and professional life. The affirmations I have described are hospitable to varieties of Christian experience and serve as catalysts for inter-spiritual dialogue, partnership, growth, and critique. Those who have other affirmations or take another spiritual path are still God's beloved children and can claim a relationship with Jesus. In sharing our contrasting positions, we may discover new aspects of our faith and find common ground amid our differences. I may challenge their ethics, politics, and doctrines, but I cannot challenge God's love for them.

A CHRISTIAN'S CONFESSION

Throughout the text, I will ask progressive and open spirited practitioners of various faith traditions to reflect on their faith and their understanding of the heart of their religious tradition. To be fair, I must ask myself these questions, as a practicing Christian, whose faith is shaped by the vision of process and open and relational theology. Matters of theology, to be authentic, must be personal as well as academic, spiritual as well as intellectual. Based on that understanding, I coined the phrase "theo-spirituality" to describe the holistic nature of theological reflection.

I confess that I could not be a Christian without being progressive and inter-spiritual in orientation. My path to returning to Christianity took me through American Transcendentalism, mystical explorations with psychedelics, Hinduism, and a popularized and accessible form of Hinduism, Transcendental Meditation. If I hadn't been there, I wouldn't be here. Over the years, I have reclaimed my evangelical Christian roots, and integrated them with progressive and process and open and relational theology and the mystical traditions of Christianity. I have embraced the power of the hymns of faith, the scriptures I memorized as a child, the importance of scripture, as well as the healings of Jesus, to shape my life and help others to find their way. I have discovered that the description "evangelical" does not need to mean "politically conservative," "racist," or "anti-science," but points to a living relationship with Jesus in which one can prayerfully affirm the mystic sentiment of the hymn "he walks with me and talks with me and tells me I am his own." I must confess that I am agnostic about human destiny. I hope for everlasting life without claiming to know its contours. The idea of non-existence makes no sense to me. I can't conceive of "nothingness" from the perspective of our amazing and wonderful universe. Yet, I know that, whether I will experience further adventures beyond the grave, I must seek to be faithful today to the way of Jesus and to future generations, seeking to be a "good ancestor" doing something beautiful for God and for the world. Trust in God's presence inspires me with each morning to chant "this is the day that God has made. I will rejoice and be glad in it." (Psalm 118:24)

While I cannot claim to articulate fully the heart of Christianity, the words "grace," "love," "presence," and "vocation" emerge as descriptions of the way of Jesus. "Amazing grace, how sweet the sound that saved a wretch like me" are more than words from a hymn. Not a spirituality of shame, but the recognition that we are loved before we can do anything or achieve anything, that we can never lose that love, and that love will bring us home to wholeness. Love beyond measure, the love that spun forth the universe, parents forth each child, and guides the galaxies and our daily steps. Presence of holiness in each place and each moment, calling us to awareness, to discover, in the spirit of Jacob's dream at Beth-El, that God is in this place and now we know it! In that presence, we discover our vocations: the place where our gifts respond to the world's needs. The vocation of the moment as well as the vocation of each season of life, finding our place as God's companions in healing the world.

GROWING EDGES FOR CHRISTIANITY

As a dynamic, diverse, and living organism, Christianity must, as Episcopalian Bishop John Shelby Spong, counsels "change or die." While there are many Christianities, and Northern hemisphere Christianity is becoming a minority in the Christian world, the heart of Christianity involves the recognition that God is always doing a new thing. God's vision joins tradition and innovation. God is our help in ages past and hope in years to come. God is calling us, as God did in the days of Jesus, to new ways of understanding our spiritual lives and the evolution of our faith tradition. My suggestions are those of a progressive process theologian, with mystical inclinations, and obviously aren't normative for Christians everywhere.

First, Christianity needs to navigate between the dynamically interdependent realities of truth and pluralism. The quest for truth, and the truths around which we center our lives, tempts us to idolatry and absolutism. Conservative Christians claim to have the way, truth, and life and that others who believe differently are lost and at risk for eternal damnation. In contrast to binary understandings of faith, faithful or centered pluralism suggests a relativity of every perspective, which leads us to assert the universality of divine inspiration and the reality that no faith tradition or Christian denomination can claim finality or completeness. This is a political as well as religious issue. The identification of religious and political absoluteness in the United States is a danger to democracy as well as the vitality of Christianity's witness. Those who claim religious finality have throughout history used their power coercively, violently, and destructively, and have contended that their "one true faith" requires the subjugation or, at least, spiritual, institutional, and intellectual separation and silencing of those who lack the fullness of truth, whether fellow Christians or indigenous peoples.

From the perspective of process and openness theology, our experiences of truth are always growing in dialogue with a changing world and a changing God. This is not just a Christian issue, given the reality of fundamentalism surfacing in Hinduism and Islam. We must join the quest to understand, affirm, and learn from the religious experiences, spiritual practices, and worldviews of persons of other faith traditions.

Second, speaking as a North American, a Northern hemisphere progressive Christian, I recognize that the numerical heart of Christianity has shifted to the

Southern hemisphere. While there are many varieties of Christianity, Christianity in the Southern hemisphere tends to be more Pentecostal, evangelical, and conservative than its northern neighbors. In certain more connectional denominations, this had led to controversy over the ethics of sexual identity. In the United Methodist and Anglican traditions, progressive Christianity's open-spirited embrace of pluralism, science, feminism/womanism, and the LGBTQ community has been under fire and threatens schism grounded in the differing ethics and worldviews of progressive and conservative Christians. As a Northern hemisphere progressive Christian, I see God's movements in expanding the circle of faith and ethics, in becoming more inclusive of the diversity of human experience. I must ask myself, "Is God present in the attitudes of Southern hemisphere movements that resemble North American conservative Christian movements I identify as reactive, intolerant, and antithetical to the way of Jesus? Can I affirm God's truth in my progressive faith without being paternalistic toward Southern hemisphere Christianities whose positions and religious experiences differ from my own, not to mention North American Christian groups I deem to be reactionary?" Issues of variety within Christianity will become more significant in North America due to immigration from the Southern hemisphere. We must find a way to affirm a lively evolving spirituality that affirms, without condescension, members of movements we perceive to be more conservative, reactive toward modernity, anti-intellectual, anti-scientific, and exclusivist than our own. While we must speak our truth and relate our experience of God's movements in our lives and in theological reflection, we must avoid the tendency to divide the world into truth and error based on progressive ideals.

Finally, I believe that today's Christians need to challenge condescending attitudes toward other wisdom traditions. If God is the source of truth in all its manifestations, then we must jettison viewpoints that suggest: 1) we have the truth and other paths are, by definition, false; 2) salvation only occurs within Christianity, or in certain branches of Christianity; 3) all religions are the same, and their differences are merely superficial; and 4) Christianity is, by definition, the pinnacle of the religious quest, the fulfillment and supplanter of every other tradition. Rather, we can faithfully affirm the wisdom of Christianity, the unique saving power of Jesus, and the grace of God, while recognizing the unique revelations and histories of other faiths, their particular spiritual practices and worldviews, and the hope of salvation and enlightenment for all people. We can witness, share, and learn in our inter-spiritual adventures.

CHRISTIAN PRACTICES.

Each chapter will conclude with unique or signature practices emerging from the respective faith traditions; practices that inform inter-spiritual relations among the various traditions. The practices I describe will be interpretive snap shots, adapted in ways that resonate with contemporary or historical Christian experience and ways Christians can take seriously practices from other faiths. Practices are pathways to experiencing the Divine presence in our lives. There are many practices that enable us to experience the heart of Christianity. Four practices stand out as unique in my understanding of the Christian vision. Each of these has shaped my own spirituality. My descriptions will be broad in scope as I seek to respond to the realities of twenty-first century technology and spirituality.

Lectio Divina.

God comes to us through imagination and intuition as well as through intellect. Revelation is both universal and personal. Scripture and other inspirational texts are living words that speak to us both personally and globally. In *lectio divina,* or holy reading, we follow a flexible pattern of reading a text silently or orally, usually a few times, letting the text sink in, and then listening to God's inspiration coming forth in the interplay of divine inspiration, personal experience, and textual content. The steps that I employ in practicing *lectio divina* include:

1.   Silence and opening to divine inspiration.

2.   Prayer for guidance.

3.   Reading or listening to the text, at least twice.

4.   Letting the text soak in silently, listening for phrases, words, images, and experiences that emerge, letting your imagination loose to experience surprising insights. Often, I take a walk to inspire a deeper understanding of the text.

5.   Identifying a phrase, image, intuition, etc., that speaks to your experience.

6.   Meditating on this phrase, image, intuition, song, etc.

7. Asking God to guide you in integrating this experience with the rest of your life. How might you embody the insight?

8. Praying for guidance for the day ahead.

I often use a short form of *lectio divina,* five minutes or less, to open the scriptures to new insights in seminar settings. In classroom settings, I have found that *lectio divina* awakens participants to see a familiar scripture or topic in new ways and to feel comfortable in challenging the text and prior understandings of faith.

Examen.

At the heart of spirituality is the interplay of "listening to your life" and "letting your life speak," phrases invoked by Frederick Buechner and Parker Palmer. In the Examen, the goal is self-awareness and God awareness. We look at a particular moment, day, or incident in our lives, and seek to awaken to the quality of our awareness of God's presence and inspiration. While there are a variety of ways to practice the Examen, here is a path that I have found inspirational:

1. Silence.

2. Prayer to be open to God's inspiration as I look at my life,

3. Gratitude for God's blessings in my life and in the world.

4. Gently looking at a particular event or at the day that has passed, exploring where I felt close or distant from God.

5. Giving thanks for God moments and confessing my failure to live according to God's vision.

6. Asking for God's guidance in transforming my life.

7. Asking God to guide me in the day ahead.

Throughout the day, take time to awaken to insights based on the practice of *lectio divina.* Live the day ahead, pausing for gratitude, self-awareness, and spiritual course correction.

Healing Body, Mind, Spirit, and Planet.

Healing was at the heart of Jesus' ministry. The deeply incarnational way of Jesus joined body, mind, spirit, and relationships. Jesus' healings addressed cells, souls, and social structures. Transcending binary understandings of purity, clean and unclean, Jesus embraced those who were marginalized and ostracized due to their physical or mental health conditions. Jesus was concerned with bringing abundant life to earth and not preparing persons solely for the afterlife. Jesus healed through words, touch, energy, distant intentionality, exorcism, hospitality, and challenge to unjust social structures. Jesus' healing ministry challenged any religious or social structure that prevented persons from experiencing the abundant life God intends for all.

We live in a different world, scientifically and culturally, from Jesus. We understand the causes of illness differently and use different language to describe illnesses. We recognize genetic, environmental, emotional, traumatic, and relational causes of illness that would have been foreign to the early Christian movement. Still, we share God's vision of wholeness and opposition to anything that subverts the image of God in humankind, whether medical or political.

Healing in the style of Jesus today is a growing edge, especially for progressive and mainstream Christians who are challenged to explore healing practices in a pluralistic technological age. Early Christian theologians asserted that wherever truth is found, God is its source. We can apply the same affirmation to healing methodologies: wherever healing and wholeness are found, God is its source. This inspires us to explore complementary and holistic forms of medicine and health care, such as yoga, Tai Chi, Qigong, herbal remedies, natural medicine, and energy practices such as Reiki and therapeutic touch. It also inspires us to employ Western healing modalities in prayerful ways: contemplation and chemotherapy, meditation and medication, and prayer and Prozac.

We need to revive traditional Christian healing practices such as the laying on of hands and the relationship between the Eucharist and healing. Beyond remedies intended to promote wellbeing and respond to illness, a growing edge for Christian healing ministry is the exploration of the environmental, economic, and political dimensions of disease and healing. The quest for social justice involves creating healthy environments and equal access to food, housing, and medical care. The quest for healing must also include responding to climate change and ecological destruction, given the reality that vulnerable persons are at greater risk from environmentally related illness than those with sufficient resources and flexibility in the workplace.

The realities of environmental destruction and injustice have been apparent during the COVID pandemic, where incidents of COVID were manifestly higher in low-income and urban communities with high populations of persons of color, on Native American reservations and Appalachian villages, and among those whose "essential work" required them to be at greater risk than white-collar employees working from home and other safe environments. The growing edges of Christian healing involve the embracing of global healing practices and the transformation of economic and political systems, as well as our personal quest to be God's companions in healing the world.

Intimacy with God.

God is personal and our spiritual lives should be personal as well, joining the intimate with the Infinite. God has a personal relationship with all of creation. Prayer forms are multi-faceted and diverse, involving awakening to God through gratitude, wonder, petition, and response. When we pray, deep is calling to deep, our hearts beat with God's heart. Our steps align with Jesus' steps, widening our circle of care from our individual prayer concerns to prayers for the world. Our prayers make a difference to us, to God, and to those for whom we pray. In the dynamic interdependence of life, our prayers create a field of force, joining us with those for whom we pray and opening the door to greater manifestations of God's vision of Shalom.

Christianity is a moving elephant. Diverse, dynamic, and forward looking. Following the way of Jesus awakens us to our role in healing the planet. Within the Christian movement, our challenges are both internal and external, calling us to embody our own Christian pluralism in welcoming ways, to affirm our experiences of Christ with conviction and humility, and to claim our vocation as God's healing partners, caring for person, community, and planet.

CHAPTER FOUR

Judaism

Judaism and Christianity are intimate siblings. Like the dynamics of many families, their relationship can be described by the phrase, "it's complicated." My late brother and I had a loving but challenging relationship. He was always my big brother and there were moments when he, in my estimation, acted like one—as a wise protector. Our relationship was complicated, but I wouldn't be the person I am today without my brother Bill. He defined in many ways, along with my parents, my initial world view and the challenges and the possibilities of my personal journey. I have throughout my life defined myself as his brother and other. Over the years, I grew in my appreciation of Bill and the challenges he faced, but no one could describe our relationship as "easy."

As I noted earlier, we can describe the relationship between Judaism and Christianity also as complicated. We might go further and say, "It's tragic." Judaism is Christianity's older sibling. Judaism gave Christianity its theological and metaphysical foundations, stories of creation, first scriptures, understanding of human nature, and vision of history. Jesus was from the lineage of David and Ruth, heroic figures of the Jewish tradition. Jesus was Jewish and so were all his earliest followers. There is no Christianity without Judaism, and Jesus the Christ is a Jewish Messiah. Jesus cannot be separated from the roots and hopes of his people. More significantly and startling, there is no Jesus without Judaism. While God has many avenues of revelation, God's Messiah, the incarnation of God's Word and Wisdom and Vision of Shalom, could only happen in Judaism, just as God's inspiration of Gautama Buddha could only have occurred within the trajectory of Hinduism. Jesus' first followers were religious and ethnic Jews, who struggled to widen their religious circle to embrace persons born in the Gentile world, and their very different understandings of religion, ethics, and deity.

Early on, like all younger siblings, Christianity sought to differentiate itself from its older sibling. Many of the first Christians, especially those who lived in the vicinity of Jerusalem, wished to remain deeply rooted and defined by Jewish law and ritual. However, the most influential streams of the Christian movement saw the new faith as global, multi-racial, and multi-cultural. This led to conflict within the Christian movement. It also led to conflicts with its elder spiritual sibling. Despite their intimacy, the first Christians, as Acts of the Apostles portrays, felt themselves bullied and persecuted by their older sibling. While much of orthodox Christian theology blamed the Jews—ironically, since the first Christians were Jews—for Jesus' crucifixion, Jesus' death was the result of the joint decision-making of the Roman leadership and the Temple establishment, which in partnership authorized the Roman military to hang Jesus on a cross. This anti-Judaism was exacerbated when Christianity left behind its Jewish ethnic roots and became a global religion. In moving forward, many Christians abandoned their roots, jettisoning the historical vision of Judaism and its God for the more ethereal, otherworldly deity of Greek philosophy.

The early Christian movement's first encounter with pluralism involved defining its relationship with Judaism. The questions posed in the first century are still active in Christian, and often tragically, in Jewish experience. Is the new Christian movement a branch of the Abrahamic tree, or does it represent a radically new and unique spiritual possibility? Must followers of Jesus be "good Jews" first, following without exception the Mosaic law, or can they disregard the Law of Moses and the Jewish tradition entirely? Is Judaism a spiritual equal or has the faith of Jesus superseded the tradition of Moses, rendering it obsolete? How shall we view the death of Jesus? Was it the result of state-sponsored violence meted out by Roman oppressors? Did it spring solely from the machinations of Jewish Temple religious leaders, or was it the result of political and religious collusion? Can Jews and Christians coexist with one another, accentuating each faith's unique gifts, or must the younger brother, like the fabled Jacob, rob his elder Esau of his legacy and inheritance? Do we still affirm the prophetic political vision, one that Jesus affirmed, with the coming of the new covenant in Jesus' life, death, and resurrection? Christian answers to these questions have led either to creative companionship or to violent persecution. Inquisitions, pogroms, and the Holocaust as well as the anti-Semitism promoted by today's Christian nationalists can be attributed to scapegoating, supersession or replacement theologies, and the denial of pluralism and the theological debt we owe our older spiritual sibling. Any form of anti-Judaism or Christian supersession must be repudiated by process and open and relational Christians.

Healthy Christianity of the future, from the perspective of process and openness theology's centered pluralism, must affirm the heartbeat of Judaism with the same appreciation and gratitude that we embrace the heart of our own faith. We are kin: the same spiritual DNA defines both of us. To deny our sibling is to deny ourselves. We must recognize the unique paths each faith has taken historically, our diverse interpretations of scripture and the Messianic age, and the saving power and illuminating wisdom of each tradition.

Siblings have different gifts and visions and often different spiritual and vocational goals. There is enough wisdom and truth to go around. Both siblings can be honored in their uniqueness. There are many facets to the running elephant, and in dialogue, we can learn and grow spiritually from each other. Just as European Americans must recognize the impact of white privilege on their lives and confess our unintentional complicity in racial injustice, Christians must do the hard work of confessing our faith's darkest hours reflected in attempts to exterminate Judaism spiritually, theologically, and existentially. We must give thanks for our Jewish past and reach out as receivers and givers of wisdom in the future. Our goal must be healing and reconciliation, and partnership and affirmation. We must now see ourselves as equal companions in working together toward God's vision of healing the earth (*tikkun 'olam*).

My dear friend and colleague at Georgetown University Rabbi Harold White often affirmed that Christianity was Judaism for the world. He saw Christianity as going beyond ethnic identity and the holy land to share the deepest insights of Judaism with the world. Rabbi White did not intend to suggest Judaism and Christianity are alike, or that Christian truth is restricted to or has superseded the Jewish tradition.

He meant to affirm the unique, though complementary, gifts of each faith in God's quest for *tikkun 'olam,* healing the earth. Still, despite the ongoing evolution of Christianity and innovative traditions beyond the people of Israel, the spiritual DNA of Christianity is profoundly Jewish. Or, more accurately, Christian spirituality results from a mixed marriage – an interfaith marriage - between Jewish spirituality and Greek wisdom. Like the results of genetic ancestry tests, Christianity today bears the spiritual and theological heritage of Jerusalem as well as Rome, Athens, Damascus, and Alexandria, and our unfolding future will always include Israel as well as the Northern and Southern hemispheres.

THE HEART OF JUDAISM

Just as there is no definitive Christianity, there is no one definitive Judaism. Like Christianity, Judaism is a multi-dimensional religion that cannot be reduced to a handful of doctrines or practices. Moreover, as was the case with my reflections on the heart of Christianity, I do not assume that the affirmations I present are all-inclusive. I must exercise the same humility I bring to Judaism that I bring to the many Christian movements. As a process and open and relational theologian, I recognize that Ultimate Reality can be experienced in many ways and that the Ultimate itself may shift its emphases to address different dimensions of history and human life. My affirmations reflect my experience of the pulse of Christianity's older sibling, grounded in its primary affirmation, the *Shema Yisrael,* "Hear, O Israel, God our Lord, is One." (Deuteronomy 6:4; see 6:4-9) God is one and our calling is to "love the Lord your God with all your heart, and with all your mind, and with all your soul." To follow this affirmation means that loving the One God permeates and orients our whole life. We are to teach our children about God's universality and intimacy; God's uniqueness and ultimacy; and God's transcendence and immanence. Judaism's radical monotheism serves as the foundation for its theology, spirituality, ethics, and politics. Dare we say that it is equally foundational for Christian theology, ethics, spirituality, and politics? The galaxies may number into the trillions, but it is one Loving and Wise, Lawful, Creative, and Personal Energy that enlivens and guides all of them.

My vision of the dynamic pulse of Judaism flows through the following twelve affirmations of faith. Many of these affirmations are also central to Christian theology, spirituality, and self-understanding.

- *The One God is creative, compassionate, and personal.* We live in a personal and moral universe. God seeks justice, and God's quest for justice is defined by mercy. Divine law, God's presence in history, the embodiment of God's will, both personal and political, is moral in nature. God seeks goodness in the ordering of the universe and in the affairs of humankind. The ever-faithful God's mercies are new every morning. God provides a way where there is no way. As personally involved in history, God hears the cries of the poor and responds with acts of deliverance, mediated through nature and human leadership. God's intimate covenantal love for Israel, chosen by grace alone, radiates outward to embrace the whole earth and its peoples.

- *Creation bears witness to divine wisdom.* The Genesis 1-2 creation stories reveal divine wisdom at work in the universe. They are not scientific accounts but reflect the poetry of Loving Creativity. God looks upon creation and pronounces it "good" in its emergence of order and beauty out of what would otherwise be chaotic. The world is good and reveals divine handiwork. Human spirituality immerses us in God's earthy artistry. Our cells and souls witness to the Poet of the Universe. The whole earth is full of God's glory, and in response to God's blessings, everything that breathes deep down praises God.

- *Value of non-human world.* The poetic cosmology of Genesis 1-2 as well as Psalm 148 testifies to the goodness of the non-human world in its variety and abundance long before humans come on the scene. The "days" of creation prior to the emergence of humankind are affirmed as "good" in God's eyes. The non-human world has value for its own sake and not just as the material for human fabrication. Nature praises God along with devout humans. The heavens declare God's glory, and so do sea monsters, winged creatures, and beasts of the field.

- *History emerges from interplay of the divine call and human response.* History is dynamic and relational, reflecting God's call to growth and morality in our personal and communal life. The great figures of the Hebraic tradition walked with God as an intimate companion. Called by God, they responded out of freedom, shaping God's vision in their unique way by following, personalizing, and at times turning away, thus creating new pathways of fidelity and eliciting novel divine responses. God calls nations, and Israel's response to spiritual, political, and prophetic leaders such as Moses, Isaiah, and Amos determines the nation's future and the next manifestations of divine providence and creativity. God's covenant with Israel reflects God's merciful choice of a small and often wayward people. The contours of the covenant reflect the quality of Israel's relationship with God.

- *The significance of personhood.* Responsiveness to God has its origins in the divine image in humankind. All humankind, in its variety, reflects God's character. While the scriptures are vague about the nature of God's image in humankind, they recognize that this image inspires creativity, responsibility, relationship, and the affirmation of each person's value. Just as God has a vision, so does every human being. Just as God makes plans for history, we are challenged to make plans and embody them in our time and place. Just as God relates to us, so we relate to one another, the non-human world, and our Creator.

The importance of personhood inspires agency and relationship. History and innovation emerge from the divine-human call and response. While God may act dramatically in the historical process, humankind is responsible for the unfolding of communities and nations. God calls forth leaders in the spiritual and political realm whose vocation is to inspire partnership with God's vision for "just such a time as this." Long before Teresa of Avila, the Jewish people knew that we are the hands and feet of God. God's vision of Shalom requires our companionship in embodying God's dream through acts of justice, mercy, and ingenuity.

Jewish mystics assert that we are creatures of eternity whose calling is to heal creation one action at a time. According to the Kabbalah, when we save one soul, we save the world. Moreover, each healing act saves the world, and enables the separate sparks of light hidden in all things to come together in the harmonious unity intended by God in creation. The Baal Shem Tov, the Master of a Good Name, who founded the Hasidic tradition, believed that every action, even the most menial and ordinary, can be dedicated to God. "Man's service with [liberating] the sparks takes place in everyday life; man can perform it in everything he does, even in the most profane bodily acts… for even the most profane deed can be done in holiness, and whoever performs it in holiness raises up the sparks. Man can serve Him in all his deeds, and He wills that man shall serve him in all. For this it is written: 'In all thy ways thou shalt know him.'"[7]

- *The significance of earthly life.* Earth matters! Judaism calls us to be earthly good rather than heavenly minded. Earth is the theatre of divine glory and human creativity. Leaving a witness, being a "good ancestor," living on in children and grandchildren and our impact on the community is the heartbeat of spirituality. This is the day that God has made. This moment is the time of healing and salvation. No far-off heaven calls. Eternity is lived in the maelstrom of politics and family life. Heaven can wait! We can live fully and abundantly in this lifetime, investing our hopes in this earth. Any heavenly hope is grounded in justice in this lifetime, the impact of our descendants and their memory of us, and the immortality of community, not individual fulfillment. "Anyone who loves God, while hating or despising his creation, will in the end hate God."[8]

- *Providence and vocation.* Earth matters and history is meaningful. God is present in the horizons of history, the movement of galaxies, and the everyday affairs of life. God moves the historical process forward toward the realm of Shalom. Divine providence can be perceived as compelling, but it never eliminates human decision-making. Abraham and Sarah, Samuel, and Isaiah had the freedom to say "no" to God's call. When God asks the angelic hosts, "Whom will I send?" the answer is not predetermined, but up to God's human companions. Saying "yes" to providence alerts us to our vocation, whether we are Sarah contemplating a pilgrimage to a new land, Ruth choosing to return to Bethlehem with Naomi, Esther taking agency to save her people in just such a time as this, or Isaiah overwhelmed by a mystic-prophetic vision. In the aftermath of the Holocaust, many Jewish theologians see providence and vocation as open-ended, sometimes fragile, and often delayed or even denied by human decisions. They recognize that God must contend with diabolical and wayward human decision-making that can go against and

---

7. Martin Buber, *Hasidism* (New York: Philosophical Library, 1948), 56.
8. Elie Weisel, *Souls on Fire: Patriarchs and Legends of Hasidic Masters* (New York: Summit Books, 1972), 32.

undermine God's vision. Still, God persists. God is still speaking, and when we hear the divine whisper and respond affirmatively, we set out on a never-ending adventure of sharing God's vision of repairing the world.

God's providence is transpersonal. People are chosen to be God's revealers and God's prophets to the nation. God also chooses communities, including the children of Abraham, to play unique roles in history. Israel is a "chosen people," called out as children of the wandering "Aramean" Abraham and Sarah, from bondage to freedom and then to be a focal point in history, a light to the nations.

God's providence includes what the Celts called "thin places," where heaven and earth meet. God appoints for Israel a promised land, first as the destination of Abraham and Sarah, then as the home after the exodus from Egypt, and ultimately in our time as the nation of Israel, a place of safety and flourishing in the wake of the Holocaust. The "thin place" of Israel, in prophetic religion, challenges the Jewish people to see their chosen status as global by making the Temple and the nation a home for the spirituality of all peoples. (Isaiah 56:7)

- *Cosmic and human law.* The heavens above, the seasons below, communities and the human heart are also shaped by divine law. In the Mishneh Torah, Maimonides or Rambam, a medieval rabbi, lists 613 mitzvot, or commandments. I recall my dear friend Rabbi Harold Saul White once noted that his grandmother referred to these as 613 ways to worship God. Certain Christians know the Ten Commandments and often have a dim view of the Pharisaic legalism described in the New Testament. While religious law, enforced in any religion, can be inflexible and enforced in ways that limit human possibility and promote injustice, law also shapes persons and communities in accordance with Divine Purpose. Pharisaic law was necessary in Jesus' time to preserve Jewish identity in the face of Roman military occupation. It was also necessary for Jesus to challenge, in the spirit of the Hebraic prophets, legalism that gets in the way of human wellbeing and marginalizes those deemed outsiders.

Still, law serves a positive function: just as planetary law guides seasons, summer and winter, and seedtime and harvest, human law guides relationships and governments, protects the vulnerable, and promotes harmony and justice. Divine law is implanted in the human spirit, and when we align ourselves with God's law in human relationships, our spirits and communities will flourish.

While law may appear to be imposed from without, the laws of God promote what Paul Tillich calls "theonomous" existence, the unity of divine and human will that promotes creative and life-affirming freedom. It is evident that our transgressions of God's purposes have led to the destruction of the environment, income inequality and food insecurity, racism, and sexism, all of which put body, mind, spirit, and community at risk.

- *The ambiguity of life.* Rabbi Simcha Bunim of Peshischa asserts that every person should have the following messages placed in their pockets. In one pocket, a note should proclaim, "for you the universe was created." The other should warn, "you are dust and to dust you will return." Life is ambiguous. There is a snake in paradise. The first couple's sin gives birth to civilization. Humans build a tower to heaven only to have it collapse and be scattered across the earth, divided by culture and language. Great achievements hide perils. Suffering gives birth to character and wisdom. Sin is real, but grace abounds. Humans turn from God's ways and God sends prophets to call them back to their destiny as God's beloved. History is the dynamic process of gain and loss, justice and greed, and achievement and threat. Yet, in all the ambiguities of life, God's providential love calls humans forward, reminding us of our mortality and insignificance, and alerting us to our divine identity and destiny.

- *Prophetic justice.* Within the ambiguities of history, God inspires certain individuals to speak for God's vision of Shalom. Prophets encounter God and discover their vocation to call humankind back to its divine purposes. Prophets experience the "divine pathos," the suffering of God, as Rabbi Abraham Joshua Heschel affirms. God hears the cries of the poor, feels the pain of the vulnerable, and calls humankind to live in accordance with God's Shalom. Heschel asserts that God exists "in a personal and intimate relationship with the world. He does not simply command and expect obedience; He is also affected by what happens in the world and reacts accordingly. Events and human actions arouse in Him joy and sorrow, pleasure or wrath… the notion that God can be intimately affected, that he possesses not merely intelligence and will, but also pathos, basically defines the prophetic consciousness of God."[9] The prophet imagines an alternative future to the world of oppression and injustice, as Christian scholar Walter Brueggemann affirms.

- *The Absence of God.* The Hebraic scriptures, or the First/Old Testament, present human experience in its many, and often contrasting, dimensions. We live in a glorious God-filled world, and yet God appears hidden and our foes appear victorious. We read Psalms of joy, "Make a joyful noise to the Lord, all the earth. Worship the Lord with gladness; come into his presence with singing" (Psalm 100:1-2) and we also ask, "My God, My God, why have you forsaken me?" The brightness of the "heavens telling the glory of God" (Psalm 19:1) finds its counterpoint in the dark night of the soul, "How long, Lord? Will you forget me forever? How long will you hide your face from me? How long must I wrestle with my thoughts and day after day have sorrow in my heart? How long will my enemy triumph over me?… How long will you hide from me?" (Psalm 13:1-2; 10:1)

Elie Wiesel captures the spirit of divine absence, describing his Holocaust crisis of faith, as he watches three fellow prisoners, including a young boy being hung by the Gestapo:

Behind me, I heard the same man asking, "Where is God now?"

And I heard a voice within me answer him, "Where is He? Here He is. He is hanging on the gallows…"[10]

Authentic faith includes pain as well as joy, absence as well as presence, mourning as well as celebrating, anger as well as equanimity. Honesty in religion embraces the totality of our emotional and relational life, and for those who choose, sharing the whole of our lives with "the fellow sufferer who understands."[11]

9. Abraham Joshua Heschel, *The Prophets, Volume 2* (Peabody, MA: Hendrickson Publishers, 2014), 3-4.
10. Elie Weisel, *Night* (New York: Avon Books, 1971), 76.
11. Whitehead, *Process and Reality: Corrected Edition* (New York: Free Press, 1978), 351.

- *The goal of history: Shalom.* All history stands under the judgment of God. The spiritual and moral arcs of history turn our attention to the contrast between God's vision of Shalom and the realities of personal and communal life. Whether described as the Messianic Age or the Realm of God, the incompleteness and waywardness of history aims toward wholeness. We look for a time when every tear is dried and the laughter of children fills the streets, when swords are beaten into plowshares and nations forsake war-making, and when everyone can experience abundant life. Human existence finds its meaning in the quest for justice. Humankind's vocation is companionship with God in *tikkun 'olam,* the repairing or healing of the earth.

A RABBI'S REFLECTION

Through the amazing miracle of digital interdependence, Rabbi Bradley Shavit Artson ("Brad"), and I met cross-country on Zoom: Rabbi Artson, from his study in Los Angeles, and I, on my patio on Cape Cod. Rabbi Artson is the Vice President and Abner and Roslyn Goldstine Dean's Chair at the American Jewish University. I had been acquainted with Rabbi Artson through his writing, most particularly his *God of Becoming and Relationship: The Dynamic Nature of Process Theology.* Our conversation began with the controversial topic of what it means to be "chosen" by God, and his understanding of what it means for the Jewish people to be called God's chosen people. In contrast to those who see being chosen by God as a special metaphysical category, as an abstraction unrelated to history, Rabbi Artson sees Jewish chosenness as concrete and relational. We can't speak of being chosen apart from reflecting on the scope of revelation. According to Rabbi Artson, the universe is "relationship-in-process… ongoing, relational, dynamic, and continuous."[12] Chosenness occurs in real time with real relationships. God chooses Israel and Israel chooses God. "Chosen is a state of being. We don't say others aren't chosen. Chosen is shorthand for 'chosen for what?'" Rabbi Artson asserted. Moreover, "there is no one way of being chosen. We are all relationally different in terms of our vocation and relationship with God." While Rabbi Artson denies that Judaism has a clear abstract and timeless "essence" about which all Jews agree, he avers that in the concreteness of life, "Jews have been 'chosen' to

12. Bradley Shavit Artson, *God of Becoming and Relationship: The Dynamic Nature of Process Theology* (Nashville: Jewish Lights, 2016), 101.

be exemplars of covenant in community." Chosenness is not exclusive: "Other peoples are chosen and choose their own paths to holiness and righteousness."[13]

According to Rabbi Artson, Judaism is not defined by a set of doctrines. Doctrines are secondary and derivative in the Jewish tradition. "Judaism is a way of life and wisdom tradition, an encounter with God that spills out into the world." In the spirit of process theology, Rabbi Artson challenges religious essentialism, preferring to see Judaism and other religious traditions as concrete, organic, lively, and changing movements. Recognizing the tendency of words to freeze reality into timeless abstractions, Rabbi Artson notes that while Judaism is not creedal, its contours can be described in terms of "believing in God, who enters into covenant through commandments. 'Do the commandments,' is God's challenge to humankind."

Augustine was said "it will be solved in the walking." The same applies to Judaism, according to Rabbi Artson. "These strings of sacred deeds, mitzvot, are given coherence and life by a process known as *halakhah,* which literally means 'walking,' or the way. Often translated as "law," it is far different from some brittle set of rules or a nitpicking obsession with detail. *Halakhah,* the Way, is communal choreography—Jews cavorting in a dance across the generations and around the globe. Our *halakhah* roots us in the ways our ancestors and sages have implemented Torah in every aspect of our lives, communal and individual. By molding our behavior to express Torah, we Jews take on the role of God's hands, reaching out to bring healing to the world, of God's breath, inspiring gratitude that allows us all to breathe in the giftedness of life and to share it with each other... Jews (from the word for Judaeans - people of Judah) are always on the way, always in process. There is no place to live in stasis, no way to be complete while alive."[14]

The Jewish tradition is profoundly processive. According to Rabbi Artson, Judaism is "an ongoing conversation. Within the Talmud, there are 5,000 debates, but only 50 are resolved! The energy is in the questioning and the answers we discover along the way." In the concreteness of the spiritual journey, "loving relationships are central. Judaism is relational, not doctrinal. It involves a complex fabric of relationships and behaviors that shape identity." The beating heart of Judaism is "telling stories and doing things together."

13. Ibid., 105.
14. The Theology of Rabbi Bradley Shavit Artson: A Video - Open Horizons

I came away from our conversation, realizing that perhaps God is the ultimate companion and storyteller, moving through our lives in inspirational ways, sharing guidance, and challenging us to love one another. Life is a call and response, in which God calls and we respond, eliciting a new divine response. Catechisms mean nothing if we are estranged from each other. Loving relationships, as Jesus and the Hebraic prophetic tradition affirmed, give life and hope to our beliefs, and inspire us to companionship with one another in healing the world.

WHAT CHRISTIANS CAN LEARN FROM JUDAISM

Healthy sibling relationships involve dynamic give and take. The wisdom of the elder is imparted to the younger. The younger goes to places the elder never imagined. To paraphrase a book by Alfred North Whitehead, religions are always "in the making," embracing, learning, and growing in relationship with each other as they share their unique emphases.

As a process theologian, I feel a great kinship with the Jewish spiritual tradition. The dynamic, relational, historical God who seeks Shalom for persons and communities is at the heart process and openness theology. Process theologians affirm the prophetic vision of social justice as well as the recognition that while all creation is "chosen" by God, and although each place is a "thin place," transparent to divinity, some places and situations are more reflective of God's vision than others. We can both claim greater spiritual depth in the give-and-take of theological conversation.

The goodness of the earth.

Christianity is the child of the mixed marriage of Jerusalem and Athens. From Jerusalem comes incarnational living, focus on embodiment, this-worldly justice-seeking, and Jesus' healing ministry. From Athens arises focus on the eternal verities of life and hope for personal immortality. Often, Christianity has been overly interested in the afterlife. For certain Christians, this world has been perceived as the front porch of eternity. "This world is not my home. I'm just passing through." To some Christians, the act of "accepting Jesus as your personal savior" is their ticket to heavenly bliss, and nothing more is required for salvation than a confession of faith or participation in the sacraments. Often, this-worldly justice has been sacrificed for the reward of eternal bliss. At best, the vision of everlasting life gives us hope for the future. At worst, this is the opiate of the masses, in which persons are encouraged to live with injustice by kings and religious leaders in this lifetime to prepare for the afterlife. While not denying the afterlife, Judaism reminds us to embrace one world at a time. Our relationship with God is known by the quality of our earthly relationships. As philosopher Martin Buber notes, "Hasidism teaches that rejoicing in the world, if we hallow it, leads to rejoicing in God… Any natural act, if hallowed, leads to God and nature needs man for what no angel can perform on it, namely, its hallowing."[15] Our commitment to being God's companions in healing the world gives birth to the prophetic spirit and social gospel.

The Necessity of Lamentation.

The Hebraic scriptures, or the First/Old Testament, present human experience in its many, and often contrasting, dimensions. We rejoice and we also lament. Healthy faith embraces the totality of experience just as God embraces the totality of creation. In February 2020, life was predictable. When they first heard of COVID-19, most persons in the USA expected life to go on as usual. We didn't expect our lives to be disrupted, as they were beginning to be in Asia and Europe. We felt immune to economic and social collapse. Now, nearly two years later, as I write these words, we live in hope for a new normal, but we are burdened by grief and loss. We are disillusioned at our nation's ineffectiveness and a former president's refusal to mount a serious response to the pandemic in the first months of the pandemic. Some lived in fear, while others lashed out violently, denying science and their responsibility to others, seeing mask wearing as an undue burden and a limit on their precious freedom. Now, as I write in January 2022, nearly two years after the first shutdown, over 800,000 have died in the United States and the numbers are still rising, and millions remain food and house insecure. With the coming of vaccines, we think we see the light at the end of the tunnel, yet we suspect that globally and nationally thousands of deaths still lie ahead of us, and we are troubled that in some quarters political machinations and intentional falsehoods have eclipsed scientific thinking. In such situations of disillusionment and despair, grief and anguish, Judaism affirms the power of lament. To heal, we need to feel our pain, we need to be empathetic toward others, we need our hearts to break at the tremendous losses our nation has experienced. We need to be disillusioned, to let go of our illusions of American exceptionalism and immunity. Lament is

---

15. Martin Buber, *The Theology of Man According to the Teaching of Hasidism* (New York: Citadel Press, 1966), 14, 20.

painful. Yet, without facing lamentation, we may not be able to change our path and to respond to the pain of persons today and prevent future pain due to our unpreparedness and injustice in resource allocation. Judaism tells Christians that slogans like "God is in control" or "Praise the Lord anyway" are hollow and spiritually dangerous if we fail to accept the darkness and tragedy of life. Lamentation reminds us, as do Biblical history and the Cross of Jesus, that God is not fully in control. God cannot determine every outcome. God needs our help to heal the world. God needs our efforts as companions in addressing injustice and disease. Out of lamentation comes a sense of responsibility, to play our role in tipping the balance of life toward the arc of justice and spiritual transformation.

Prophetic restlessness.

Affirmation of the goodness of the earth and God's presence in history, in juxtaposition with the reality of suffering, often the result of political and economic policies, inspires prophetic restlessness and challenge to social injustice. In light of God's vision of Shalom, we must challenge anything that stands in the way of our siblings' experiencing abundant life. We can yearn for everlasting life, seek equanimity in our spiritual lives, and yet be passionate about social transformation. The social gospel is not an appendage to spiritual maturity but the heart of a fully committed and intimate relationship with God. In the spirit of the prophets, our relationship to the Jewish prophet and healer Jesus sensitizes us to the pain of the world and turns us from abstract eternity to experience divinity in the cries of the poor, the destruction of non-human species, and denial of human rights. To be a Christian, faithful to Biblical spirituality, we need to reclaim the prophetic vision of Shalom and affirm that as we have done unto the least of these, we have done unto God.

CHRISTIANITY'S GIFT TO JUDAISM

Christianity and Judaism need to meet, like all siblings, on common ground: sharing wisdom with one another, learning from one another, forgiving and accepting forgiveness, giving and receiving in good faith with no need to change the other, and growing toward God's dream of Shalom. The most definitive Christian affirmation, the incarnation of Jesus, builds on the Jewish vision of God's good creation and, beyond that, recognizes the holiness of each moment. Each moment is God-filled, embodying God's love, and calling us to love one another. The incarnation reminds us that love and grace are at the heart of God's relationship to the world. God's love overcomes all alienation and opens the door for each moment, becoming a "thin place," where heaven and earth permeate one another. Justice is real. Ethical and relational waywardness has consequences for persons and nations. Still, the final word is grace, and grace is definitive of Christianity at its best—not grace for some, but grace for all, since all of us participate in the waywardness and wonder, the tragic beauty, of humankind. In all things, God is working for good. The ongoing divine-human call and response is personal, situational, and global. God not only creates the world; God responds to the world, adapting to our decisions. God's love overcomes human waywardness and constantly enables us to begin again and again. Now is always the time of salvation. Jewish spirituality and Christian process theology join in affirming that God needs our efforts to heal the world. We are, as Teresa of Avila counsels, the hands and feet of God.

A JEWISH SPIRITUAL PRACTICE

Words matter. Words reveal the wise and loving energy of the universe. God's *dabhar*, creative word, energizes and enlivens all creation and every person. As the *Shema Yisrael* proclaims:

Hear, O Israel: The Lord is our God, the Lord alone. You shall love the Lord your God with all your heart, and with all your soul, and with all your might. Keep these words that I am commanding you today in your heart. Recite them to your children and talk about them when you are at home and when you are away, when you lie down and when you rise. Bind them as a sign on your hand, fix them as an emblem on your forehead and write them on the doorposts of your house and on your gates. (Deuteronomy 6:4-9)

Jewish spirituality invites us to repeat the words of God's name throughout the day as a type of mantra to deepen and focus our faith, a way of moving from the surface to the depths of life and infusing every moment with God's presence. Christians can repeat throughout the day words like: "God," "Christ," "Adonai," "Yahweh." These words are more than a talisman or calming influence; they also connect us with the Living Word, which inspires, energizes, and protects, and gives us confidence in the long road to justice.

CHAPTER FIVE

Zoroastrianism/Zarathushtrian Religion

American philosopher and pioneering psychologist William James described the quest for justice and peace as "the moral equivalent of war." James believed that our inner spiritual battles and our quest for justice were more demanding and more essential for human survival than our external military victories. Twenty-five hundred years earlier in Persia, today's Iran, the prophet and spiritual guide, Zarathustra (Zoroaster, in Greek) proclaimed that history and human life is a battle between good and evil and light and darkness. Although Zoroastrianism (from the Greek translation of the religious tradition of Zarathustra) or Zarathushtrian/ Zarathushti faith, has fewer than 200,000 adherents today, 10,000 of which are in the United States and Canada, we can discern the impact of Zoroastrianism on the formation Judaism, Christianity, and Greek philosophy through the impact of its cosmological and ethical vision emphasizing the ongoing fight between good and evil, light and darkness, the reality of divine judgment, postmortem paradise and punishment, angelic and demonic beings, and the final (eschatological) victory of good over evil.[16] The exact origins of Zoroastrianism are in doubt. Some sacred texts date to 1500-1000 BCE, contemporary with the Rig Veda, the primordial scriptures of Hinduism. Even the date of Zarathustra's life is a matter of

---

16. Zoroastrianism is also known as Mazdaism, based on the ultimate deity, Ahura Mazda.

controversy, ranging from prior to 1000 BCE to the axial age of religious transformation, seventh and sixth centuries BCE.

Little is known about the prophet Zarathustra (Zarathushtra), whose name means Golden Light. Zoroastrians describe his birth as miraculous, like that of Jesus and Buddha, and his childhood as extraordinary. He was from childhood a God seeker, for whom the veil between divine and human was transparent. As a young adult, he challenged the practices of the Iranian religion in which he was raised: polytheism, animal sacrifice, excessive clerical power and affluence, and religious superstition.

Zarathustra's quest for God was both intellectual and contemplative. Similar in spirit to the intellectual quest for the divine in Hinduism's Jnana yoga, Zarathustra found God's presence in observing the cosmological and moral order of the universe. Zarathustra came to believe that all life has its origin in the Dynamic Creativity of the One God, whose wisdom and intelligence is present in all creation. His contemplations led him to experience God in terms of God's attributes as the voice of conscience, the moral order of the universe evident in the heavens above and the human spirit. The One God Ahura Mazda, aware of his spiritual dedication, supplied Zarathustra with life-changing glimpses of divinity in the world of creation and human life, and called him to be a prophet, speaking on behalf of the Creator. Zarathustra discerned these divine attributes in his life and embedded in human existence and shared a path of human holiness and ethical integrity in Iran for the remainder of his life. Zarathustra was a spiritual teacher and a prophet, challenging injustice and religious privilege. While praying in his oratory, Zarathustra was slain at age 77, by an enemy of the movement, 47 years after his first direct experience of God's attributes.

In the spirit of the Hebraic prophets, Zoroaster experienced God's wisdom speaking through his moral experience, inspiring him to challenge the religion and ethics of the indigenous Iranian religions. The orderly motions of the heavens, reflective of the world's soul, were mirrored in the inner ordering of the human soul. The light of God shined in all persons, but most especially in the lives of the righteous ones, those who followed the way of life and light. In aligning ourselves with God's moral order, we become God's emissaries and co-creators in bringing harmony and peace to the world, confronting evil in ourselves and in the historical process. Zoroastrian mysticism is ethical and prophetic, and involves becoming as divine as possible in mortal life, through embodying, in our thoughts and actions,

God's attributes of wisdom, justice, mercy, and goodness. We advance God's cause in the world through worship and ethical action.

While once Zoroastrianism was the primary religion of Iran, the religions of the Greek, Christian, and Islamic invaders eventually displaced it from its birthplace. Today, the majority of the Zarathustra's followers live in India, with small communities in Iran, Europe, and North America. Despite its numerical insignificance, the teachings of Zarathustra and his followers with its arduous pathway to wholeness and its focus on personal responsibility is an appropriate counterbalance to the "cheap grace," practiced by many Christians, whose vision of salvation focuses on what we have received from God rather than on our responsibility to incarnate divine mercy and justice in daily life and political involvement.

Compared to New Testament theology and spirituality, Zarathustra's faith most resembles the spirituality of the Letter of James, "faith without works is dead." Spirituality is lived out in our daily integrity, generosity, fidelity, and compassion. To both James and Zarathustra, our salvation or spiritual wholeness depends largely on what we do in our daily battle against the powers of evil, not just on what God does for us apart from our efforts. Some scholars believe that the images of light and darkness in the Prologue of John's Gospel (John 1:1-14) find their origins in Zoroastrian cosmology and ethics.

Zoroastrianism impacted Christianity by its affirmations of the existence of angels and demons, the ongoing conflict between good and evil, post-mortem judgment, heaven and hell, and the final battle to end human history. Zoroastrianism or Zarathushti faith surfaces each Christmas with the story of the Magi. The coming of the Magi, most likely followers of Zarathustra, is at the heart of our stories of Jesus' birth. Following a star, they sought to honor the light of the world in its battle against the forces of darkness. (Matthew 2:1-18) Today, the light of Zarathustrianism still shines, radiating from India and Iran to illuminate the whole globe.

THE ETHICAL FAITH OF ZOROASTRIANISM/
ZARATHUSHTI FAITH

Zoroastrianism, referred also as Zarathushti faith by many of its adherents, proclaims a strenuous ethical faith, grounded in its vision of God, the Giver of Light, in whom no darkness dwells. God's perfection is the source of all goodness, beauty, order, and intelligence in the universe. The created universe is good, but possesses the polarities of light and darkness, health and illness, and good and evil, whose interactions lead to conflict in our lives in the historical process. Evil comes from choices in the creaturely world that lead us from light to darkness. The reality and impact of moral evil emerges from the decisions of demonic beings, as well as humans, acting freely in defiance of divine order and righteousness. The ethical faith of Zarathustra can be described by the following principles:

- *The Unity and Universality of God.* Ahura Mazda, the Ultimate Reality and Supreme Wisdom, is one, creative and dynamic in nature, parenting all creation. God is universal, manifesting God's attributes in all creation. Zarathustra rejoices in God's being: "Not only did I conceive Thee, O Mazda/ as the very first and last/As the Most Adorable One/As the Father of the Good Thought/As the Creator of the Eternal law of Truth and Right/Of the Lord Judge of our actions in Life."[17] God's light dwells within all creation as its deepest reality and the goal of its existence. Divine creativity is constantly active not only in the emergence of the universe but also in the ongoing historical process. Divine wisdom and creativity give birth to the soul of the universe, bestowing value and beauty on the human and non-human world. All reality emanates from the All Good Creator, whose words and actions are just and holy, without moral ambiguity. Among God's creations is the world of polarity: there is the angelic world, aligned with God's vision "on earth as it is in heaven," and the demonic realm, whose existence is grounded in the binary nature of life. God does not create evil, but like Judaism, Christianity, and Islam, Zoroastrianism affirms that nothing, not even the demonic, can exist apart from God's universal creativity. There is ultimately no "other" coequal to or independent of God, but rather beings who have

---

17. Farhang Mehr, *The Zoroastrian Tradition* (Costa Mesa, CA: Mazda Publishers, 2003), 30.

the freedom to go against God's vision, bringing forth chaos and destruction, rather than creativity and joy.

- *Ongoing Creation.* Creation is dynamic and continuous in nature. Reflecting God's creative wisdom, cosmic and human history involves the interplay of divine order and human action, aiming at the final victory of God's light. Although God's victory is ultimately assured, cosmic and human history is a battlefield in which the followers of good and evil, whether humans and angels, or faithful demigods, and evil demons, contend with one another. We participate in the moral evolution of the universe by practicing good thoughts, words, and acts for the benefit of all. Our moral acts and ritual sacrifices enhance the embodiment of Ahura Mazda's way in our lives and in the world. Similar to the image of divine-human call and response of process-relational and openness theology, Zoroastrians believe that our choices can accelerate or delay the embodiment of God's vision, the moral arc of history.

- *The Moral Order of the Universe.* God has embedded a moral order within the cosmic and historical process. Ahura Mazda, the Ultimate Reality, seeks to create order in all things. The divine law, Asha, is inherent in our nature, the universe, and non-human life. We know the good, and yet may be led astray by demonic forces as well as by the devices and desires of our hearts. Still, as Theodore Parker was to claim in the quest to abolish slavery, the moral arc of the universe aims toward justice. Humans are not passive in the historical process. According to Zoroastrianism, we are, in many ways, God's moral agents in seeking justice and order in our personal relationships and community responsibilities. We have a responsibility to take care of the planet, not just human affairs. The non-human world's well-being depends on our choices. We are world-shapers, co-creators with God, playing our role in healing or destroying the planet. In the quest for personal and global righteousness, followers of Zarathustra are commanded to treat the non-human world with respect. God's creations are good and orderly, deserving of our respect and protection. Accordingly, Zoroastrianism is often touted as the first ecologically sensitive religious tradition.

- *The Angelic and Demonic.* While God is not the origin of evil and suffering, the world of time and space is a battleground between the forces of good and evil. Within cosmic history, there are polar realities that lean toward God's goodness and order, or toward personal and cosmic disorder. Zoroastrianism has been described as the integration of theological monotheism and ethical dualism. God is one, and yet good and evil contest each other throughout history. Within the created universe, there is a "great chain of being," which includes angelic and demonic beings, humans, and the non-human world. These angelic and demonic entities constantly struggle with one another to gain the upper hand in history and will be at war with one another until the Final Battle in which good triumphs over evil.

  The origin of the demonic is unclear in a universe created by an unambiguously good deity. The emergence of the demonic appears to reflect the polar nature of reality, existing at every level of the universe and revealed in the binary division of light and darkness, male and female, birth and death, creation and destruction, and youth and age. Our calling in the contest of light and darkness, good and evil, is to promote God's cause, grounded in the recognition that our actions tip the balance toward the victory of God's light in the world.

- *Law of Consequences.* Biblical wisdom affirms that as we sow, so shall we reap in this life and the next. (Ephesians 6:8) Buddhism and Hinduism speak of the inexorability of ethical cause and effect in terms of karma that shapes our current life, grounded in previous incarnations, and conditioning our future incarnations. Perhaps influenced by the binary morality of Zoroastrianism, Islam speaks of a post-mortem judgment: souls weighed in the balance, tipping toward good or evil, and bliss or punishment. Zoroastrianism affirms the significance of every decision. Every choice brings us closer to, or further from, divine order. Our choices shape our character and the lives of our communities. Nothing is lost in terms of our present experience and future destiny. God is light and we approximate God's light by dedicating our lives to God. Acts of kindness, fidelity, and sacrifice to God lighten the soul's burdens, while brutality, infidelity, self-interest, and allegiance to the demonic pollute our souls, weighing them down, preventing us from fellowship with God. Like Zoroastrianism, process and openness theology recognizes our role in creating our destiny: the embodiment of God's vision of possibility is contingent on our willingness to follow God's way. Process and openness theology affirms the universal aim toward wholeness and the role of humankind in advancing or stalling the moral and spiritual arcs of history. While God's vision is ongoing and ultimately victorious, God needs our companionship in bringing forth God's realm on earth.

- *Afterlife.* Followers of Zoroaster believe in both resurrection and the contrast of blissful and painful afterlives. In the wake of our physical death is the "last judgment," in which we face the consequences of our actions. There is a moral continuity between this life and the next. One life leads to one death, one judgment, and one eternity, experienced in either a heavenly or hellish environment. We cannot escape the outcome of our actions, which follow us as sure as night follows day, or age follows youth. According to Zoroastrianism, bliss or damnation await us, depending on the quality of our decision-making, and whether we followed the better or evil angels of history. Despite the necessity of spiritual purification, heaven is our destination, and companionship with God is our ultimate goal. At the end of history, all souls, righteous and unrighteous, will be resurrected, purified of their sins, and able to participate in the final victory of Ahura Mazda.

- *Eschatology.* The battle between light and darkness, good and evil, and order and chaos goes on throughout history. The moral arc, embedded by God in history, leans toward justice, and inspires God-oriented angels and humans. Eventually, cosmic and planetary history achieve their resolution in the victory of good over evil. The Zoroastrian imagery of the final battle of good and evil served as a template for emerging apocalyptic, or end of the world, imagery in the Hebraic scriptures and New Testament book of Revelation. God's ultimate victory is assured, but in the meantime, we must fulfill our role as God's co-creators in the historical process. Zoroastrian eschatology speaks of the culmination of history as a time of earthly refreshment. Eventually all souls, after their rehabilitation and refining, will experience the fullness of life on a transformed earth.

CONVERSATION WITH A ZARATHUSHTI

In my quest to dialogue with a follower of Zarathustra, my first thought was to reach out to my former student and congregant at Georgetown University, Gregory Han, a Presbyterian (PCUSA) minister who served at the time as Director of Interfaith Relations and Education for the Interfaith Ministries of Greater Houston. Greg suggested that I contact Mr. Kai Dotiwala, a leader in the Zarathusti (Zoroastrian) community of Houston. Mr. Dotiwala is owner of an environmental company, focusing on issues of sustainability related to the petroleum industry.

Mr. Dotiwala was born in the Zarathushti faith and raised in Pakistan, went to college in the United States, and has been involved in responding to American environmental issues for over 35 years. In high school, Mr. Dotiwala was always interested in different belief systems, including atheism and agnosticism, while also being firmly anchored in his own Zarathushti faith.

Although his parents were active members of the Zarathushti community, he was still seeking his religious path. In his twenties, he made a commitment to claim the path of Zarathustra as the center of his life, personally, relationally, and professionally. Indeed, Mr. Dotiwala sees his focus on environmentalism as a reflection of his Zarathushti faith. One of the attributes of the Divine, Ahura Mazda, involves protecting the environment.

The heart of his faith as a Zarathushti involves a commitment to its ethical structure. Similar to the New Testament Letter of James, the Zarathushti tradition asserts that spirituality without ethics is of no value. According to Mr. Dotiwala, the everyday ethics and long- term impact of the Zarathushti ethical structure involves "opening to a good mind, which leads to a commitment to the progressive spirit, aiming at good dominion, that is, creating a good environment. When your environment is good, based on your commitment to human progress, then at death you reach immortality." While the Zarathushti community believes in the soul's survival beyond death, the immortality we seek involves immortality of influence, "leaving a positive footprint beyond yourself in this world."

When I asked Mr. Dotiwala what he might share that is unique in the Zarathushti faith tradition to someone from another faith or a seeker, he responded that most Zarathushtis would say "good thoughts, good words, good deeds." While this is important to the Zarathushti tradition, Mr. Dotiwala noted that "no religious tradition says bad thoughts, bad words, bad deeds." He prefers to focus on the actual words of Asho Zarathushtra envisioned in the Gathas, what he describes as a "unique value proposition," a term often used in business. "From the very beginning, there are two spirits at work in the world, life and non-life. The progressive spirit (mentality) Spentamainyu chose life. The other the regressive spirit Angramainyu chose non-life. You can be alive and not truly be living." In contrast to a lifeless existence, being fully alive, aligning with the spirit of life, involves bringing "more life to the world and supporting the human moral and social progress." In all our actions, Mr. Dotiwala counsels, we should constantly ask, "Does this action contribute to human progress or good? Does this action deter or harm human progress or regress the impact of the good spirit in human life? The goal of human life is for human beings using their free will to move Ahura Mazda's (God's) good creation to that ultimate harmony and to bring Nature to, 'Freshokerati' ('Making Wonderful.' or 'Resurrection.')."

Seeking to be congruent with the goals of Ahura Mazda, the Lord of Wisdom, "we should aim at wisdom in all that we do." Aligned with Divine Wisdom, we promote the moral and spiritual arcs of the universe, leaving a positive impact long beyond our lifetime.

WHAT CAN CHRISTIANS LEARN FROM ZOROASTRIANISM

Zoroastrianism sees spirituality as strenuous, and our moment-by-moment decisions as critical for our personal growth and community wellbeing. For the followers of Zarathustra, there is no such thing as "cheap grace," to quote German theologian Dietrich Bonhoeffer. God makes demands on us ethically. Spirituality involves the charge to "walk the talk." We must choose between light and darkness in every thought, word, or action. Following the way of Ahura Mazda requires us to walk in the light, and live mindfully in terms of our domestic, professional, and recreational activities. The path of light is the narrow way, forged with awareness of the surrounding moral and spiritual pitfalls and precipices.

Zoroastrianism's focus on the path of light and power of choice challenges Christians to evaluate their spiritual and political citizenship in terms of the way of Jesus. We are responsible for both good and evil in the social order. Our lifestyle and politics can be a matter of life and death for our human and non-human companions. The strenuous ethical path indicts us as complacent bystanders when we assume that Draconian immigration policies have nothing to do with us, or that we have no role in responding to the realities of climate change, economic injustice, white privilege, virus prevention, and conspiracy theories. Our choices make a difference, and our apathy or empathy in terms of others' suffering deadens or enlightens our spirits. With process and open and relational theology, Zoroastrianism challenges us to fulfill our vocation as God's companions in healing the earth and tipping the creative process from chaos to order and evil to good.

CHRISTIANITY'S GIFT TO THE FOLLOWERS OF ZARATHUSTRA

Zoroastrianism's strenuous ethics needs to be counterbalanced by Christianity's emphasis on grace, God's acceptance of our fallibility, and God's willingness to take the initiative in healing and forgiveness. Given the impact of the environment, including the influence of cultural norms, economics, and family of origin, on personality, character, and ethics, judgement must be balanced by unconditional love. The free choices of saint and sinner alike depend on the impact of others' decisions. Process and open and relational faith affirm that God's moral and spiritual arc gracefully heals us, challenging and confronting our failures in light of God's unconditional and all-inclusive love.

Grace abounds. While there are consequences to our behaviors, both personal and planetary, and we shape our character by our decisions, God's grace brings wholeness when we lack the resources to care for ourselves.

A ZOROASTRIAN PRACTICE

Zoroastrian spirituality involves walking as a child of light. Darkness abounds and our calling is to bring God's divine light and cosmic order into the various sectors of our daily lives. In that spirit, throughout the day, pause a moment, breathing slowly and deeply, experiencing the light of God flowing in and through you, filling you to the brim, body, mind, and spirit. From that sense of fullness, ask God's help to see the light and be the light in the hour ahead, at which time you will pause again and let God's light illuminate you. Walking in the light, you will do your part to defeat the powers of darkness one act at a time.

CHAPTER SIX

Islam

In our reflections on the relationship of Judaism and Christianity, we discovered that the relationships of religious siblings can be complicated and contentious. In many ways, Islam has done unto Christianity what Christian leaders have done to Judaism. Islam sees Mohammed as the "seal of prophecy," the final and complete revealer of God's nature among the Abrahamic religions. To orthodox members of the Islamic community, following the words of Muhammed and his first followers, the message of the prophet Muhammed, given in the Quran, is the complete and perfect revelation, surpassing all others including those given to Moses and Jesus. To orthodox Muslims, there is no need for any further revelation, and all previous revelations suffer by comparison. Islam corrects the idolatrous and polytheistic notions of the Trinity and the identification of Jesus as God's Son. Though Christianity and Judaism are also people of the Book, traditional Muslim theology asserts that Judaism, Christianity, and their scriptural witnesses are filled with imperfections, due to human interpretations, while the messages of the Quran come directly from Allah, the One God.

Reading other peoples' critiques of your religion can be both painful and helpful. When Christians read Muslim critiques of the New Testament, including orthodox Islam's belief that the Christian doctrines of the Trinity and Incarnation are inherently idolatrous, our discomfort may be an antidote to anti-Judaism in our own religion. We may see these critiques as inaccurate and unjust, just as some of our critiques of other religious traditions are shaped by our own spiritual biases and belief in the superiority of our revelations and, thus, may also be judged as inaccurate and unjust by the practitioners of other faiths. Having been given "a taste of our own medicine" by Islam, we might become more sensitive and empathetic in relationship to Judaism. We need to be reminded that all religions are finite and evolving. They both reflect and distort the ultimate reality. The true light that shines in everyone is prismatic, coming to and through each of us, and our religious traditions, in ways shaped by our culture, history, and personal context. There is always more light to be experienced. Accordingly, we should dialogue with other faiths in a spirit of appreciation, affirming their highest aspirations and not their basest behaviors and looking for the deeper truths beneath doctrines that are problematic to us.

Following the Quran, the Muslim holy book, many Muslims assert that the message of the Christian Savior Jesus has been superseded by God's verbal revelation to the prophet Muhammed. Jesus is one prophet among many and not metaphysically or spiritually unique. Although Muslims have historically been tolerant of religious diversity within Muslim-majority lands, many orthodox Muslims consider Christians and Jews spiritual inferiors and see these faiths as purveyors of evil due to their connection with secular Western culture, the Israeli occupation of Palestine, and attempts of Christians to convert Muslims to their faith. Even if these critiques are theologically inaccurate representations of our faith, they remind us of "historical" Christianity's imperialistic understandings of persons of other faiths as spiritually and morally inferior to us, eventuating in the belief that non-believers are lost in this life and the next. The venom some fundamentalist Muslims spew on Christianity has been more than compensated by conservative Christian leaders, many of whom state that Christians pray to the true God, while Muslim prayer is idolatrous. Just a few minutes before typing these words, I encountered a quote from a well-known Southern California evangelical pastor, who referred to Islam as the devil's religion. To such preachers, Allah is a false god, Muhammed (Mohammed) a false messenger, and Islam a pathway to eternal damnation. In the mind of these Christians, like certain Muslim fundamentalists, there is no room for dialogue with other faiths. Conversion or elimination are the only options for unbelievers and infidels.

Christian-Muslim relationships have been further complicated by political and military interactions extending over 1400 years. Both religions have been plagued by a crusade mentality and have gone to war over control of sacred sites. Both have in the heat of battle seen the other faith as demonic, destructive, and idolatrous. Killing a Christian or Muslim infidel has been at times a ticket to eternal beatitude. September 11, 2001, solidified anti-Muslim feeling in the Western World. Terrorist violence is falsely viewed by many Western Christians as normative among Muslims. To them, *jihad* is identified with violence, despite the long history of just war theory in Islam. Moreover, the primary understanding of *jihad* is as a spiritual not military struggle, the human struggle to be fully committed to Allah in heart, mind, and soul.

In responding to other faith traditions, it is imperative to follow Jesus' words, "Do not judge so that you may not be judged…why do you see the speck in your neighbor's eye but do not notice the log in your own eye?" (Matthew 7:1, 3) This is especially challenging in Christian-Muslim relationships in which our diverse faith traditions are intimately connected with contrasting cultural and political perspectives and interests.

Tragically, religious viewpoints often undergird violence, ostracism, and polarization. This is evident in American Christian nationalism and the Muslim al Qaeda and Taliban. Whether Christian, Hindu, or Muslim, fundamentalism leans toward separating the world into binary categories of truth and error, saved and unsaved, and friend and foe, forgetting our inherent fallibility, as well as our common identity as God's beloved children. Binary thinking leads to persecution of opponents, who because of their apostasy, are deemed unworthy of ethical consideration.

In the religious world, and most especially in Christian-Muslim relationships, we must look at spiritual heights as well as demonic depths. We would do well to remember the words of President George W. Bush following a mass murder in Dallas, Texas: "Too often we judge other groups by their worst examples, while judging ourselves by our best intentions." Our critiques must always be balanced with empathy and grace.

PINNACLES OF ISLAM

Like Judaism and Christianity, Islam is not monolithic. Its religious bandwidth ranges from orthodox legalism to unbridled and ecstatic mysticism and scorning of Western secular culture to a creative synthesis of Islamic wisdom with science, gender equality, non-religious literature, and global spirituality. There are growing numbers of progressive Muslims, who see faith in Allah as evolving, science-affirming, welcoming of pluralism, and culturally liberating. Progressive Muslims dialogue with members of other faiths as equals, sharing and receiving wisdom in interfaith settings. Focusing on the highest aspirations of Christianity's younger sibling, we can see the high points or pinnacles in the contours of Islam that serve as the basis for creative conversations, give and take, and spiritual growth in Christian-Muslim relationships. Among the pinnacles of Islam is the following list, not intended to be exhaustive, but a way to provide a point of contact in inter-spiritual relationships and with the insights of process and openness Christian theology.

- *The Reality of Revelation.* Islam begins with a word from God to Muhammed (570-632 CE) calling him to be a prophet, proclaiming God's Word and Wisdom to the Arabian peninsula and ultimately to the whole earth. Spiritually sensitive, and critical of the polytheism, violence, immorality, and divisiveness characteristic of the peninsula's tribal culture, Mohammed sought a deeper experience of the Holy to transform the religious and cultural life of the area. Every year, Muhammed took monthly retreats to seek divine guidance, and on one of these retreats, he experienced God speaking to him through an angelic personage, telling him to "Proclaim!" Like the Hebraic prophets, Muhammed was initially reluctant to accept his mission. "I am no proclaimer," he exclaimed in response to the angelic summons. Muhammed believed that the task was too large and that he lacked the piety and resources to be God's prophetic messenger to humankind. Time after time, the pious businessman heard the divine summons, "preach and proclaim" God's truth until he relented, claiming his role as God's human mouthpiece to Arabia and to the world. In the words of the angelic messenger:

Proclaim in the name of Your Lord who created!
Created humankind from a clot of blood.
Proclaim: Your Lord is the Most Generous,
Who teaches by the pen.
Teaches humans what they knew not.
(Quran 96:1-3)

Revelation came to the Prophet Muhammed in words just as it had to the Hebraic prophets. This spoken revelation was to be written down and circulated to the Arabian peoples, the descendants of Hagar and Ishmael, the son of Abraham and Hagar, the stepbrother of Isaac. As Muhammed heard the angelic revelations over the next two decades, he repeated them to auditors who transcribed them word for word into what now is the Quran.

Islam asserts that God speaks to human beings and directs the divine message to historical individuals whose calling is to share God's word with the world. To Muslims, Muhammed is the final prophet, of a line that begins with Abraham, extends through Moses and the Hebraic prophets, and includes Jesus of Nazareth. Not set apart metaphysically as many Christians portray Jesus, Muhammed's uniqueness is in God's choice of him to be the seal of the prophets, and his affirmative response to God's call and the angelic witness. Not considered to be the "savior," Muhammed is nevertheless unique in his personal integration of the roles of prophet, movement leader, mystic, politician, military strategist, husband, father, and merchant. In many ways, Muhammed and Mary, the mother of Jesus, are similar recipients of the impossible tasks of birthing a divine holy book and a divine baby, respectively! Muhammed becomes the epitome of Islam, the "surrender" or "submission" to Allah, the willingness to follow God's way even if it conflicts with current social and religious values just as Mary of Nazareth willingly submits to God's vocation for her, regardless of the costs to her reputation and well-being.

- *The Holy Book.* The words of Allah, spoken through an angelic messenger and received by Muhammed, reflect the Uncreated Quran, God's eternal and heavenly message to humankind. In the divine gift of the Quran, meaning "recitation," the Arabian people received their Book, the final and complete installment for the Peoples of the Book, embracing and honoring, and yet going beyond in its fullness, the Jewish and Christian scriptures. Preserved from error, the Quran provides all that is needed for spiritual integrity, relational health, and political conduct. It is the truth that leads to joy in this lifetime, and Paradise in the next. In contrast to progressive, scholarly, and contextual approaches to scripture, orthodox Muslims, like fundamentalist Christians, assert the perfection of their texts. Conservative Muslims' attitudes toward the Quran could be summarized by substituting the word "Quran" for the fundamentalist Christian's scriptural mantra, "the Bible says it, I believe it, and that settles it." Other, more progressive Muslims as well as Sufi mystics view Mohammed's encounter and experience of relationship with God as more significant than the written words of the Quran. Progressive Muslims, like progressive and process and openness theologians, see their holy book as the interplay of revelation and receiver, not a perfect and timeless document.

- *The One God.* Following the traditions of Judaism and Christianity, Islam proclaims a radical monotheism. "There is no God but Allah and Muhammed is God's prophet," so proclaims Islam. God transcends the universe and is beyond our imaginations in wisdom and sovereignty. There is no other like God (Allah), completely One and Centered, Powerful and Merciful, the Creator and Determiner of all things. Orthodox Muslims challenge the Christian vision of Trinity and the unique status of Jesus as God's Beloved Child. Words like "Father" or "Parent" limit God's unique transcendence. Following the apophatic path or imageless way, Islam considers any attempt to visualize or portray God as idolatrous in nature. Words alone cannot describe God. Images localize and distort the divine. The only appropriate words to describe God come from Allah through the perfect and unchanging verbal and written revelation, the Quran.

  The One God is known by many finite and fallible names, but the word "Allah" stands alone as descriptive of the divine. God speaks to Muhammed. Muhammed is God's storyteller, spiritual guide, law giver, and revealer of Allah, "the God."

- *Divine Power.* At the heart of Islam's vision of God is God's power. Whereas most Christians assert that God is love and Jews proclaim God's infinite loving kindness, most orthodox Muslims believe that the Quran describes *power* as the primary characteristic of the Divine. God's power is infinite and all-determining. Similar in theological perspective to the stark omnipotence of the Genevan Reformer John Calvin, Islam asserts that everything is in God's hands. The moment of birth and death, sickness and health, victory and defeat all come from the hand of God. It is common for Muslims to say, "if Allah wills it," as they embark on a project or hope for a positive outcome to an endeavor. Awe and fear before the Sovereign God are the appropriate creaturely responses. Still, though God is all-powerful and judges the living and dead, God is also described as "the Holy, the Peaceful, the Loving, the Guardian over God's servants, the Shelterer of the orphan, the Guide of the erring…the Very Forgiving, whose love for us is more tender than that of a mother-bird for her young."[18]

The transcendent and all-powerful Allah is seldom described in parental terms such as "father" or "mother." Still, Muslims believe that God cares for the weary and downtrodden, provides guideposts to ethical living for this life, and promises joy in Paradise.

- *Divine Intimacy.* Islam affirms the infinite qualitative distance between God and creation. God is God and we aren't! God is supreme and we are mortal and fallible, creatures of a day. But God's infinity does not preclude intimacy. Allah is closer than the vein on your neck. God knows every whisper and every secret. God records everything on land and sea, or in the solitude of the human spirit.

- *Human Responsibility and the Reality of Judgment.* Although orthodox Muslims believe God is all-determining, they also assert that we are responsible for our behavior. All things are noted by the All-Seeing One, whose justice goes beyond status and position. The scales of justice fairly and accurately evaluate each of us in terms of our faith and ethics. Each action moves us toward or away from God's plan for our lives, and toward or away from God's Paradise. Eventually, there will be a reckoning in which we must look at our lives as God does. On the day of reckoning, we must face the reality of our actions, in terms of intent and consequences.

18. Ameer Ali, *The Spirit of Islam* (London: Christopher's, 1923), 18.

We will face paradise or pain, based on our submission to God's will in our decision-making.

There are a growing number of progressive Muslims, such as progressive-process Muslim theologian Farhan Shah, who affirm the freedom and creativity of humans to inject new realities in the world. God influences but does not determine human behavior.

- *Absolute Dependence on Allah.* While Jews and Christians often see the problem of divine-human relationships in terms of disobedience, Muslims locate the primary fault of humankind as a failure to recognize our complete and utter dependence on God. God is awesome and we are mortal. God determines all things, and any agency we have depends on God's providence. Rugged individualism and independence defy the Creator of the Universe. Our calling is to submit to God's will and, in this submission, discern our duty as God's obedient subjects. We need to let God be God, lean not on our own understanding, and follow God's spiritual laws without question.

- *Walking the Talk.* Islamic spirituality affirms the wisdom of the New Testament Letter of James, that faith without works is dead. Islam seeks to knit together our lives in terms of our daily commitments. Foundational for every commitment is trust in God, "There is no God but Allah, and Muhammed is his prophet." In times of crisis, Muslims are enjoined to call upon God, "There is no God but Allah." Putting God at the heart of daily life provides the perspective necessary to face success and failure and the complexities of life and death.

At the heart of Muslim spirituality is daily prayer, performed five times each day. Similar in spirit to Benedict of Nursia, and monastic Christianity's praying the hours, Islam's five daily times of prayer keep our eyes on Allah, remind us to submit to God's will, and remind us that we live our lives moment by moment in relationship to the All-Powerful, All-Knowing God. Our daily commitments require us to be generous in our care for others. Charity, the donation of 2.5 per cent of assets to the poor and destitute, the food insecure and unsheltered, is mandated for those who follow Allah. Finally, Islam recognizes the spiritual importance of retreat and fasting to deepen our spiritual lives (Ramadan); and pilgrimage, spiritual journeys to Mecca, as a way of claiming spiritual roots and deepening faith.

- *The Interplay of Religion and Politics.* The personal is political, and the political is personal according to Islam. Muhammed was a mystic and spiritual leader. He was also a military leader, an administrator, and a politician. A military tactician, he was not eager to go to war, but when pushed, entered the fray valiantly and wisely, defeating his political and military opponents. Moreover, like John Calvin, a thousand years later, Muhammed believed that government and law should be conducted in accordance with the insights of the Quran and its interpretations.

We can never separate faith and public policy. Sometimes this has led to aberrations, for example, in theocracies that have quashed all dissent and encouraged human rights abuses. However, the joining of faith and politics among the Peoples of the Book, especially progressive Islam, Judaism, and Christianity, has inspired the abolition of slavery, civil rights protests and legislation, economic justice, environmental activism, and expanding human rights to include women and the LGBTQ community. Islam has affirmed that all Muslims, regardless of race, are siblings and equal before Allah. While this affirmation has been, like many Christian moral imperatives, often aspirational, rather than concretely embedded in social institutions, the ideal social structure reflects Allah's bias toward justice and equality for all humankind.

- *Postmortem Paradise and Punishment.* Islam's tendencies toward binary theology and spirituality are most pronounced in the literal and irrevocable separation of the righteous from unrighteous in the postmortem realms of heaven and hell, both of which are described in graphic detail. What happens in this unique and unrepeatable lifetime is important, insofar as this earth is, to use John Calvin's imagery, the theatre of God's glory. This life is also the front porch and proving ground for our eternal destiny. Our relationship to God and our neighbor tip the scales of justice toward heaven or hell. Paradise is visualized as a spiritual oasis from scorching desert heat. Paradise is a place of joy and celebration, bountiful food and refreshment, comfort and joy, and eternal bliss. In contrast, hell resembles the unbearable heat of the desert, unrelenting and everlasting. While more graphic than many orthodox Christian images of heaven and hell, these dual post-mortem states remind us that what we do in this lifetime matters. Wealth without morality leads to spiritual destruction and eternal punishment. Piety and obedience, ethical behavior, and sacrifice in this lifetime receive their eternal reward in Paradise.

- *Mystical Movement.* Islam is a religion of the book. Still, for some Muslims, the Book is not enough. We don't want to speak or hear about God; we want to experience God. The Sufi tradition affirms Allah's universality and intimacy. As one Muslim poet affirms: "When the ocean surges/ Don't let me just hear it/Let it splash inside my chest." Inspired by the religion of Love, Sufis went beyond legalism and parochialism to see God everywhere and in all things. God can equally be found in a mosque, temple, church, and ashram. As the poet-mystic Rumi avers, there are a hundred ways to kneel and kiss the ground. There are hundreds of paths to God, and we gain from hearing the stories and experiencing the faith of fellow seekers, regardless of religious tradition. God is more than a lawgiver or sovereign; God is a lover, a companion, a friend of the spirit, whose love activates our love and expands our circle of compassion to all creation.

A VOICE OF PROGRESSIVE ISLAM

Farhan Shah is one of the leading voices of progressive Islamic theology. Currently working on his Ph.D. dissertation related to process theology and the Islamic spiritual teacher Muhammad Iqbal (1877-1938) at the University of Oslo, Farhan Shah and I experienced the profound interdependence of life through our Zoom conversation joining Norway and Cape Cod. For Farhan Shah, curiosity, humility, and compassion are central to theological reflection. Curiosity challenges us to explore the insights of other faith traditions with a theological "beginner's mind." Reality is always more than we can imagine. We need to be humble about our perceptions of others' faiths. All understandings of God are finite. Accordingly, Farhan Shah believes "every interpretation—including Quranic interpretations— needs to be open-ended." While we all share common existential concerns, we need to "cherish the differences among religious traditions." We all have the same issues, regarding mortality and meaning, and we understand them in different ways. Experience joins us with one another while abstract doctrinal thinking separates us. We may articulate our experience differently, but, ultimately, we are joined in our quest for meaning and significance.

The heart of Islam, according to Farhan Shad, is the affirmation of God's compassion and of human freedom and responsibility as God's co-creators in healing the world. God is supremely compassionate, and essentially love, according to progressive Islam. In Arabic, the word for compassion is "womb." According to Farhan Shah, "We all live in the womb of God. We all live in God's life." In the spirit of process panentheism, God is in all things and all things are in God. "Divine breath is in every creature, not just humans."

Farhan Shah and I concur about the disastrous impact of Islamic and Christian fundamentalism in terms of their binary understandings of truth and error, literal understanding of scripture, and focus on abstraction, and doctrine, as definitive, rather than on concrete experiences. "Perhaps," Farhan Shah stated, "the pandemic may end up being a blessing as well as a tragedy. The pandemic reminds us that we are interdependent, members of God's beloved community, despite the differences in our religious traditions. Crisis, etymologically, means 'decision.' These times are also novel opportunities to join hands to work for a sustainable existence, both human and nonhuman. To create a future which we can gladly embrace rather than flee in despair."

All I can say as a fellow spiritual seeker, a Christian theologian, is "Amen. Let it be so."

WHAT CHRISTIANS CAN LEARN FROM ISLAM

The heart of Christianity beats with the grace and mercy of God. "While we were yet sinners, Christ died for us," proclaims the Apostle Paul. Grace is seen as God's unmerited and, at times, undeserved gift from God. Grace is real and transforms lives. Yet, as in our conversations with Zoroastrianism, often our understanding of the grace of God leads to what German theologian Dietrich Bonhoeffer describes as "cheap grace," that is, we can receive God's love without significant amendment to our personal or political behaviors. In New Testament religion, the Letter of James, along with the message of the Hebraic prophets, serves as an ethical counterbalance to extreme interpretations of Paul's theology of grace. Holistic spirituality requires works as well as faith, reflected in an ethical and interpersonal response to the grace of God. Zoroastrianism, Islam, and Judaism remind Christians to act and to give as well as to receive, to change the world as well as to depend on God's activity to save us.

In the same spirit, Islam's five pillars - the affirmation of the oneness and sovereignty of Allah, daily prayer, financial generosity to the poor, the Ramadan fast, and the pilgrimage to Mecca—remind Christians that faith is a matter of day-to-day choices in lifestyle and lived values, not just belief. Authentic faith must transform our personal relationships and political involvements. We can't claim to love the child in the manger and separate children from their parents at USA borderlands or give God glory and praise while being apathetic about global hunger and climate change. We can't affirm "God is love" or "the truth will set you free" while intentionally spreading false conspiracy theories about political and business leaders and election results, often leading to acts of violence and terrorism, or practicing vigilante justice, often based on racial superiority.

Although Islam has also, at times, neglected to embody God's mercy through acts of violence perpetrated by al Qaeda and the Taliban, the spirit of Islam embodies the affirmation that faith must be expressed in spiritual practices and acts of mercy. The word "Islam" means peace as well as surrender. Submission to God requires a healthy and moral lifestyle. To be faithful, we must walk the talk as well as talk the talk.

CHRISTIANITY'S GIFT TO ISLAM

While challenging to its own fundamentalists, the heartbeat of Christianity is dynamically flexible in ritual and scripture. You can be a Christian and claim seven, two, or no sacraments. Alfred North Whitehead asserted that the pure conservative goes against the nature of the universe. The same applies to the spiritual journey. Living faith is a growing faith. Jesus grew in wisdom and stature. Muhammed received revelations over two decades. A living God does new things: faithful, God's mercies are new every morning. A living faith is also an ever-expanding faith, moving from local to global, and stable to the cosmos.

The Christian movement is a story of spiritual and theological evolution. In expanding its message to the Gentile world, the Christian movement embraced Greek philosophical concepts and let go of strict Jewish rituals. In contrast to Islam's preference for the Quran in its original language, Christianity has embraced translating its scriptures into the vernacular, both in native tongues and paraphrases appropriate to different cultural settings, such as Eugene Peterson's *The Message,* Clarence Jordan's *Cotton Patch Gospels,* and *The Living Bible* as well as biblical texts appropriate to children, teens, and persons in recovery. The heart of Christianity is dynamic and changing in telling the "old, old story" of Jesus in new and creative ways in response to changing cultural, scientific, and political contexts.

This spiritual dynamism is now emerging in progressive Muslim communities and among progressive Muslim theologians who proclaim the equality of women and sponsor worship services where women and men worship together. These groups engage in mutually enriching dialogues with persons of other faiths, and understand God the Infinite as intimate, relational, and constantly in process, changing God's vision in relationship to the world's changes. Muslim mystics have also been willing to modify traditional perspectives in favor of direct experiences of the holy. Christians and Muslims alike can embrace a god of change and glory, whose intimacy is expressed in loving, concrete, and evolving relationship with the world.

AN ISLAMIC SPIRITUAL PRACTICE

Muhammed's encounter with an angelic messenger, giving birth to the Quran, resulted from the interplay of his yearly retreats, and Allah's initiative in choosing him as prophet. Mature faith is the gift of grace and effort. The All-Merciful One calls each one whether in five daily prayers, similar in form to the Benedictine hours of prayer, the muezzin, the public call to prayer, or in urges to go on retreat, or make a pilgrimage to a sacred site, such as Mecca, Jerusalem, Iona, Scotland, or the Via Santiago in Spain. Faith comes alive through dedicated daily and yearly practices.

In the spirit of Benedict's Christian monasticism and the five daily prayers of Islam, consider taking several times for daily prayer. When I was in my final pastorate on Cape Cod, I would stop and pray hourly when the steeple bells rang. During my morning walks on Craigville Beach, I paused to pray for our congregation and its mission when I saw the church's steeple on the hill above the beach. I now pause a moment for prayer as I walk by friends' homes in my Bethesda, Maryland, neighborhood, and stop to open to divine guidance when I turn on the headline news on cable television. Throughout the day, you can pause, take a few deep breaths, take your spiritual temperature, and reorient your spiritual GPS. You may wish to recite a Psalm such as Psalm 23 (The Lord is my shepherd), Psalm 100 (Make a joyful noise to God all the earth), Psalm 46:10 (Be still and know that I am God) or Romans 8:38-39 (Nothing can separate me from the love of God). You may also wish to reflect on a phrase from Rumi or another Muslim mystic to deepen your spiritual life. These moments of regular prayer will deepen your faith, calm your spirit, and expand your sense of kinship with the world.

CHAPTER SEVEN

Bahai

The Biblical tradition is a journey of hopefulness. In a time of national tribulation, with the future in doubt, the prophet Isaiah imagines the age of the Messiah, God's Chosen One, who will usher in a new world order, the age of Shalom.

> *The wolf shall live with the lamb,*
> *the leopard shall lie down with the kid,*
> *the calf and the lion and the fatling together,*
> *and a little child shall lead them.*
>
> *The cow and the bear shall graze,*
> *their young shall lie down together;*
> *and the lion shall eat straw like the ox.*
>
> *The nursing child shall play over the hole of the asp,*
> *and the weaned child shall put its hand on the adder's den.*
>
> *They will not hurt or destroy*
> *on all my holy mountain;*
> *for the earth will be full of the knowledge of the Lord*
> *as the waters cover the sea.*
> (Isaiah 11:6-9)

Each Sunday morning, worshippers at the Cape Cod church I pastored prior to my retirement and Christians everywhere yearn for God's Peaceable Realm as we pray "thy kingdom God, thy will be done, on earth as it is in heaven." (Matthew 6:10) We share this hope with people of other faith traditions. We see the promise of God in terms of the transformation of ourselves and our society to more resemble God's Just Order. Other Christians expect something more dramatic. They look forward to the cataclysmic end of our current world, the dramatic return of Jesus, and the setting up of God's realm as an earthly kingdom. Our world, they believe, is so mired in sin that transformation can occur only after complete destruction of the earth and its civilizations. God's faithful followers, presumably persons like themselves steeped in binary and end times theology, will be saved while unbelievers, including progressive Christians and faithful agnostics as well as devout members of other faith traditions, will be left behind to endure the tribulation and terror of an apocalyptic nightmare.

Many of us have a radically different vision of the future from the apocalyptic soothsayers and their prognostications, regularly proven wrong and regularly revised, of doom and gloom. We believe that God will not abandon but recreate the world. God calls the world forward through God's movements in the spiritual and moral arcs of history.

The hope of a new world order is still alive in the twenty-first century, not as a dramatic as a global catastrophe but as the coming together of the world's nations in peaceful harmony through a federation of nations. Many persons see the world of independent, conflicting, self-interested nations as unsustainable in terms of global climate change, nuclear weaponry, massive starvation, threat of pandemic, and the disparity between the wealthy nations and the majority world. The pandemic has been a time of reckoning for nation-first ideologies. We are all in the same storm and staying in our separate boats has added to the personal and economic carnage of the pandemic. We must change our ways before the ecosystem and economic order collapses.

Despite the realities of institutional and international conflict, the world is lured forward by the fragile dream of peace on earth good will to all, a world of swords beaten into plowshares, of flourishing democracies, and conflict resolution among nations. We see the emergence of this dream in the birth and failure of the League of Nations and the political ambiguity of the United Nations, essential yet often parochial and ineffectual. We see this hope in Martin Luther King's dream of the Beloved Community in which all persons, regardless of race, walk hand in hand.

Now more than ever we need images of hope that guide nations toward peace and unity, joining persons across race and religion and putting an end to state-sponsored violence, economic injustice, and environmental destruction. Religion can be a source of unity as well as division. The divisive power of religion, or policies justified by false understandings of religious truths, is obvious in the Holocaust, racism inspired by a handful of Bible verses, the Israeli-Palestinian conflict, the "troubles" in Northern Ireland, Islamic terrorism, the rise of religious nationalism among Hindus in India and Christians in the USA, and science denial in a time of pandemic. Still, despite the ambiguity and violence of religious history, virtually every faith tradition lives in hope for a new age where justice and peace abound. The quest for an age of peace, the divine institution of a new world order encompassing all humankind and healing the earth is alive and well and at the heart of the Bahá'í faith tradition.

The faith of Abraham's children is prophetic in nature. God raises up prophets and messengers to respond to respond to the crises of history. God calls humankind, singling out unique individuals, to speak God's word of challenge, warning, and comfort. God chooses but people must respond to fully mediate God's word to humans in their historical context. Prophets and teachers, and messengers and divine leaders, such as Abraham, Zarathustra, Moses, Isaiah, Amos, Hosea, John the Baptist, and Mohammed, transform the world, despite their human limitations in time and space, and sometimes insight. Even Jesus the Christian Savior and Messiah roots himself in Israel's prophetic tradition, proclaiming as his mission statement the words of Isaiah 61:1-2, slightly modified by the Nazareth preacher:

> *The Spirit of the Lord is upon me,*
> *because he has anointed me*
> *to bring good news to the poor.*
>
> *He has sent me to proclaim release to the captives*
> *and recovery of sight to the blind,*
> *to let the oppressed go free,*
> *to proclaim the year of the Lord's favor.*
> (Luke 4:18-19)

In the 19th century, the world awaited a divine revelation that would usher in planetary healing. In 1844, William Miller prophesied the end of the present world, and followers donned white robes in expectation of Jesus' return. In that same year, the Bahá'í faith asserts that God revealed God's vision of the future to Siyyad 'Alf Muhammed, later known as the Bab, the Gateway to the Messenger of the Age to Come. In Persia, today's Iran, during a time of cultural chaos and foreign imperialism, there was passionate expectation among Muslim seekers that the Hidden Imam would return to usher in a new world, vastly different from the ambiguity and alienation, the injustice and oppression, of the present age.

Bahá'í faith proclaims that God is causing the emergence of another world order. This new world order will reflect the Peaceable Realm of Isaiah in which swords would be beaten into agricultural implements, and humankind would learn war no more. Bahá'í faith believes that during the 19th century, God sent two messengers, similar in purpose to John the Baptist and Jesus, a forerunner and a fulfillment, to proclaim the era of world unity. This time, the light would emerge from Iran and encompass the whole earth.

The Bab, Siyyad 'Alf Muhammed (1819-1850) discerned Allah's unique presence in his life and declared himself the one who was promised. The Bab taught a path of progressive Islam, open to science, culture, and religious reformation, the call to go beyond religious parochialism and the affirmation of the essential unity of the world's religions. As the name Bab or "Gateway" suggests, the Bab saw himself as the forerunner of the Coming Manifestation of God on earth.

Like John the Baptist, the Bab's calling was to prepare the way for one greater than himself. Prophetic teachers typically rouse the ire of those intent on preserving the status quo, the old-time religion and its politics of power and persecution. The Bab was imprisoned and executed at age 30, after planting Bahá'í's message of a coming new world order.

In his late twenties, Mírzá 'usayn-'Alí Núrí, known as Bahá'u'lláh (1817-1892), became a follower and an avid proclaimer of the message of the Bab. He too experienced persecution and imprisonment for his faith in God's coming world. During an extended time of incarceration, Mírzá 'usayn-'Alí Núrí received a direct message from God, revealing his true destiny and title, "Him Whom God Will Make Manifest." Bahá'u'lláh proclaimed a message to the world's leaders that a

Great Peace will emerge, and that they must be the leaders in realizing God's realm on earth. "It is not for him to pride himself who loveth his country, but rather for him who loveth the whole world. The earth is but one country, and mankind its citizens."[19] Bahá'u'lláh envisaged a new world order and provided moral and institutional pathways toward that goal. He recognized that each of us needs to live into the world about which we dream. We need, as Gandhi said, to be the change we want to see in the world. We need to see God's light and then, as Jesus says, become the light of the world to come. We must embody the values of equality, forgiveness, hospitality, and integrity as harbingers of God's coming realm.

Bahá'u'lláh's message was met with contrasting responses: indifference, due to its perceived impracticality, and violence, because of its revolutionary spirit. Bahá'u'lláh, believed to be the Manifestation of God for our time, endured the fate accorded to prophets throughout the ages: he was arrested, exiled, and eventually lived the remainder of his life near Haifa, Israel, where he proclaimed the simple message, "Let not a man glory in this, that he loves his country; let him glory in this, that he loves his kind."[20]

THE ONE WORLD OF BAHAI FAITH

In many ways, the emergence of the Bahá'í faith in the evolution of Islam parallels the emergence of Progressive or Liberal Christianity in the evolution of Christianity. Both nineteenth-century movements sought to break through parochial understandings of Christianity and Islam, respectively, to embrace a global spirit. Both movements recognized the universality of religion, beyond Islam and traditional Christianity, respectively. Both movements emphasized the ethical and social aspects of religious faith and created their own versions of the social gospel affirmation that religion cannot be separated from social welfare. The political is personal, and the personal is the political. Belief must become manifest in the quest for peace and justice. Both movements see the spiritual adventure as progressive and evolutionary, denying the finality of their own positions and open to new revelations, including those from science. In this section, I will reflect on five aspects of Bahá'í faith's unitive vision.

---

19. William S. Hatcher and J. Douglas Martin, *The Bahá'í Faith* (Wilmette, IL: Bahá'í Publishing, 2002), 40.
20. Ibid., 46.

- *Divine Unity.* The affirmation of divine unity is at the heart of the Abrahamic traditions. From the actions of one Reality, all creation springs. There is God and there is no other all-encompassing spiritual being. God is the sovereign reality, beyond and within all things. "Out of utter nothingness God created all things...rescuing from the abasement of remoteness and the perils of extinction...The unity of the Living, the Ever-Abiding God–a unity which is exalted above all limitations, that transcendeth the comprehension of all living things."[21] Humankind in all its variety can be described as the fruits of one divinely nurtured tree, each fruit as the gift of God's wise creativity. The unity of God inspires us to seek human unity.

- *Divine Manifestation and Revelation.* Human spiritual and planetary evolution results from the impact of God's Manifestations in human history. Throughout history God has brought forth teachers and healers, fully reflecting divine wisdom, appropriate for their time and place. Bahá'u'lláh, the parent of Bahá'í, is not the only, or the final, divine revelation to humankind. Bahá'u'lláh was preceded by God's Manifestation in Abraham, Zoroaster, Moses, Buddha, Jesus, and Mohammed. While Bahá'u'lláh's truth propels humankind to world unity, other Manifestations of the One God will appear in the future to bring completeness to God's work in the world. History is the progressive revelation of God's vision. All revelations or manifestations of God share the same truth, wrapped in the unique and relative garments of their time, place, and culture. All are equal in revealing God's truth. God's spirit dwells equally and fully in all of them.

Differences among revelations are the result of the unique needs and customs of the world's diverse communities in the quest to embody God's truth in our world. Truth is one and its manifestations are one despite their revelational variety. "The purpose of God in creating man hath been, and will ever be, to enable him to know his Creator and to attain his Presence."[22] Accordingly, "God's purpose in sending His Prophets unto men is twofold...to liberate the children of men from the darkness of ignorance, and guide them to the light of true understanding. The

---

21. Ibid., 74-75.
22. Ibid., 101.

second is to ensure the peace and tranquility of mankind, and provide all the means by which they can be established."[23] This goal applies to every person and race without exception.

Unlike us, the Manifestations of God, while fully human and mortal, are "chosen" by God for the task of revelation, according to Bahai faith. Their souls pre-exist their human incarnation, whereas our souls emerge at conception. They have a direct encounter with God whereas ours is mediated by creation or in holy texts. These Manifestations of God call us to claim our agency in cleansing the "mirror" of spiritual perception so that we can reflect God's attributes as fully as possible.

- *Human unity.* Humankind is the crown of creation and God's agent of transformation. One God brings forth one people, despite our varied cultures and religions. Our task is to be God's leaders in reuniting the social order to reflect God's transcendent unity in the relations of persons and nations on earth. Our calling is to promote the social evolution of humankind, beyond nation states to global unity. Unity does not mean uniformity: the varieties of race, culture, religion, and gender flow from God's creativity. Male and female are equal and should have equal roles in determining the planet's future.

- *Planetary Unity.* We are created through and for divine unity. Humanity's origins are one, and humankind is essentially united despite its wondrous diversity. Spirituality is political and global as well as personal and local. Creation is bending toward a global unity in which war and international strife will end. While nations will continue to exist in the world to come, they will be similar in relationship to states functioning in concert within the United States, centers of authority ideally operating within a much larger sovereign global federation which inspires their ultimate earthly allegiance. Only through international community and the subservience of nationalism to planetary unity will we find peace, economic justice, an end to hunger, and environmental healing. During this time of protest and pandemic in the United States, the dangers of disunity have become abundantly clear. We are all, as the saying goes, in the same storm. Our survival and flourishing depend on us claiming our places

23. Ibid., 105.

in the same boat. In many ways, the Baháʼí vision of planetary unity is similar to the eschatological, future-oriented, vision of history of Jesuit mystic-priest-paleontologist Teilhard de Chardin, who believed that God is drawing us toward the Omega point, a sense of global consciousness that unites and energizes all creation. Whereas much of global and personal evolution has been unconscious, Baháʼí asserts that planetary evolution is now in the hands of humankind, intentionally responding to God's call of the future. In the spirit of the New Testament message of Revelation, the achievement of planetary unity will be preceded by a time of tribulation, due to our failure to live out God's vison of unity. This time of tribulation, the result of human ignorance and waywardness, will inspire among the world's peoples a commitment to realizing world unity. Eventually God's will for earth will come to pass and we will beat swords into plowshares, forsake war making, and work together to heal the earth.

- *Universal Salvation.* The unity of God and the world demands unity of human destiny. The binary separation of heaven and hell detract from God's ultimate healing goal. Baháʼí faith affirms that the human soul emerges at conception and continues eternally beyond the grave. God's attributes are present in every human life, luring us, despite our waywardness, to reflect God's vision in our values and behavior. After death, all persons continue their evolution toward God. In this life and the next, our salvation is the result of divine grace and human effort. Neither the world nor individual humans can find fulfillment apart from sustained and committed corporate and individual effort.

A BAHAI CONVERSATION

The writing of this text has enabled me to connect with friends and colleagues, old and new. During my seventeen years as Protestant University Chaplain at Georgetown University, I pastored students from every denomination and theological persuasion as well as agnostics, atheists, and seekers. One semester, I sponsored a small seekers group that met for questions and conversations over breakfast every Tuesday morning. One of the mainstays of this group was Krista, who always asked intellectually astute questions and shared insights and questions from her spiritual journey. A student in the School of Foreign Service, Krista was drawn toward East Asia: she was an avid student of Japanese and Chinese languages, cultures, and religion, she spent her Junior "year abroad" in Japan. During her year abroad, she found what was for her a path with a heart. She found a spiritual home in the Bahá'í faith.

Twenty-seven years after her graduation from Georgetown University, we had a chance to reconnect as peers who could share our faith journeys with one another. Now living in Fort Worth, Texas, and coordinating a program in Chinese studies at an independent school, Krista maintains a strong commitment to Bahá'í faith as a path to reconciliation and world unity.

Raised a Lutheran, she appreciated the pious, reflective, and socially concerned faith of her parents. Not locked into their own faith tradition, her parents invited her to learn about other religious traditions. This openness inspired her college spiritual quest, not only in the varied programs of the ecumenical Protestant community I pastored at Georgetown, but in explorations in a variety of faith traditions. While at Georgetown, Krista met a Bahá'í student from West Africa who became one of her best friends and recalls thinking "I've near heard of this. This faith sounds too good to be true." Krista wanted to learn more.

Krista recalls that when she first attended the Tokyo Bahá'í Center near Sophia University college where she was studying during her year abroad in Japan, she felt like she was "home" as she encountered people coming together from all over the world. She experienced a heart-felt welcome and, more importantly, she felt inspired by her encounters with the Bahai writings. She found the Bahá'í focus on the unity of religions, the equality of all races and of women and men as well as the unity of spirituality and science revelatory. Her feelings of belonging increased during her time in Japan. As Krista recalls her movement toward Bahá'í now nearly thirty years ago, "I never felt so much at home. Maybe I should join." Following her spirit, Krista identified herself as Bahá'í, committed herself to Bahá'í spirituality, and is, three decades later, an active participant in a small Bahá'í community in Fort Worth, Texas.

In the spirit of Bahá'í, Krista did not feel the need to abandon her Christian faith but sees her Lutheran upbringing as part of a larger circle of human unity. Krista avers that "each day is an adventure in discovering how I impact the world, as I seek to honor everyone and see all people as one." Her favorite quote from Bahá'u'lláh is "the earth is but one country and mankind is its citizens."

Not highly doctrinal, Krista lives her faith one day at a time through simple spiritual practices. "I pray every morning and evening and read from the Bahai scriptures each day." She shared the contents of her book stack with me in which the writings of Bahá'u'lláh sit side by side with the message of Buddhist monk Thich Nhat Hanh. Similar to progressive, process and open and relational Christians, Krista embraces the Bahá'í affirmation of the universality of inspiration. "Faith is a sense of unity and connection and that includes all humankind." As our conversation concluded, I was grateful for Krista's spiritual journey and the opportunity I had as a university chaplain to contribute to the spirituality of scores of students, now as adults sharing their faith with their own children.

WHAT CHRISTIANS CAN LEARN FROM BAHAI

Tragically, from the beginning, Christianity has been a schismatic religion. Once the faith of the martyrs, Christians have martyred, that is, excommunicated, declared heretical, and killed, millions for differences in theology, practice, institutional authority, and race. Centuries of anti-Judaism, culminating in the Holocaust and still alive and well in attacks on synagogues, have marred Jesus' vision of God's all-embracing love. The intimate connection of Christianity and racism, revealed in centuries of slavery and the dehumanization of persons of color, as well as today's Christian nationalism, is a tragic consequence of authoritarian religion, scriptural literalism, and the assumption that there is only one pathway to truth. The genocide of First Americans and other indigenous peoples was justified by colonialist Christians claiming to bring their true light to the First Americans' darkness just as the Hebrews brought God to the benighted Canaanites. The Crusades and the Inquisition manifest the demonic nature of religious absolutes and the confining of truth to our authorized channels.

Beginning with the Reformation, and in the past century, hundreds of denominations have emerged, often declaring the falsehood of their neighbor's faith, based on the most inconsequential differences. We cannot understand the Protestant Reformation's profound theological insights without also remembering the bloody battles between Roman Catholics and Reformers, including religiously sanctioned capital punishment in Geneva and elsewhere, and the hounding of Anabaptists by Catholics, Lutherans and Calvinists alike. Moreover, the rise of anti-Semitism made it easy for German Christians four hundred years later to align themselves with Hitler's "final solution."

As Christians, we must confess the sin of theological, institutional, and sacramental dogmatism and disunity. We must remember, with Reinhold Niebuhr, the limitations of our most deeply held truths, as well as the truth hidden in what we perceive as our neighbor's falsehood. Humility is the heartbeat of religious pluralism and spiritual evolution.

The progressive and universalistic spirit of Baháí reminds Christians that we need to excel in love for one another, making love rather than doctrinal purity our goal. Baháí reminds us that God's revelations take many forms historically. While there may be levels of revelation and inspiration, the great wisdom traditions, including those of indigenous peoples, African spirituality, and pagan earth-based spirituality, emerge from and reveal God's presence in the world. We—and all traditions—have our truths and treasures in jars of clay. All spiritual traditions have treasures to share, and all spiritual traditions are finite and open to further growth. We can learn from diverse understandings of God and the spiritual path. We can grow from the profound monotheism of the Abrahamic religions as well as the non-theistic spirituality of Gautama Buddha. While our calling is to seek the truth, heresy-hunting in any form is an anathema to the spiritual evolution of individuals and the race.

While there are nuances, and sometimes great differences, in the teachings of the great Wisdom Givers or Manifestations, the world's spiritual leaders all point to the ultimate truth of Oneness. God is one. God's message is one light refracted in many ways. We are one despite are apparent differences. We are all pilgrims on the path toward divinity.

Following the wisdom of Baháí and process and openness theology, Christians and persons of other faith traditions need to recognize diversity as a gift from God, not as a fall from grace. God brings forth the varieties of religious experience. God parents forth all the colors of the rainbow, diverse expressions of spirituality and sexuality, and the many gifts of a multi-cultural world. Let us celebrate the One in the Many and the Many in the One.

CHRISTIANITY'S GIFT TO BAHAI FAITH

Baháí faith proclaims God as the organ of spiritual evolution and the energy aiming toward the emergence of world unity. God is active and creative in bringing forth Manifestations or Revelations to respond to the historical and contextual needs of humankind. God will continue to bring forth Prophets in the quest for wholeness. God calls to humankind through the words of prophets, and we respond by following their teaching.

An area under-emphasized by Baháí is the character of God's experience of the world. Like many Christian scriptures, the Baháí focus on what God does unilaterally omits the human and creaturely impact on God. Process and open and relational understandings of God proclaim the interdependence of God and the world. God's love is responsive as well as creative. God receives as well as gives in relationship with the world. In the Christian tradition, Jesus is the ultimate revelation of relatedness. God's love for the world is reflected in God's cruciform suffering and redemptive joy. God is the fellow sufferer who understands, an intimate companion who celebrates.

Progressive and process-relational and openness Christianity can help Baháí expand its understanding of God's loving quest for planetary unity as a social process of call and response. God's Manifestations are not unilateral and abstract but contextual and shaped by God's experience of the world. Divine and human love is relational, feeling the joy and sorrow of those whom we love. God in Christ, the God of process and openness theologies, is the Ultimate Empath, experiencing our lives from the inside and responding in ways that encourage personal evolution and wholeness.

A BAHAI PRACTICE

Baháí asks us to think globally as well as to act locally. Our individual spiritual evolution is connected to looking beyond our individual lives, family, nation, and religion to planetary wholeness. Our lives radiate beyond ourselves in space and time, and our actions should reflect our commitments to wider and wider circles of care. In this exercise, based on my interpretation Baháí theology, the personal and global are joined.

After a time of stillness, involving the practice of breathing deeply and feeling your connection with life within and around you, imagine your breath in terms of a light that fills you with every inhalation. Feel the fullness of God's presence in you. Feel your connection with God's revelations throughout the ages, inspiring and supporting you. Experience your sense of safety and completeness. When a few minutes have passed, begin to consciously join breathing in and breathing out, similar in form to the teachings of Buddhist teacher Thich Nhat Hanh. With each in-breath, experience God and God's creation supporting you. With each out-breath, feel your positive impact on wider and wider circles of life, present and future. Feel your contribution to the well-being of your family and immediate companions, your community and religious organization, your nation, and the planet. Feel your unity with your human and non-human companions. Visualize the world as one living, breathing, diverse reality.

As you conclude this meditation, take time to reflect on one act that will expand your positive impact on the world. In what ways can you, in your realm of activities, promote global unity? Interpersonally? Institutionally? Nationally? How can you bring greater love and greater oneness to the world? Ask God's blessing in giving you the insight, energy, and commitment to be an agent in healing the earth.

CHAPTER EIGHT

Hinduism

At the heart of theological and philosophical reflection is the contrast between the One and the Many. Hinduism asks metaphysical questions—and metaphysics can't be separated from spirituality—such as: Is reality one or is it plural? Is there an eternal spiritual or material substrata to reality or is the manifold plurality of phenomena the ultimate? Is there an unchanging and eternal reality beneath the changes of life or is change the nature of things? Is there one deity or does the Holy have many manifestations?

The interplay of the One and the Many is a political and communal issue as well as a theological and metaphysical issue. The Great Seal of the United States of America proclaims E Pluribus Unum, "out of many, one" or "one, out of many" as a sign of the unity of the thirteen original colonies and the six nations from which the United States emerged: England, Ireland, Scotland, Germany, France, and Holland. Sadly, missing are the First American Nations, the victims of genocide, and the peoples of Africa, brought to the USA against their will.

Throughout its history, the USA has struggled with diversity and pluralism with respect to race, ethnicity, politics, gender, economics, and sexuality. The country was torn asunder by the Civil War, threatening the very existence of the union.

Today, national unity is being threatened by polarization, incivility, demagoguery, conspiracy theories, denial of democracy, and alternative "facts."

Is it possible to affirm with integrity both diversity and unity, whether it be in the body politic, in opinions about the nature of the universe, or in the character of God? Is it possible that the diversity present in the universe reflects diversity in God's nature? Is it possible that the Trinitarian vision of God points to the wondrous dynamic multiplicity of the Holy and its reflections in all creation? Could the vision of a Trinitarian God inspire us to affirm the diverse unity of creation and humankind in all its manifestations?

The contrast of the One and the Many is at the heart of Hinduism, the name of which comes from its spiritual origins along the Indus River. Some Hindu devotees speak of as many as 330 million gods. Even in the West, we know some of their names: the Holy Trinity of Brahma, the Creator; Vishnu, the preserver; and Shiva, the transformer. Not to mention, Shakti and Kali, the feminine creative and transformative energies of the universe. Ganesh, the Elephant God, known for his power to destroy any obstacle in the way of success, is invoked when a new project is begun. Many of us are familiar with Krishna, the powerful and playful manifestation of Vishnu, through the Hare Krishna mantra, chanted by his robed devotees, and popularized in the music of Beatle George Harrison. Yet, there is also the vision of unity within Hinduism: One Reality, Brahman, infinite in being, consciousness, and bliss, which undergirds all the changes of the phenomenal world, and which is manifest in Atman, the deepest, eternal reality of human existence.

My experiences with Hinduism go back to my high school days in the San Francisco Bay Area. Hindu teachers emerged with the coming of the Summer of Love, seeking to share and meditation and chanting, and the good news of Brahman and Krishna, with the affluent and extroverted West. I first read of the Unity beneath change in my encounters with the Transcendental philosophy of Ralph Waldo Emerson, and later the Upanishads and the Bhagavad Gita. I heard the chants of "Hare Krishna, Hare Rama," in George Harrison's "My Sweet Lord," released in 1970, my first year of college, and I encountered several swamis as a high school senior on a quest for enlightenment through meditation and psychedelics. I marched with Krishna devotees through Haight-Ashbury and Golden Gate Park in San Francisco.

In October 1970, as a first-year college student, I learned Transcendental Meditation at Berkeley, California, which began a fifty-plus year journey through TM, Centering Prayer, Lectio Divina, Walking Prayer, Mindfulness Meditation, and Breath Prayer. In response to those who denounce Hindu polytheism as idolatry and see meditation as short-circuiting our relationship with Jesus as Savior, I testify that "I wouldn't be a Christian without Transcendental Meditation." Through the mysterious providence of God, the week after I learned Transcendental Meditation, I quit drugs, alcohol, and meat, and returned to a progressive Christian congregation, whose free-spirited faith enabled me to reclaim the name "Christian" and set on the path of theological reflection, teaching, and ministry. From my teenage encounters with Hinduism, I learned that God has many faces and that there are many faithful paths to encountering the Holy. I discovered the reality of changeless divinity giving birth to the finite world of change and change bringing life to the changeless. Although I remain agnostic as to the exact nature of the afterlife, the integration of my evangelical roots with Hindu philosophy and Christian and Jewish mysticism have given me a sense of confidence that within all the changes of life, there is an Eternal Reality that survives our deaths, and that the life will continue and expand the holy adventure of this lifetime. In my own creative synthesis of the One and Many, and Change and Changelessness, I have come to experience Alfred North Whitehead's vision of the interplay of eternity and temporality, and unity and plurality, found in the hymn:

> *Abide with me*
> *Fast falls the eventide.*

In the Hindu vision, we can embrace, without contradiction, change and changelessness, pleasure and self-denial, chanting and contemplation, withdrawal and social activism, and divine unity and holy diversity. Unity doesn't mean uniformity. The 330 million Hindu gods may be too modest a number to describe the ever-changing, ever-evolving, ever-creative, and ever-plural nature of the Holy in a trillion-galaxy universe.

THE SPIRIT OF HINDUISM

Although the roots of Hinduism, found in the hymns of the Vedic sages, are over 3000 years old, Hinduism has no founder and few boundaries. There are many paths in Hinduism, also known as the Sanatana Dharma, the eternal way. In fact, Hinduism delights in plurality as much as in unity, often absorbing the insights of other traditions in its pantheon of gods and pluralism of religious practices. Every authentic spiritual teacher has, at one time or another, been defined as an avatar, a manifestation of God, by Hindu sages. Hinduism affirms the *apophatic* understanding of divinity, described as Nirguna Brahman, the Infinite and Indescribable One, but also the *kataphatic* approach, Saguna Brahman, the various, embodied, imagistic, and personal Deities. There is in the generous spiritual universe of Hinduism, a path for everyone and eventually, life after life, all paths lead to the One, as all streams, rivers, snow, and rain flow to the Ganges. Hinduism makes the following spiritual affirmations:

- *Divine Oneness.* Beneath every phenomenon and all change is changeless unity. Brahman, the ultimate reality, is described as *Sat, Chit, Ananda*—infinite and pure Being, Bliss, and Consciousness. Never changing, Brahman is the sea in which all things are droplets. Buried under the lively panorama of becoming is pure and unchanging Being, birthless and deathless, soul without end.

- *A Universe of Gods.* There is a god for every time, every place, and every occasion. At least 33 crores or 330 million gods. From unity comes plurality. Brahma, Vishnu, and Shiva and their countless manifestations draw humans toward the Holy in ways appropriate to time, place, gifts, and personality. In the quest for Brahman, we meditate on the Eternal within all things, and seek to go, with Plotinus, from the alone to the Alone. In the world of diverse deities, we pray, chant, dance, and play. There is embodiment and incarnation. Avatars, ranging from Buddha and Krishna to Jesus and beyond, emerge whenever the world needs transformation. The visible, personal, intimate, and lively gods consort with humankind and deliver us from ignorance, in the world of *maya,* temporality, illusion, and *lila,* divine play.

- *You are Divine.* While Jews and Christians speak of humankind in God's image, Hindus believe that, deep down, all of us are truly Divine. The Universal Soul, Brahman, and the Personal Soul, Atman, are the same reality. One is the ocean, the other the waves; one is the river, the other the droplets. The relationship of Atman to our phenomenal life can be compared to the relationship of people to their clothing. Some say, "the clothes make the man," but the clothes aren't the man. What's truly real is the person beneath the clothes, not the clothing they wear. The same applies to the relationship of Soul to body. The Soul is the real person; the body is the superficial reality. When we identify ourselves with the body, we forget who we are. We become lost, anxious, fearful of both life and death. While many Christians believe the human problem is sin or disobedience, Hindus see the main problem of life as ignorance of our true self. We are like the lion raised by goats. We bleat and eat grass and are frightened by predators, when in fact we need to look in the mirror and see our true lion selves, birthless and deathless. Liberation comes from realizing our true nature as Infinite and Eternal, pure consciousness, being, and bliss, fully Divine in nature.

- *An Expansive Universe.* Hindus live in a spacious universe. In contrast to the young—earth and human-centered dogma of fundamentalist Christians, Hindu cosmology posits billions of galaxies, with billions of planets, existing for billions of years. In the constantly changing universe of phenomenal beings, we have the opportunity for millions of lifetimes, incarnations, on our way to enlightenment. Universes come and go with each new day of the Hindu trinity of Brahma, Vishnu, and Shiva. All things must pass. Yet within the arising and perishing of the universe, we make our way to self-awareness, life after life, on the pathway to knowing who we are.

The universe as the play of God (*lila*) is our playground as reflections of the divine. Joy and suffering exist but they are ultimately shadows of the real thing, Brahman/Atman. In the play of life, nothing lasts and nothing ultimately matters. History is simply a tale of divine and human discovery, signifying nothing ultimate or lasting in and of itself but being the stage for self-realization. In contrast to Jewish and Christian understandings of history, the rise and fall of empires is purely superficial, not the theatre of divine call and human response in the quest for God's realm on earth as it is in heaven, as Jews and Christians assert.

- *Many Paths to Holiness.* All paths lead to divinity. The many paths to liberation (moksha) reflect diverse personalities, social settings, and levels of spiritual evolution. The path of Jnana yoga involves the quest for self-awareness, through intuiting intellectually our unity with God. "Thou art That," translated as "you are Brahman," says the Jnana yogi describing the quest to pierce the darkness of ignorance in quest of the true light of Infinity. For the activist, there is Karma yoga in which one sees each act as a pathway to liberation. Doing our duty without attachment to the results propels us forward on the quest to enlightenment. In the Hindu scripture, the Bhagavad Gita, Arjuna is ambivalent about going to battle. He winces at the carnage he will put into motion. The God Krishna/Vishnu advises him to fight on, for to do his duty is to awaken to divine reality. The soldiers on the battlefield, Krishna observes, were never really born, nor will they ever die, despite the outcome of the battle in terms of deaths and casualties. The soul is deathless, despite the appearance of death. Fight on! Win the day! Do the right thing without worrying about results, and you will find spiritual freedom, you will know who you are.

The strenuous path of Raja yoga involves deep contemplation and spiritual exercises to strip away the layers of illusion to experience our True Self. Similar in emotional style to evangelical Christianity, Bhakti yoga involves devotion to God. In the West, the most popular form of Bhakti yoga is identified with the worship of the playful and powerful Krishna, the lover of thousands of *gopikas,* cow-herding girls, enamored of the Lord Krishna's beauty and companionship. We are not God, but we find ourselves in intimate relationship with God. As Bhakti wisdom asserts, "I don't want to be cake; I want to eat cake. I don't want to be God; I want to love God." In singing and chanting, in dancing and praying, we are taken out of ourselves and become united with God as lover and Beloved.

- *Spirituality for All Seasons.* Hindus believe that each season of life is filled with possibilities for joy and fulfillment. Not unlike Erik Erikson's stages of life, Hinduism sees the seasons of life as spiritual and vocational in nature. As a child and youth, we discover that our calling is intellectual and professional growth. From childhood playfulness, we learn teenage skills and prepare for adult responsibilities. In adulthood, we enjoy the quest for pleasure, power, and prosperity. During this time, our calling is to be fruitful and multiply, to conquer the world and birth children, enabling them to continue the adventures of new incarnations. When the first grandchild is born, our calling is to retirement, often described in terms of becoming a forest dweller, living far from the madding crowd. Retirement is a time for soul searching, for deepening our sense of the Infinite, and not merely a time for rounds of golf, cocktail parties, and sea cruises. The real journey now is the exploration of the inner geography, the discovery of the divine within, the Infinite in our finite lives. The final adventure is that of the *sannyasin,* the preparation of the spirit for unity with God. Free of all constraints and obligations, the sannyasin sets their sights on the Infinite. Knowing no gain or loss, the *sannyasin* prepares to put off this mortal coil, toss away their outer garments, and embody Infinite Atman in the world of fleshly finitude.

- *Life After Life.* With the exception of a minority of theological and spiritual outliers, most Jewish and Christian visions of the afterlife affirm the significance of this lifetime and decisions we make for our post-mortem adventures. We have one lifetime followed by adventures in immortality, shaped in good measure by our beliefs and behaviors in this lifetime. According to the mainstream Christian vision, there is one life, one death, and one spiritual home awaiting us. While we may evolve in the afterlife, this evolution does not require further earthly adventures. We do not return to the world for further spiritual growth.

In contrast, Hinduism believes there are "many lives and many mansions." The Eternal puts on and takes off its earthly raiment from life to life. We have been here on earth before, and we return for new incarnations until we experience unity with Divinity, sloughing off ignorance of our true nature to reveal our identity as Atman/Brahman. Our current incarnation is shaped by our values, self-awareness, and behavior in our past lives. What we do in this lifetime will shape the life to come. Karma is the impact of our actions in this life and the next. We reap in this lifetime what we have sown in our previous lives. The doctrine of karma explains that it is no accident that some are born healthy while others are born with disabilities. It is not a matter of chance that some are born into wealth and others born into poverty. Gifts and talents in this lifetime emerge due to impact of our past life decisions. In this moment and this lifetime, we can mend our ways, we can pursue spiritual values and live ethically, doing the right thing and letting go of results as preparation for a more evolved future lifetime.

Hinduism doesn't speculate on how many incarnations, or experiences of transmigration, are necessary to experience full and sustained unity with our True Self. Hinduism promises that our incarnation as humans, while weighed in the balance from lifetime to lifetime, awakens us to the possibility of spiritual liberation. We may have experienced many lifetimes in the non-human world, but birth into a human psychophysical organism is a great gift and responsibility. For Hindus, the wages of ignorance of our true nature, is rebirth, while the reward of self-awareness is the cessation of birth, and full unity of Atman and Brahman.

A JOURNEY TO HINDUISM

Like myself, Jeffery Long, Professor of Religion and Asian Studies at Elizabethtown College, in Elizabethtown, Pennsylvania, began his religious quest at an early age. Growing up Roman Catholic in small town Missouri, Jeffery was a seeker by disposition. He recalls that his family was religious, but their faith involved hard work and morality rather than doctrinal absolutes. His parents supported his interest in science fiction and dinosaurs. Jeffery's youthful theology was shaped as much by the cosmic visions of "Star Trek" and "Star Wars" as the teachings of the Roman Catholic Church.

At age eleven, his world was turned upside down when a truck accident left his physically active, Vietnam veteran father a quadriplegic. After eighteen months of struggling with paralysis, his father placed his wheelchair in the path of a speeding train and was killed instantly. His father's suffering and death led Jeffery to ponder the afterlife. He found the teachings of his church unable to explain his father's death and destiny. The doctrine of purgatory made no sense; his father and family had already lived through purgatory. The idea of hell was morally repugnant to him as he began to ponder the possibility that this lifetime is part of a greater adventure involving spiritual evolution over many lifetimes.

Jeffery found a pathway toward wholeness and an open door to Hinduism through popular culture, through Beatle George Harrison and the film "Gandhi." Just as the Beatles' and Beach Boys' interest in Hindu spirituality inspired me to learn Transcendental Meditation in 1970, film and music introduced Jeffery to the riches of the Hindu tradition, a path with a heart as Carlos Castaneda's Don Juan avers. In viewing "Gandhi" and listening to Harrison's Hindu-influenced songs, Jeffery encountered the Bhagavad Gita. The words of the Hindu holy book resonated with his spirit. Long before Amazon, initially Jeffery's quest for the Bhagavad Gita was thwarted; there were no copies in the public library. Synchronously, he discovered a copy of the Gita at a flea market in the local United Methodist Church parking lot. The words of Krishna, a manifestation of Ultimate Reality, to the warrior Arjuna leaped out at him:

Those who are wise lament neither for the living nor the dead. Never was there a time when I did not exist, nor you, nor all these kings; nor in the future shall any of us cease to be. As the embodied soul continually passes, in this body, from boyhood to youth, and then to old age, the soul similarly passes into another body at death. The self-realized soul is not bewildered by such a change.[24]

In his further readings of the *Bhagavad Gita,* Jeffery found truth and healing and a coherent vision of the afterlife:

That which pervades the entire body is indestructible. No one is able to destroy the imperishable soul...For the soul there is never birth nor death. Nor, having once been, does he ever cease to be. He is unborn, eternal, ever-existing, undying and primeval. He is not slain when the body is slain...As a person puts on new garments, giving up old ones, similarly the soul accepts new material bodies, giving up the old and useless ones...Knowing this, you should not grieve for the body.[25]

Jeffery jokingly describes himself as a "born again Hindu." For many years he claimed the identity of a Hindu-Christian. Now he sees himself as a Hindu with

---

24. *Bhagavad Gita: As It Is,* with translation and commentary by A.C. Bhaktivedanta Swami Prabhupada (Los Angeles: Bhaktivedanta Book Trust, 1972), pp. 21-24. The original verses are *Bhagavad Gita* 2:11b-13.
25. *Ibid,* pp. 26-29; original verses 2:17, 20, 22, and 25b

Christian roots. While he has not repudiated the Roman Catholic tradition, just as I have not repudiated my evangelical Baptist roots, he now sees them as part of a larger story, the universalistic vision of Hinduism and its affirmation that the Holy comes to us in many ways.

Since 2005, Jeffery has been formally affiliated to the Vedanta tradition established by the nineteenth-century Bengali sage and saint, Sri Ramakrishna Paramahamsa. In describing his spiritual journey, Jeffery affirms "I didn't change sides. I believe in the universal truth that the great sages have taught. Of the existing world religions, Hinduism most closely approximates what I see as the universal matrix that encompasses and includes the core insights of all religions."

WHAT CHRISTIANS CAN LEARN FROM HINDUS

Many Paths to God. Although Hinduism, like Christianity, has been plagued by the marriage of spirituality and nationalism, the generous spirit of Hinduism is a gift and a challenge to the monotheistic tendency to limit orthodoxy to one path, profession of faith, or practice. The many paths of Hinduism remind persons of faith that the fullness of Reality and human experience invites many legitimate spiritual paths. All paths are finite and in accord with a particular perspective. Spiritual awareness invites us to humility in our judgment on other spiritual practices and traditions.

Hinduism reminds us that inflexible orthodoxy runs contrary to the diversity of the universe and human existence. We can find God in prayer and protest, solitude and community, action and contemplation, and praise and political involvement. Moreover, the grandeur of the universe and of its Creator remind us that diverse visions of Divinity complement and supplement one another. Contradictions and contrasts abound. We have the obligation to judge the adequacy of doctrines and practices in their portrayal of the Divine, as well as in their fruits in acts of kindness, justice seeking, peacemaking, and reconciliation. God is always more than we can imagine. Whether seen as personal or impersonal, the Divine emerges intimately in every person's experience, and may be found through a variety of paths.

The various paths are not a fall from grace or a plunge into confusion but reflect the dynamic and intimate call and response between God and the world, emerging from different cultures, technologies, topographies, communities, and human experiences and idiosyncrasies. God desires abundant life, and abundant life joins the personal and universal, the intimate and the Infinite. Could it be, as process and openness theology asserts, that the variety of religious experiences and traditions is a reflection of God's desire that all find the fullness of life.

The Importance of Meditation. As I noted earlier, my life was transformed when I learned Transcendental Meditation. While monks and mystics within Christianity have always taught forms of contemplative prayer, the coming of Hinduism and Buddhism to the West inspired Christians to reclaim their spiritual heritage. Many, like myself, practice hybrid techniques, joining Christian centering prayer, *lectio divina,* and the Examen, with Buddhist walking prayer, Hindu meditation, and Chinese and Japanese healing practices. Our Christianity has been enriched by our inter-spirituality.

Hinduism serves as a witness to the importance of solitude and stillness in spiritual growth. The activism of Christian social involvement needs to be balanced and deepened by times of quiet prayer and mindfulness.

CHRISTIANITY'S GIFT TO HINDUISM

In the dialogue between Christians and Hindus, one of the greatest contrasts is their respective visions of history and its significance for the human adventure. The spaciousness of history and the vision of the creation and history as, to an extent, illusory in nature, have led Hinduism to downplay the significance of historical events and the importance of social transformation for spiritual growth. While Mahatma Gandhi's political activism is an exception, much of Gandhi's inspiration came from his understanding of the life of Jesus and his teachings in the Sermon on the Mount and the concept of civil disobedience articulated by Henry David Thoreau. The prophetic spirit of the Hebrew prophets, the ministry of Jesus, and the social gospel and liberation theology movements in Christianity, challenge Hinduism to look outward as well as inward, and to abandon traditions of injustice embedded in the caste system and understandings of reincarnation which counter the quest for justice in this lifetime. Reincarnation, like the promise of heaven, can work against social change. The oppressed can be told, usually by the comfortable, politically powerful, and affluent, to delay social change and justice-seeking in favor of the next incarnation or heavenly reward.

The spirit of process-relational and openness Christianity says that this life matters. What happens in the economy and politics matters to human spiritual flourishing, and to the embodiment of God's vision in the world. Christians and Hindus alike need to go beyond individual visions of spirituality and the after-life. In the interdependence of life, our future incarnations, or our ability to experience God in this lifetime and beyond, depend in good measure on our social and political status. The mystic, as one of my spiritual mentors Howard Thurman says, must challenge everything that stands in way of human flourishing.[26] The simplicity of life necessary for spiritual evolution must be a choice. While some spiritual seekers, such as Francis of Assisi may choose to abandon their affluence, progressive and process-relational and openness theologians hold that poverty, resulting from inequality and social injustice, is not a choice, and destroys bodies as well as spirits. Social justice and environmental consciousness are requisite for spiritual transformation in the 21st century. Despite its temporality and fragility, this world is our home, and our earthly lives are more than the clothing we put on and take off daily.

A HINDU SPIRITUAL PRACTICE

Over fifty years ago, I received a mantra to repeat as part of my Transcendental Meditation (TM) practice. The popularity of TM led to a resurgence in interest in Christian meditation practices, pioneered by Thomas Keating, Basil Pennington, and John Main. These forms of Christian contemplation or Centering Prayer, like Hindu mantras (Om, Om Shanti), are intended to be search lights for our inner divinity, the Christ within, or Atman. Repeated regularly, and letting go of distractions, these mantras take us from the superficial surface to the divine depths of life. They enable us to experience our inner holiness and connection with all life, as well as awaken us to divine guidance in daily life.

In the spirit of TM and other Hindu-based meditative techniques, you may choose to explore a Hindu mantra such as "Om" or "Aum" (the divine) as you inhale and "Shanti" (peace) as you exhale. You may also choose a mantra or centering word from the Christian tradition, repeating slowly as you breathe gently, such as

---

26. For more on Howard Thurman's blend of mysticism and social action, see Bruce Epperly, *Prophetic Healing: Howard Thurman's Vision of Contemplative Activism* (Richmond, IN: Friends United, 2020).

"Je-Sus," inhaling on the first syllable, exhaling on the second syllable. You might choose to repeat the words "peace," "light," "love," God," and let your breath follow.

For those who are now of retirement age or beyond, such as myself, I encourage you to learn more about the Hindu notion of *sannyasin,* or forest dweller, who chooses to let go of many of life's responsibilities to focus on Eternity. This doesn't mean letting go of your responsibilities to the social order and future generations or declining your vocation to be a "good ancestor." It does mean disengaging from what is unimportant, letting go of the detritus and the disturbing, to focus on your Spirit. It means to seek the peace of everlasting life in a changing world. We are mortals, dusty as well as eternal, and in spiritual disengagement, we prepare for the great letting go of the small self to awaken to the Great Self (the dynamic divine within, the Atman, the resurrection life) that is our deepest reality and destiny.

CHAPTER NINE

Buddhism

When I was in graduate school in the mid-1970s, I was introduced to breath prayer by Congregational minister Allan Armstrong Hunter. In Hunter's prayer, as you inhaled, you "spoke" silently the words, "I breathe the Spirit deeply in." As you exhaled, you filled your mind with the words, "And blow it gratefully out again." Thirty years later, I encountered a similar life-changing prayer in Vietnamese Buddhist monk Thich Nhat Hanh's book on mindful living, *Peace is Every Step*:

> *Breathing in*
> *I feel calm.*
> *Breathing out*
> *I smile.*

These days, I use these prayers interchangeably to focus spiritually and respond creatively to the stresses of life. I have encouraged newly minted professors and preachers-in-training to breathe deeply and prayerfully for a centering moment before they begin their sermons or classes. Peace is only a breath away.

Buddhism is a path of calm compassion and mindful exploration that has inspired many inter-spiritual pilgrims in North America. The Dalai Lama and Thich Nhat Hanh have enriched millions of spiritual seekers by their global spirituality, intellectual acuity, and personal integrity. Many Christians like me have benefitted by from practicing Buddhist prayer and sitting meditation. We have been intrigued and challenged by the humorous, irreverent, and intuitive legends of Zen Buddhist monks. We have found inspiration from the global compassion of Bodhisattvas who, like Jesus, sacrificed the equanimity of enlightenment to plunge into the world in all its tragic beauty to bring healing to all creation.

Like Christianity, Buddhism is a multifaceted religion. There is the strenuous spirituality of Gautama Buddha and the Theravada monastic tradition.[27] There is also the diverse and graceful spirituality of the Mahayana, "greater vehicle," movement which includes mindfulness meditation; Zen sitting meditation and intuitive riddles or koans; and the devotional practices of Amida and Shinran Buddhism. Similar in spirit to Bhakti devotional yoga, Shinran and Amida Buddhists find salvation by simply calling on the name of Buddha, trusting the merit of Buddha or, a bodhisattva, to escape the wheel of death and rebirth.

During my college years, I was invited to a Buddhist church in San Jose, California, the worship of which reminded me of the progressive Christian congregation I attended at the time. My Buddhist classmate told me that deliverance from earthly tragedy, and unity with Buddha resulted from simply calling on Buddha's name (Namo Amida Butsu) in faith and confidence. As I heard his testimony, his words reminded me of the confessions of faith characteristic of my evangelical childhood. The many faces of Buddhism, like the diverse yogas of Hinduism, provide pathways to wholeness in response to the variety of personal, experiential, and intellectual types of followers.

Like Christianity, Buddhism receives its name from the title given to its energizing spirit. Christ is the Messiah, the Chosen and Anointed One, God's Savior of the World. Buddha, who lived approximately from 567 to 487 BCE, is the Enlightened, or Awakened One, who chose to become the Waymaker, who delivers humankind from suffering and rebirth.

Once upon a time, seekers came to Gautama Buddha, trying to understand his true identity. "Are you an angel? A god? A teacher?" they queried. Buddha responded, "I am awake." Gautama Buddha's path to awakening took him from privilege to poverty and then to letting go of all spiritual attachments and, ultimately, enlightenment. The son of a great king in India, Siddhartha Gautama, was destined to

---

27. The Theravada tradition considers itself the "way of the elders," reflecting the meditative simplicity of Gautama Buddha.

the life about which virtually everyone dreams: power, pleasure, prestige, wealth, a beautiful wife, and fame. He enjoyed the lifestyle of the rich and famous. The world was his oyster. When he was a baby, a fortune teller predicted that if he stayed in the palace as a child and youth, he would become one of the great kings of India. On the other hand, if he encountered the harsh realities most people face, he would abandon political power to become a great spiritual teacher. Wanting to preserve his political legacy, his father ensured a life of comfort and protection for his young son. Gautama married, had a child, and lived into young adulthood shielded from the pain of the world. Yet, he felt an inner movement, one he couldn't quite define, for something more, something beyond power and prestige.

Spiritual awakening is often the work of a deeper providence, one we cannot shield ourselves or our children from. At age 29, when Buddha finally ventured forth from the palace and encountered an aged man, he discovered that his wealth couldn't protect him from the aging process. All things must pass: youth succumbs to age, and health to sickness. The next day, he encountered a sick person and recognized that illness can strike at any time, rendering the healthiest of us disabled and dependent. On the third day, when Gautama quietly escaped the palace, he happened upon a corpse, and the realization that death is the fate of all flesh, including princes and kings. On the fourth day, Gautama met a monk, and discovered an alternative to privilege and power. Back home, Gautama could no longer be satisfied with his lifestyle of wealth and power. Eventually he left the palace, his wife and his child, to pursue spiritual deliverance from the vicissitudes of life.

For six years, Gautama sought spiritual awakening and equanimity, but no path, not even mortification of the flesh, could satisfy his questioning spirit. At age 35, determined to become enlightened, Gautama vowed to sit under the Bo Tree under which he experienced spiritual awakening. Like Jesus, he experienced the temptation to turn his back on the world, and to claim enlightenment solely for himself. But, also like Jesus, Buddha stayed the course, experienced spiritual liberation, and chose a life of compassionate teaching, not hoarding enlightenment but sharing it with the world for the next forty-five years. At eighty, and preparing to die, Gautama Buddha, the Enlightened One, gave his own Great Commission to his followers: "Behold, O monks, this is my last advice to you. All component things in the world are changeable. They are not lasting. Work hard to gain your own salvation. Do your best." He enjoined his followers to be lights for themselves, seeking their enlightenment, and then as part of the Sangha, the community of monks, give light to the world.

Like Christianity, Buddhism became a path for the world, and is active on every continent, with approximately 500 million followers, including millions of North American practitioners and students. Although Buddhism has nearly died out in India, the wisdom of Buddha moved southward to Vietnam, Cambodia, Myanmar, and Thailand, and northward to China and Japan, before the crossing oceans and mountains to bring enlightenment to the Western world.

THE GLOBAL SPIRIT OF BUDDHISM

Followers of Gautama would be the first to tell us that the spirit of Buddhism transcends doctrine. Experience trumps orthodoxy. You can't confuse the finger pointing to the moon with the moon itself. As Buddhist wisdom notes, if you are hit by a poisoned arrow, you don't ask who shot the arrow, or its composition. You call a call a doctor and receive medical treatment. In that spirit, the heartbeat of Buddhism can't be encompassed by any theological formulation. Still, despite its pragmatic and experiential orientation, Buddhism, like every other wisdom tradition, has its own unique spiritual and theological contours.

- *The Experiential Nature of Religion.* Buddhism is proof that belief in God or specific doctrines or rituals are not requirements for a religious movement. Gautama focused on experience and challenged anything that blocked the path to spiritual awakening. A contemporary of the Hebraic prophetic tradition, Gautama was a prophet whose direct experience of the Holy inspired him to jettison the Hindu cosmology, social order, temple and ritual system, and priesthood. Like Socrates and Confucius, he was agnostic about the nature of Divinity, and believed that direct experience is more important than doctrinal orthodoxy. Pragmatic in spirit, Gautama Buddha identified the causes of suffering, and proposed a cure. Experience in its complexity is primordial in the quest for enlightenment; doctrines and cosmologies are secondary and often get in the way of the quest for enlightenment.

- *The Truths of Life.* Gautama Buddha's Four Noble truths diagnose life's problems and provide a path to healing. The First Noble Truth is that life is suffering, Buddha asserts. This is not world denial, but recognition that, in a world of perpetual perishing, we experience pain in childbirth, growing up, adolescence, aging, and dying. We experience pain in disappointment and grief. The Second Noble Truth is that our suffering is caused by the desire to control reality, freeze-frame positive experiences and, ironically, negative experiences as well, to hold on to what is ever-changing. Life is perpetually perishing. All things, even our most joyful experiences and proudest achievements, must pass. Or, as the soap opera says, "Like sands in an hourglass, so are the days of our lives." Attachment and desire bring pain, while "going with the flow" brings contentment and equanimity. The Third Noble Truth is that suffering can be alleviated. There is hope that we can escape desire and suffering, and the round of death and rebirth. The Fourth Noble Truth is that there is a pathway to enlightenment and joy, the Eightfold Path. Transformed values and behaviors lead to transformed experiences and liberate us from the wheel of ignorance and rebirth.

- *The Importance of Right Beliefs and Behaviors: The Eightfold Path.* Mosaic law says that God has placed two paths before us: the path of life and the path of death, and then enjoins us to choose life. In similar fashion, the Eightfold path is Buddha's path of life that delivers us from suffering and ignorance and brings us from death to life. Enlightenment is not accidental, but emerges from practical behaviors, involving our world view and life focus, intentionality, employment, speech, attitudes toward life, relationships, and daily habits, and commitment to contemplative living. Soren Kierkegaard once stated that "purity of heart is to will one thing." That is the point of the Eightfold Path, to shape your daily decisions and behaviors toward the goal of enlightenment. Later Buddhists would describe this as mindfulness, open-spirited awareness of the quality of your life, moment by moment, in the quest for spiritual awakening. In a similar fashion, many Christians practice the Examen, the reflection on one's daily life as a means of discerning one's spiritual progress, opening to God's wisdom, and correcting anything that diminishes our commitment to God.

- *The Interdependence of Life.* Buddhism sees one of the greatest metaphysical, political, and spiritual evils of life as attachment to independent, individualistic existence. Reality is relational and dynamic: always connected and always changing. As Whitehead says, and Buddhists affirm, the whole universe conspires to create each moment of experience. All things are connected in a dynamic ecology of life. We create one another through our thoughts and actions. Our joys and sorrows are one reality, touching all of us. Empathy and compassion are the primary ethical virtues. I cannot be fully happy until all sentient beings find happiness. When an enlightened one forgoes nirvana until all sentient beings are enlightened, these great souls—Bodhisattvas—affirm the wisdom of Martin Luther King, who asserted, "Whatever affects one directly, affects all indirectly. I can never be what I ought to be until you are what you ought to be. This is the interrelated structure of reality." In speaking of our response to global climate change, environmentalist Bill McKibben asserts that "the best thing an individual can do is to quit being an individual."

- *A World of Change.* Central to Buddha's vision of reality and subsequent Buddhism is the recognition that the self is a dynamic rather than a stable entity. Even the use of the word "self" suggests stability when it is actually an illusion in the constant flow of experience from one moment to another. Process theology and Buddhism both assert that the self is constantly arising and perishing, moment by moment, and day to day. Every moment of experience arises out of its environment, synthesizes its experience into a unitary reality, and then perishes to give birth to the next occasion of experience. The dynamic and momentary self can be compared to one candle being blown out and then in a split second, giving light to its emerging successor. Experience, in all its incredible dynamism and complexity, is all there is. The unchanging Christian soul or Hindu Atman is an illusion. Our sense of self is not an eternal deposit beneath the surface of life, but instead, a constantly changing phenomenon grounded in the perception of a shared history and series of experiences from one moment to another. As Whitehead avers, the process *is* the reality. In contrast to the notion of an enduring substance, Buddhism affirms a continuation of energy and experience, more, or less, enlightened, and more, or less, burdened by the impact of past actions, or karma, that migrates from life to life. Healthy spirituality goes with the flow of life, observing and letting go, while being immersed in healing the world.

- *Nirvana.* Whereas Christians describe heaven or the realm of God as the eschatological or post-mortem goal of existence, Buddhists speak of the spiritual quest culminating in Nirvana. Nirvana is literally translated as "blowing out," the extinguishing of the energy that propels us from one life to another. Negatively put, Nirvana means that the cycle of death and rebirth comes to an end. The dynamic, arising, perishing self, compelled by the impact of its thoughts and actions, its karma, ceases, never to be born again. Whereas the apostle Paul says, the wages of sin is death, the Buddhist monk affirms that the wages of ignorance is rebirth. This contrast has led to the humorous meme, "Jesus saves. Buddha recycles."

Positively understood, Nirvana means the expansion of self to embrace the well-being of all creation. In the spirit of Jesus, spiritual growth involves growing in wisdom and stature, and moving from self-interest to world loyalty.

- *Compassion: The Way of the Bodhisattva.* In Charles Sheldon's social gospel classic, *In His Steps,* followers of Jesus are challenged to ask, "What would Jesus do?" whenever they have a serious decision to make. In like fashion, Buddhists are invited to ask, "What would the Buddha do?" in their quest for enlightenment. A critical moment in Buddha's spiritual journey involved his choice to share the path to enlightenment or to retreat to a monastery. Historically, Buddhists have taken one of two spiritual paths, the path of the Arhat, the life of the solitary monk, and or that of the Bodhisattva, the choice of an enlightened one to defer Nirvana until all sentient beings are enlightened. The compassionate Buddha or Bodhisattva, like the Savior Jesus, sacrifices equanimity and calm to plunge into the maelstrom of conflict and suffering. Buddha's spiritual journey serves as the example for our own quest for enlightenment. Spiritual stature embraces, rather than avoids, the pain of the world. Enlightenment moves us from apathy to empathy. Paul's hymn to the self-sacrificing Christ, who gives up eternal joy to become one of us, suffering as we do, could easily describe the goal of the compassionate Buddha. (Philippians 2:5-11)

- *The Intuitive Way of Zen.* The following encounter captures the spirit of Zen, or the Buddhism of sitting meditation and intuitive wisdom. A university professor visited a Zen master to discover the essence of Zen. While the master served tea, the professor talked profusely about his understanding of Zen. As the professor rambled, describing his intellectual credentials, the Zen master poured the visitor's cup to the brim, and then kept pouring. Taken aback by the master's behavior, the professor exclaimed, "The cup is full. Nothing more can go in." The master replied, "You are like this cup. You have so many ideas that nothing more can go in. How can I tell you anything about Zen unless you empty your cup?"

While Zen Buddhism appreciates good literature and parabolic sayings, Zen seeks to go beyond thought and concept to experience our deepest dynamic and interdependent spiritual self. Doctrines get in the way of reality and often lead to violence. Consider the mayhem caused by the relationship of fundamentalist Islam and Christianity to political violence and suppression of diversity. Fundamentalists, so enamored by their concepts, live by abstractions and not reality. They see people who differ from themselves as cardboard figures without souls, lost and wayward, hell-bent on damnation, thus deserving no ethical consideration.

Zen *koans,* or parabolic sayings, take us beyond the rational and controlling mind, pierce our ordinary way of looking at reality, and awaken us to our true nature. This experience is known as *satori,* or breakthrough. Some of the best known *koans* are "what is the sound of one hand clapping?" or "what did your face look like before you were born?" According to Zen, each of us must be a light unto ourselves, finding our own spiritual way. Even holding onto the Buddha can be a problem if you look for a dogmatic, authoritarian belief system, and not your dynamic, relational, experience. The iconoclastic Zen monk goes so far as to say, "If you meet the Buddha on the road, kill him."

- *Ordinary Spirituality.* One of the most well-known Zen Buddhist sayings is "Before enlightenment, I chopped wood and carried water. After enlightenment, I chopped wood and carried water." Like the Protestant affirmation of the priesthood of all believers, Zen Buddhist spirituality affirms the unity of the sacred and the secular. Every task can be holy, and every encounter can be a pathway to enlightenment. Following the principle of right livelihood, any task for anyone from student to retired volunteer, can contribute to our enlightenment. Enlightened people bring beauty and compassion to ordinary tasks. Enlightenment does not deliver us from ordinary responsibilities. Enlightenment adds zest to everyday tasks. Washing dishes, grading papers, preparing sermons, caring for children and grandchildren, and cooking meals. Enlightenment is here on earth. You don't need to wait to the afterlife for awakening; it's already here.

BUDDHISM IN PROCESS: CAN CHRISTIANS BE BUDDHISTS, TOO?

Recently I had the opportunity of hearing Jay McDaniel lead a seminar, sponsored by the Cobb Institute, "Can Christians Be Buddhists, Too?" Jay is one of my oldest friends and someone whose intellectual and spiritual acumen I have appreciated for over four decades. As graduate students, at Claremont Graduate School, we were roommates from 1975 to 1977. During that time, Jay was reflecting on the relationship between Buddhism and process theology. Over the years, Jay has been a leader in process theology, the author of many books on theology, spirituality, and ecology, editor of "Open Horizons" and a convener of the "Process and Faith" websites, as well as a pioneer in bringing process thought to China, and now emeritus Professor in Religion at Hendrix College in Conway, Arkansas.

In his seminar, Jay shared his journey toward integrating Buddhism and Christianity in his spiritual life. Raised as a United Methodist in Austin, Texas, Jay saw love at the heart of Christianity. God was love and in loving one another, we become more Christ-like. As a college student, Jay became influenced by evangelical Christianity and discovered something troubling about himself: the more "orthodox" he became, the more defensive and dogmatic he also became, and sadly the less loving he became, especially to those who didn't follow God's ways as articulated in evangelical understandings of the Bible.

According to his recollections, Jay first became interested in Buddhism during his senior year in college. In his words, "I was looking for an alternative to a form of fundamentalist Christianity into which I had briefly fallen; and I found that alternative in the writings of the late Catholic writer, Thomas Merton…He was a monk living in a monastery in Gethsemane, Kentucky, who wrote voluminously on many topics, including war and peace, social justice, contemplative prayer, mysticism, and Buddhism. Merton's interest in Buddhism struck a chord in me because I, like he, was drawn to forms of spirituality that emphasize 'letting go of words' and 'being aware in the present moment.' Protestant Christianity often seemed too wordy to me. Buddhism pointed to a world beyond words. One reason I especially liked Merton was that he was sensitive to the fact that Christianity, too, points to a world beyond words."[28]

Merton inspired him to seek a deeper love, one that for Merton joined the wisdom of Buddhism and Christianity. While in seminary and graduate school, Jay took courses in Buddhism and had the opportunity to be a companion and English tutor to a Buddhist roshi, a Zen master or spiritual guide, "Gensho," with whom he spent nearly every day for a year as the monk sought to immerse himself in American culture. During this time, Jay began practicing Zazen, or sitting meditation, and has been a practitioner of Zen Buddhist meditation for over forty years. According to Jay, "Zen had something that I needed in my spiritual journey." In the process, Jay discovered what Vietnamese monk Thich Nhat Hanh describes as "living Buddha, living Christ." He is active in his local Episcopal church and daily practices Zen meditation.

Jay was then and still is uncomfortable with the phrase "double belonging," a description of persons who participate in practices from two different religious traditions. "Even as I felt like I was experiencing two different worlds each day, I did not feel that I belonged to two countries and had two passports. Rather, I felt like one person who was receiving nourishment from two intravenous tubes: one the dharma of Buddhism and the other the wisdom of Christ. I borrow this metaphor from a wonderful Zen teacher in the United States, Susan Jion Postal. Intuitively I knew the two medicines were compatible, but I was trying to figure out how they were compatible with my mind. Moreover, I knew that if I had to choose one medicine over another, I would choose Christ. I was not all Buddhist and all Christian, or half Buddhist and half Christian, but rather a Christian influenced by Buddhism. Fortunately, the two fluids did indeed feel compatible and mutually enriching, so I wasn't forced to choose. Each had a healing quality that could add to the other."[29]

28. Jay McDaniel, "Can a Christian be a Buddhist Too?" (Can a Christian be a Buddhist, Too? - Open Horizons)
29. Ibid.

Jay's spirituality is motivated by three important questions: 1) the reality of a personal God who hears our prayers, 2) the Buddhist affirmation of *anatta* or no self, that is, the self is constantly in process, arising and perishing, with no permanent unchanging ground, and 3) the interdependence of life. Jay believes that process theology enables him to integrate Buddhism and Christianity as complementary spiritual paths, enriching one another intellectually and spiritually. Process and openness theology sees the personal God as dynamic, relational, and the ultimate model of selflessness. God is creative-responsive love, receiving as well as giving and constantly immersed in the world of change. In contrast, to the unmoved mover of Aristotle, influential in Christian theology, who is distant and unchanged by the world, the God of process and openness is the most moved mover, inter-dependent, passionate, and ever-changing. As the author of Lamentations asserts, God's love endures forever, God is faithful, and God's mercies are new every morning. Jay avers that the personal God of process theology can be described as the cosmic Bodhisattva, who defers enlightenment until everyone experiences enlightenment or liberation from suffering. Indeed, I (Bruce) believe, that the life of Jesus superlatively describes the spirit of the Bodhisattva.

According to Jay, "Buddhism is a constant reminder that every moment is an opportunity for enlightenment. From Buddhism, I believe we can be non-judg-mental, embracing the moment as it emerges, fulfilling our spiritual vocation as a partner in bringing wholeness to the world in which all of us are connected."

Jay affirms that we can be both Christian and Buddhist, and that the God revealed in Jesus goes beyond the boundaries of institutional and doctrinal Christianity. "Faith in God is trust in the availability of fresh possibilities. And life in God lies in being present to each situation in a kindly way, open to surprise, honest about suffering, and seeking wisdom for daily life. I saw this kind of faith in 'Gensho.' He did not have an image of God in whom he placed that faith. When God becomes an ocean, we must sit loose with images, too, lest we make idols of them. Still, we can have faith in something more, maybe even someone more: someone who listens and seeks our well-being. This is a faith to which I am drawn, moment by moment, as I try to walk with Christ, with help from Zen."[30]

---

30. Ibid.

WHAT CHRISTIANS CAN LEARN FROM BUDDHISTS

Experiential Religion. As a theologian, I recognize the importance of reflection on our vision of reality, the nature of God, human freedom, providence, and ethical analysis. I also realize the danger of inflexible understandings of God, scripture, ritual, and doctrine. Fundamentalist and authoritarian religious perspectives often lead to authoritarian politics, ostracism of divergent positions, and persecution. Fundamentalism privileges abstractions over concrete experience. Doctrinal absolutism substitutes the finger pointing to the moon for the moon itself.

Gautama Buddha focused on spiritual experience rather than doctrine. Thich Nhat Hanh describes Buddhism as a practice, rather than a religion focusing on doctrines. More important than our thoughts about God is self-awareness and spiritual awakening. More fulfilling than the recipe for cake is eating the cake itself. Spirituality involves cultivating experiences of the divine, not thoughts about God. Although Buddhism takes seriously our worldviews, it also counsels doctrinal flexibility. Buddhism's pragmatic spirit is an antidote to doctrinal and political absolutism, and the identification of our viewpoints with divine truth. Experiential humility delivers us from the absolutist perspectives characteristic of Christian exceptionalism and its attendant aberrations, such as Christian nationalism, conspiracy theories, and political idolatry.

Radical Interdependence. Buddhism is an antidote to the rugged individualism characteristic of North American Christianity. Tragically, Christianity has conformed to Western individualism, rather than transformed the West with its image of the interdependent body of Christ. Buddhist interdependence reminds us that we are all in this together. Independent existence is an illusion, whether it relates to economics or salvation. Success and failure are relational. Our economic and spiritual wellbeing depend on the wellbeing of others.

Individualistic understandings of spirituality lead to binary understandings of heaven and hell, the divisions of orthodoxy and heresy, and the chasm between the saved and unsaved. In contrast, dynamic interdependence inspires compassion. Buddhist Bodhisattvas, like the sacrificial Christ, identify their individual well-being with the healing of creation, inviting us to go from self-interested individualism to world loyalty.

CHRISTIANITY'S GIFT TO BUDDHISM

Historically Buddhism has given little attention to social justice issues. As a result of his involvement in social issues, and eventual exile, Thich Nhat Hanh has advocated for an "engaged Buddhism," that joins contemplation with action to promote justice in public policy and economics. Grounded in the Hebraic prophets, Jesus' Sermon on the Mount, and the twenty-and twenty-first century social gospel and liberation theology movements, the interplay of spirituality and social change is at the heart of progressive Christianity and process and open and relational theology. The personal is the political, and the political is the personal. According to Christian spiritual guide Howard Thurman, the mystic challenges any social or political practice that stands in the way of persons experiencing fulfillment. Inspired by the social activism of Jesus and the prophets, civil rights activists joined prayer and protest. Motivated by the vision of prophetic healing, they challenged racism and injustice, while seeing the divine in those whom they opposed. Given the impact of prophetic spirituality, Buddhism's vision of the interdependence of life can be a catalyst to world-transforming activism, joining contemplation and confrontation, to challenge racism, economic injustice, and global climate change. The interdependence of life reminds us that we are all in the same storm and need to see ourselves as all occupying the same boat. Social conditions shape spiritual growth, and spiritual teachers need to promote a social order conducive to the quest for enlightenment.

A BUDDHIST SPIRITUAL PRACTICE

On Easter night, Jesus breathed on his disciples and said, "Receive the Holy Spirit." Centuries before Jesus, the Psalmist proclaimed, "Let everything that breathes praise God! Praise God!" The simplest and most universal activities, inhaling and exhaling, can be the source of the greatest spiritual insight. Breathing mindfully and slowly grounds and centers, reduces stress and restores calm. It also connects us compassionately with all creation.

Like many other Buddhist teachers, Vietnamese Buddhist monk Thich Nhat Hanh counsels us to breathe mindfully. In fact, every breath can be a prayer and an encounter with the holiness of the moment, if we devote our breaths to the planet and our neighbor. In the spirit of Thich Nhat Hanh, I will share some of the ways I use breath as part of my spiritual life:

- I take a few gentle breaths before I begin a talk, seminar, or sermon, or even a writing project.

- I breathe and open to insight when I log onto my computer, especially when it takes longer than I expect.

- I breathe gently and deeply when I experience myself become stressed or busy.

- I breathe before I post a response on Facebook or respond to a point of contrast or conflict at a meeting.

- I breathe prayerfully as I gaze at my wife reading beside me, sharing deeply my love for her.

Every breath can become a prayer for those who awaken to the everlasting and holy now in which we live and move and have our being.

Thich Nhat Hanh advises us to use the following statements as we breathe calmly and deeply:

> *Breathing in, I calm my body.*
> *Breathing out, I smile.*
> *Dwelling in the present moment,*
> *I know this is a wonderful moment.*

When we breathe compassionately, we move from apathy to empathy. One compassionate breath prayer, *tonglen,* involves our willingness to identify and then heal the suffering of the world. After a time of spiritual centering, gently inhaling and exhaling, during the time of pandemic, I slowly breathed in the pain of persons suffering from COVID-19, those who are dying, and those who are grieving. I experience my connection with their suffering, moving from apathy to empathy. We are one, and my desire is to ease their suffering. I breathed out comfort and healing to those who suffer, surrounding them with love and seeking their happiness.

CHAPTER TEN

Jainism

One of the most important theological and ethical questions involves humankind's place in the universe and the relationship between the human and non-human world. Is human life continuous with the non-human world, as the theory of evolution suggests, or are humans, created in the image of God, qualitatively different from the non-human world, as many conservative Christians assert? Does the non-human world have value apart from human interests or does it merely exist to benefit humans? Is nature intended for our exploitation or does it inspire our reverence? Do our behaviors in relationship to the non-human world have moral implications? Does God's image, and care, extend beyond humankind? Do non-humans have souls?

With the growing necessity of taking seriously global climate change and humankind's destruction of nature, it is imperative that we focus on the extent of our moral responsibility to non-human creatures and to the natural world. Process and open and relational theologies hold that whatever exists, and whatever can experience, has inherent value and, accordingly, deserves our ethical consideration. Non-human life matters to God, whose eye is on the sparrow, and who rejoices in the praises of creation. As scientific studies indicate, trees and flowers may communicate at a rudimentary level with one another and with insect species, giving credence to the vision of a living universe. Moreover, there is growing evidence that our emotional lives may influence the growth of flowers, and that, as Japanese scientist Masuro Emoto asserts, human consciousness may even have an impact on water crystals.

Long before the times of Jesus and the emergence process-relational and openness theologies, the religion of the Jains, grounded in the insights of Mahavira and his spiritual predecessors, affirmed that every creature has an internal life force, or soul (*jiva*), that is eternal and unchanging. Possession of such a soul is not limited to humankind, but is found in domestic and wild animals, and whales and fish of the sea, as well as in microbes, trees, rocks, and water particles. In a world in which all creation has an inner spirit, every being deserves respect and reverence, and *ahimsa,* non-violence or non-injury should guide our every interaction. While life is robbery, that is, survival requires some degree of destruction, we must minimize destruction, by embodying a lifestyle of non-injury characterized by vegetarianism, care for insects, respect for ponds and water, and constant vigilance. Recognizing that the soul is present in all things, Jain monastics walk lightly on the earth sweeping the ground in front of them to avoid any harm to insects in their path, believing that harming even the smallest mite causes pain to the creatures and hinders their own spiritual evolution.

Jain spirituality owes its origins to the twenty-fourth Way Maker, or Way Crosser, Mahavira (599-527 BCE), an older contemporary of Gautama Buddha. Like Gautama, Mahavira was raised surrounded by great wealth, but found comfort and opulence unable to satisfy his spiritual quest. At age thirty, Mahavira left home, family, security, and social standing behind to become an ascetic. He went so far as to renounce clothing, wearing nothing but air for a garment, affirming, "I will look upon all creatures as equals. I will speak only truth. I will possess nothing. I will take nothing from others. I will practice lifelong celibacy."[31] Mahavira considered ant and human equal, both possessing an eternal soul despite belonging to different species.

After twelve years of meditation and asceticism, Mahavira experienced enlightenment and then committed himself to a complete withdrawal from the passions of this lifetime, eradicating fully the impact of karma and embodiment on his soul. Like Gautama, Mahavira attained enlightenment while meditating under a

---

31. Andrea Diem-Lane, *Ahimsa: A Brief Guide to Jainism* (Walnut, CA: Mount San Antonio College, 2016), 25.

tree. According to legend, the 24th Way Crosser, or Tirthankara, explained his enlightenment:

I am all-knowing and all-seeing possessing an infinite knowledge. Whether I am waking or standing still, whether I sleep or remain awake, the Supreme Knowledge and Intuition are present with me—constantly and continuously.[32]

Following his enlightenment, Mahavira, like Francis of Assisi who preached to wolves and birds some eighteen hundred years later, gave his first sermon to both humans and non-humans, explaining that *ahimsa,* or non-injury was the way of enlightenment for all sentient beings. Mahavira believed that carnivorous animals can speed their enlightenment by becoming vegetarians. Long before Charles Darwin, Mahavira challenged the foundations of what was to be known as the Darwinian theory of evolution through competition and survival of fittest. He felt that conflicts among non-human animals emerge from their passions and ignorance and can be rooted out by positive relationships with sages. Evolution occurs as much through cooperation as competition. At seventy-two, Mahavira gave his final sermon to his followers, summarizing the five principals of Jainism: non-violence, truthfulness, refraining from theft, self-control, and detachment from worldly possessions. He told his followers not to grieve at his death because death is an illusion, the soul, or *jiva,* of humans and non-humans alike is immortal.

THE ASCETIC VISION OF JAINISM

Like Buddhism and Hinduism, Jainism joins metaphysics and mysticism. Aligned with the eternal nature of things and, thus, transcending the bondage of the material world, we experience enlightenment, and are freed from the negative karmic impact of embodiment and reincarnation. At the heart of Jainism are the following practical principles, aimed at liberating all creatures from violence, passion, and attachment to the physical world.

- *The Eternal Soul.* Beneath and within every physical being dwells an eternal soul, *jiva.* In a universe that has neither beginning nor end, nor a creator god, individual souls are joined with matter. There are souls in obvious beings: humans, chimpanzees, right whales, and dolphins. There are also souls hidden in what most people deem unlikely places: in

---

32. Ibid., 13.

mosquitos, gnats, rain drops, human sweat, quarks, microbes, and even human secretions. In the physical realm, all souls are sheathed in matter. Although there is no beginning to *ajiva* (matter), its nature is inherently ambiguous. Matter is necessary to creation, eternally emerging alongside soul. Matter allows us to navigate the physical world, but it is also the source of passion and ignorance. Our thoughts and actions within the embodied realm can bind us more completely to the burden of physical existence and condemn us to the cycle of death and rebirth. The impact of our mindless and destructive actions covers the soul, in the same way that moss, mold, or lichen covers trees, flat surfaces, and submerged vessels, disguising it from ourselves and blinding it to its own existence. Each of our actions adds to our subtracts from this karmic burden. Matter, also shaped by karma, provokes passion, anger, and attachments, which only further imprison us.

In the moral universe of Jainism, the most soul-masking and self-imprisoning behavior is the destruction of our fellow beings. When we hurt another, we harm ourselves. As I noted earlier, we cannot avoid some level of destruction. Life requires death, but our commitment to spiritual growth necessitates minimizing our destructive behavior as much as possible. I observed a good but unavoidable example of inadvertent karmic bondage when I participated in a Jain celebration at Claremont School of Theology. As I walked back to one of my companion's car, I noticed that the windshield was covered with insects who perished due to the unintentional impact of his driving on a freeway. Despite unintended carnage like this, we can minimize our karmic burden by touching the earth lightly, leaving as little personal footprint as possible.

- *Reverence for life and non-injury.* Jainism asserts that the major spiritual issue of life is violence toward our fellow creatures, grounded in ignorance of our true spiritual nature and the impact of our actions on others. Jains ask, "How wide is your circle of compassion? How broad are our ethical obligations? What are we going to do about it?" Small circles of compassion end at our family, nation, or species, while larger circles of compassion inspire us to embrace the whole earth.

Process-relational and openness theologians and contemporary ecologists recognize, that even though we live in an omnivorous planet, we have an obligation to care for the non-human world. In the spirit of Psalm 148's world of praise, process-theologians affirm that the myriad of non-human creatures experience their environment, have varying degrees of creativity, and respond to God's presence, albeit in simple and repetitive ways. Jains go a step further. There are souls (*jivas*) in the smallest droplets of water and in the microorganisms of our bodies. The ubiquity of soul challenges us to an all-encompassing ethic of *ahimsa* and reverence for life. Whatever exists is currently participating in the long journey of spiritual evolution. Every creature, even the most carnivorous, is longing for enlightenment. Within the lion is a vegetarian waiting to come forth! Though it may take millions of incarnations, eventually all creation has the opportunity for enlightenment and escape from the impact of matter and karmic bondage.

Jains believe in a version of "what goes around comes around." Karma may not be instant, as John Lennon suggests, but our behaviors toward other creatures, our infliction of violence through war, diet, farming, fishing, and other destructive pastimes clouds our own spiritual vision, blinds us to our true nature as eternal soul kin to all things, and heightens the passions that lead to death and rebirth. We are even accountable for what we do unconsciously, unavoidably, or accidentally. While Jain ethics appear to be negative as well as positive, focusing at first glance on non-injury and non-violence more than compassion and care, its ethical vision inspires compassion toward all life.

Even the droplets of water are on a journey of spiritual evolution. Caught up in the illusions of the survival of the fittest, wolves, snakes, and sharks are, deep down, seeking to go beyond violence to compassion. Legend has it that Mahavira led a venomous snake to non-injury and subsequent enlightenment like the later Francis of Assisi's conversion of a vicious wolf from enmity to friendship with the citizens of the village of Gubbio.

Jains typically do not eat meat, fish, or poultry. These organisms are complex and multi-sensory. They also contain millions of microorganisms which are destroyed by our eating habits. Jains typically restrict their diet to organisms that have only one sense, fruits and vegetables, thus minimizing violence and suffering as well as karmic bondage by their consumption. These days, we are discovering that eating lower on the food chain helps preserve the environment while contributing to our own physical and spiritual wellbeing. Positively speaking, and going beyond strict asceticism, reverence for life awakens us to a living, loving, and longing universe in which all creatures are pilgrims, and none are strangers. Our souls enlarge to embrace creative relationships with the universe around us. Freed from competition and injury, we can claim our oneness with all creation.

- *Liberation from Matter.* Despite their reverence for life and affirmation of the universality of soul, hidden within each creature, Jain spirituality counsels the spiritual seeker to avoid attachments to the perpetual perishing and passion inspiring world of the flesh and matter. The marriage of soul and matter is eternal. From the very "beginning," that is, from all times in a universe that has no beginning, soul has been joined with matter. Soul has been embodied throughout myriads of lifetimes, from crystals to humans. Individual souls, infinite in number, have emerged, living countless lifetimes connected with matter. Necessary to existence, matter and embodiment are also a prison for the soul, as the philosopher Socrates suggested, provoking attachment, ignorance, separation and alienation, violence, and passion. This is true among microorganisms as well as human beings. Individual souls travel through countless bodies, some simple like water droplets, others complex like humans and higher non-human animals, on the quest, mostly unconscious, for enlightenment. In this current incarnation, humans are uniquely poised to break free from the cycle of passion, violence, separation, and life and death. Through a commitment to integrity, honesty, chastity, non-possessiveness, and non-injury, we open the prison gates to experience the liberation of soul-filled existence. We cleanse the doors of perception as well as our digestive systems, and become intentional pilgrims toward the universal, passionless, non-injurious existence of Jain ascetics. Liberated as much as humanly possible from injuring other beings, the Jain ascetic heals, purifies, and eliminates their karmic bondage, still living in the flesh but no longer of it, no longer a victim and prisoner of passion, attachment, and sensuality. The ascetic experiences equanimity and spir-itual maturity by aiming at non-action and non-injury and minimizing all potentially destructive encounters. Enlightened existence leads to freedom from the impact of karma and matter, and freedom for unity with all creation.

A JAIN CONVERSATION: NON-VIOLENCE AS A WAY OF LIFE

Dr. Sulekh Chand Jain is one of the most influential figures in North American Jain spirituality. A mechanical engineer by training, Dr. Jain has taught at MIT, worked at General Electric, and founded his own company. Dr. Jain has served as Secretary and President of the Federation of Jain Associations of North America. Born and raised in the religiously pluralistic India, Dr. Jain lived in a world of porous religious boundaries. He often reads portions of the Bible, Bhagavad Gita, and Buddhist sutras as well as Jain holy books to edify his spiritual journey. As a young man, he realized the Jain spirit that no tradition has a monopoly on truth. He avers that "I do not belong to any congregation. All congregations belong to me." When he was growing up, Dr. Jain remembers going to "Christian churches and Buddhist and Hindu as well as Sikh temples."[33]

Dr. Jain brought this spirit of interfaith appreciation to the United States, working to unite Jains, Hindus, and Sikhs in joint religious ventures, including shared temples, and participating in a variety of interfaith organizations. "No one has a monopoly on the truth. No one knows the whole elephant," Dr. Jain noted, "we can only know the truth partially. The human mind can't describe the totality of Reality. Religions need to learn from each other." Dr. Jain's approach nurtures both a spirit of humility and lifelong spiritual seeking, looking for truth wherever it is found, regardless of religious tradition. For example, Dr. Jain states that "when I look at Jesus, I see one of the greatest teachers of ahimsa, non-violence, even on the cross." Dr. Jain adds that "most of the Ten Commandments are also about non-violence."

As Dr. Jain reflects on the heart of Jainism, he identifies three principles that have shaped his daily life and spiritual aspirations. First, non-violence in everything we

33. For more on Dr. Sulekh Jain's work, see https://sulekhcjain.wordpress.com/about/ - including his free book, *The Ahimsa Crisis*.

do. For most people, Dr. Jain reflects, non-violence involves food: what we eat and how our food is produced. Our spiritual goal is not to commit violence on any being in our occupation, lifestyle, and consumption. A lifelong vegetarian, Dr. Jain is now a vegan, living simply and out of that simplicity reducing the pain of the non-human world. Dr. Jain believes that we should encounter every being with compassion and empathy. At the deepest level, Jainism is about interdependence with all life forms, the recognition that despite our apparent difference, we are all one.

The second principle around which Dr. Jain shapes his life is "fellowship with others," and the practice of forgiveness. Forgiveness involves not only giving forgiveness when I have been wronged, but "asking for forgiveness when I may have wronged others."

The third principle that reflects his commitment to Jain spirituality as bridge building with other persons and spiritual traditions. Bridge building reflects our commitment to non-violence in personal, business, and institutional relation-ships. Dr. Jain's spirituality has fostered a lifelong leadership in bringing people together from various religious traditions, seeking unity and partnership where others might see difference and division. Deep down, we are all joined with each other. "We must meet people from other religions, knowing that truth is larger than any tradition and that in bridge building, we are apostles of non-violence." Taking seriously Dr. Jain's religious vision is a necessity if we as humans are to respond to the current crises of climate change, racism, economic injustice, and sustainability. Our religious differences can be the source of cooperation rather than division.

WHAT CHRISTIANS CAN LEARN FROM JAINISM

Christians have often succumbed to radical anthropocentrism. Many Christians believe that the *imago dei*, "the image of God," separates us completely from the non-human world. They believe salvation and eternal life pertain only to human-kind, while non-humans are intended by God to be objects of human domination, existing solely for our good pleasure. In the eyes of many Christians, most espe-cially "bible-believing" Christians, there is a chasm between humankind and the non-human world, which has become, in their economics and behavior, the object of human artifice and exploitation. In contrast, Jainism proclaims the universality of spirit, and teaches humankind to revere all creation. Our vocation is to minimize suffering in the non-human world.

Christians need to follow Francis of Assisi, Albert Schweitzer, and Jainism in embracing God's presence in the non-human world. While we can't avoid harming other creatures, our relationships need to be grounded in reverence for life. We need to live in the spirit of universal affirmation of all creation, and let this guide our lifestyles, faith communities, and politics. Reverence for life challenges us to form an environmental spirituality, and to respond boldly and creatively to human-caused global climate change.

CHRISTIANITY'S GIFT TO JAINISM

Jainism affirms the eternity and universality of ensouled existence. All things have a *jiva,* a deathless spirit, hidden beneath layers of matter and karmic debris. Yet, there is a deep individualism in Jainism despite the universality of soul. Moreover, matter is ambiguous: it may be perceived as beautiful, but the perception of beauty is problematic, in that it may bind us to earth, and excite passions that lead to further karmic bondage. The ideal life transcends the earth, focusing on liberation from the prison of karmic embodiment.

While Jains appropriately affirm a philosophy of non-injury, process and openness Christianity complements this with a philosophy of embodied affirmation and appreciation that leads to individual acts of compassion and social concern. Our economic and political involvements can cure or kill and heal or destroy and harm. Progressive forms of Christianity and Judaism affirm a prophetic reverence for life in which our individual well-being is connected to the well-being of our social order and the healing of the earth. Process and openness forms of Christianity affirm the world of the flesh, while challenging us to go beyond individual self-interest to world loyalty, to love the flesh of others (not just their soul) enough to eradicate structures of injustice and oppression. Persons' bodies, as well as their souls, matter. As the Black Lives Matter movement asserts, black bodies matter, especially in light of the impact of centuries of slavery and discrimination. Christianity and Judaism bring a social dimension to soul liberation, recognizing that the social order can liberate or enslave human spirits. Prophetic passion can seem too earth-bound and concerned with history for Jain ascetics; and at times prophets can become overly attached to their concepts of a just world order. Still, the notion of social liberation (economic, political, feminist, womanist, LGBTQ+, animal, and so forth) complements and expands the moral scope of the more individualistic and ascetic Jain vision. Enjoy life, delight in sight and sound, and work for justice, but also affirm the importance of undying spirit that transcends the things of the flesh.

A JAIN SPIRITUAL PRACTICE

The Jain spiritual tradition perceives the presence of God in every creature. Beneath the material disguise is holiness. Our vocation is to minimize the suffering of every creature. From a Christian perspective, we can speak of the inner light, or Christ, disguised in all creation. Benedictine spirituality counsels, "Greet everyone as Christ." In this spiritual practice, try to embody the Jain vision of universal divinity. Cleanse the doors of perception, as William Blake counsels, and see the infinity of every creature you encounter. Look beyond the external visage and see the holy. Experience your kinship with trees, osprey, companion animals, rocks, flowers, water, and air, and everything you encounter. See all life as one. In response to this vision, practice respect and reverence for all life forms.

Consider whether the question of the soul's universality is an invitation to explore your lifestyle. Do you need to simplify your life to respond to the negative impact of consumerism on the non-human world? Do you need to reflect on your diet and its relationship to animal suffering, especially in factory farms? Prayerfully consider what might be a change in behavior or lifestyle in response to the wisdom of Jain spirituality.

CHAPTER ELEVEN

The Sikhs

My first encounter with the Sikh religion occurred in the summer of 1970 when I attended a seminar led by the Sikh guru, Yogi Bhajan (1929-2004), who taught a syncretistic blend of Sikhism and new age spirituality that especially appealed to the hippie community. To a long-haired blond Californian spiritual seeker on the verge of his first year in college, the message of Yogi Bhajan was intriguing. Yogi Bhajan spoke of the Aquarian Age, and saw Guru Nanak, the first Sikh Guru, as a forerunner of the age of peace, harmony, and understanding. The fact that Sikhs didn't cut their hair appealed to my long-haired contemporaries, even though none of us wanted to hide our hair within the Sikh turbans.

In the fifty-plus years since that time, the Sikhs have been at the periphery of my studies. Like many theologians, I saw Sikhism as a synthesis of Hinduism and Islam, indeed, a reform movement within Hinduism similar in form to the Protestant Reformation's transformation of Western Christianity. Over the years, as I have gotten to know Sikhs personally and professionally, I have come to see Sikhism as a religion with its own spirit, and not a footnote or appendage to Hinduism.

The Sikh tradition owes its origin to Guru Nanak (1469-1539), the first of the ten Gurus, whom God called to be prophets to Punjab, a state in northern India, and the world. A contemporary of the Protestant Reformers, Martin Luther and

John Calvin, Guru Nanak sought to reform Hinduism and Islam, challenging the Hindu caste system, religious parochialism and possessiveness of truth, superstitious ritualism, and priestly corruption. He championed a spirituality that transcended parochial religious traditions in favor of belief in the One Universal God. Born the son of an accountant, he possessed a unique spiritual personality even as a child. His older sister saw the divine light flowing through him. An early childhood teacher was amazed at his spiritual insight and proclaimed, "Your son is an Avatar…destined to be a world teacher."[34] From a Sikh perspective, these pronouncements are self-evident. Already in childhood: Nanak possessed the characteristics of a Guru, chosen by God to be the embodiment of Divine Light. In his young adult years, as was customary, Nanak married, raised a family, and served as a government official, all the while growing in his perception of God's presence in his life and his future mission as an embodiment of Divine Truth. While Sikhs take seriously spiritual practices in the path to liberation, Nanak's marriage reflects the Sikh belief that God is found in daily life, raising families, domestic responsibilities, work, and military action, not in the solitude of the monastery. We can, as W. H. Auden avers, love God in the world of the flesh.

While bathing one day, Nanak received the call to be a Guru, set apart to be God's teacher, teaching the Divine Name to the World. In the Sikh religion, there is "But One God; he sends his emissary called Guru, who is the embodiment of Divine Light. God then delivers His message (Gurbani) through his emissary, the Guru."[35] For the remainder of his life, some forty years following this transformative experience, Nanak traveled through India, Ceylon, Persia (Iran), Tibet, and Arabia (Mecca), sharing the Good News of Divine Light. He taught of God's love for and affirmation of each person, regardless of caste, occupation, or gender. Prior to his death, Nanak passed on his vocation as Guru to one of his disciples, Lehna, Guru Angad Dev Ji. Although Nanak did not choose one of his biological sons to be Guru, the line of eight Gurus beyond the second Guru was hereditary, though not necessarily passed on to the eldest son. Two hundred and nine years after Nanak's calling to be a Guru, Guru Gobind Singh affirmed that the Guru's role would now be invested in the writings of the Ten Gurus and other spiritual teachers, as a living, written word and final teaching for the Sikhs, the Adi Granth or Guru Granth Sahib.

34. *Sikh Religion* (Detroit: Sikh Missionary Center, 1990), 14.
35. Ibid., 23.

THE SIKH SPIRIT

The Sikh spiritual tradition makes a unique contribution to religious experience and the history of religions. Although founded as a reform movement emerging from Hinduism and Islam, Sikhs see themselves as a distinct religious movement, differing in kind from the Protestant Reformation in Christianity, which maintains its continuity not only with Western and Roman Catholic but also with Orthodox Christianity. We will explore some of the prominent features of Sikhism, a religion of 25 million adherents, nearly 300,000 of which live in the United States, through the following affirmations.

- *The Guru is the Living Word of God.* Hinduism has a long tradition of viewing gurus as insightful spiritual teachers, able to convey insight and wisdom to their students. Sikhs expand on this understanding of guru as spiritual teacher. According to Sikhism, the ten Sikh Gurus, beginning with Guru Nanak in 1499 and concluding with the death of Guru Gobind Singh in 1708, are revelations of God's presence in humanity. The word "guru" means Divine Light and Gurus serve as God's Light in the world, fully enlightened, and leading humankind from darkness to light. The Guru is the embodiment of God in whom the Light of God shines fully, visibly, and completely. The Guru's body is "a platform from which God Himself spoke and delivered his message."[36] Sikh's affirm that Guru Nanak and his nine successors can be described by the following affirmations: "O Nanak, Jot of Nanak (Light of God) and God are one," "I am primal God and thou art Guru God," and "In the body of Guru God revealeth himself."[37] Similar to the Gospel of John's affirmation of Jesus, Sikhs see their Gurus as the "word made flesh." Trusting the Guru's words, embracing the Guru's spiritual wisdom, and chanting the name of God pave the way to salvation, deliver us from the burdens of karma, and free us from the wheel of transmigration, death, birth, and rebirth. The Living Word of God (Nam) enlightens all creation, revealing God's Truth in a human body.

- *The Living Words of God.* As his earthly life was ebbing, the final human Guru, Gobind Singh, conferred the role of Guru upon the words of the

---

36. Ibid., 7.
37. Ibid., 8.

ten Gurus and other teachers, now collected in the Adi Granth or Guru Granth Sahib. According to Sikhs, the Guru Granth Sahib preserves the Light of God and is seen as the Living Guru forever. Like the Quran, the Guru Granth Sahib is the Holy Word of God, perfect, preserved from error, and God's eternal wisdom relevant to every age. There is no room for additions, subtractions, or amendments to the original text. God speaks from the words of the Adi Granth directly to the spiritual seeker, providing the path to enlightenment. Whether we encounter an embodied or a written Guru, Sikhs affirm the words of Guru Nanak: "Those who encounter the Guru achieve an indestructible word of God. The Guru bestows divine knowledge and unveils the mysteries of the three worlds…Without the Guru's help we cannot burn to nothingness the ashes of self-love…Through faith in the Guru the true self is known."[38] Moreover, "the Word is the True Guru, and the True Guru is the Word."[39]

- *One God, One Humanity.* With Jews, Christians, and Muslims, Sikhs affirm the absolute unity of God. All things come from God's hands. God is present in every creature and all creation. Accordingly, every human being reflects God's presence and has an equal opportunity in this lifetime to experience enlightenment and freedom from transmigration or rebirth. Indeed, humanity is uniquely poised, regardless of caste or gender, to intentionally move from darkness to light and from transmigration to liberation. The unity of God is the ground for the unity and equality of humankind, and the Sikh's fervent opposition to the caste system. There is no spiritual monopoly or superiority; all can be enlightened, and all religions can be paths to God. As Guru Nanak asserted, "There is no Hindu. There is no Muslim." According to Sikh history, Guru Nanak dressed as a Muslim pilgrim and traveled to the great mosque, where pilgrims perform devotions. Later that night, contrary to custom, he went to sleep with his feet pointed toward the Kaaba, the Holy Shrine of Islam. When a Muslim religious leader kicked him, accusing him of impiety, and exclaimed, "Why is this infidel sleeping with his feet towards the House of God?" Nanak replied, "Turn my feet in the direction in which God is not." Whereupon the priest spun Nanak around, only to discover

---

38. Andrea Diem-Lane, *The Sikhs* (Walnut, CA: Mount San Antonio College, 2014), 10.
39. *Sikh Religion*, 246.

that the Kaaba turned around to follow the Guru's feet. The omnipresent
God welcomes all of God's children as equals. Muslim and Hindu, man
and woman, and Brahmin and laborer, eat together at the Sikh dinner
table. Sikhs saw women as equal and opposed, *sati,* the Hindu practice of
self-immolation of women at their husband's death. In contrast to Muslim
mosques which have only one entrance, Sikh temples have four entrances
as a visible affirmation that God can be approached by many ways and
that, in contrast to Hinduism, all castes can enter as equals before God
and in our human relations. Sikh social ethics promoted the political and
economic equality of the lower castes, based on God's presence in every
life regardless of station, ethnicity, or profession.

• *The Solider-Saint.* Guru Nanak's Christian contemporary Martin Luther
spoke of the priesthood of all believers. Luther believed that the domestic
life—including, marriage, politics, and employment—were just as
significant in our spiritual journeys as the monastic and priestly lives.
We can serve God in virtually any occupation, including the military.
A Christian can wield the sword faithfully just as a Christian can raise
a family or celebrate the Eucharist. The Sikh tradition concurs, recognizing the vocation of the "soldier-saint," a virtuous soldier, who fights
not to gain territory but on behalf of their faith. Because Punjab was the
gateway to India, it was often attacked by both Hindus and Muslims,
bent on displacing the Sikh community and its religious, political, and
military leadership. Fighting for their faith, Sikhs became courageous
and skillful military professionals. Yet unlike most military strategists,
the Sikh military leaders fought purely defensive wars and following a
military victory, of which there were many "miraculous," Sikh military,
religious, and political leaders returned territory to those whom they
had vanquished. Sikhs saw war as an ethical enterprise with moral limits,
similar in spirit to the Christian "just war" theory. God can be glorified in
any occupation. Illumination can occur in the battlefield as well as in the
temple. According to a Sikh spiritual teacher, "A Sikh is a saint because he
worships the All-Pervading Divine Spirit and on whom that Spirit shines
day and night like the full moon. A Sikh is a soldier because he is ever
ready to take up arms to uphold righteousness."[40]

---

40. *Sikh Religion,* 202.

- *Chanting the Name of God.* Devotion and praise are present in virtually every religious tradition. Our awe at the universe, at God's love, and at our moments of transcendence, even at our very existence, invokes praise and delight in God's name and nature. For Sikhs, God's name (Nam) creates and sustains the universe and is embodied in the lives of the Gurus and in our praises. Sikh spirituality reflects the Bhakti, or devotional spirituality, of Hinduism and mirrors the worship and praise of evangelically spirited Christians, whose faith centers on Jesus and inspires shouts of joy and thanksgiving. Sikhs believe that chanting God's name dispels all darkness and releases us from the bondage of karma. Praise also has an ethical component. Praising the Creator leads us to honor creation and see the holiness of our fellow humans. We honor whatever our praiseworthy God has created and, in honoring God, choose to respect and promote the well-being of our fellow humans, challenging caste, economic inequality, racism, inhospitality as unworthy behaviors for those who claim to love God.

A CONVERSATION WITH A SIKH: HOW CAN I KEEP FROM SINGING

The North African theologian Augustine of Hippo once asserted that when you sing, you pray twice. On the eve of the twentieth century, philosopher Friedrich Nietzsche averred that people no longer believe because believers no longer sing. Sikhs, like the Baptists of my childhood, know how to sing their faith. It was not surprising that when I reflected on the Sikh tradition with Jan Protopapas, that both of us emphasized the importance of song and music in our spirituality. Jan's website describes her as "a Canadian American ethnomusicologist, educator and scholar of South Asian and Sikh sacred music studies. She is also a recording artist, musician, and composer…[who] weaves together the academic, emotive, and sensual elements of her research and aims to share her passion with both the scholarly world and the …. world."[41]

Jan and I share common spiritual origins in conservative and evangelical Christianity, where music was at the heart of our faith. In her case, the Brethren in Christ; in my case small town American Baptist churches. Both of us sang hymns,

41. www.janprotopapas.com

children's melodies, and praise songs in our youth and we still sing them today. In the churches of our youth, we found love and connection, and though we took other paths as adults, our childhood faith still beats within us. I often surprise my wife when she hears me singing revival hymns around the house. Jan regularly sings hymns and praise songs to her ninety year old mother. Her mother even joins her in singing bits of pieces of "I Have Decided to Follow Jesus" in Hindi. Both of us have discovered that the deep vibrations of faith, transcend the boundaries many erect to protect religious orthodoxies and ensure the loyalty of the faithful. In music, there is a universal voice singing a myriad of melodies, the voice that set the Big Bang in motion and still guides the galaxies and stars and human hearts. In Sikh theology, this divine voice is referred to as the Shabad, the primordial sound of God

Jan's first significant encounter with the Sikh tradition, and what she describes as "the sonic metaphysical traditions of India," occurred as a college student studying abroad in India in the late 1980s. She had been drawn to India's language and music and discovered that she had an affinity for the languages of India. Jan recalls, "I knew [in a way deeper than rational understanding] I needed to go to India."

A providential experience crystalizes her encounter with the religions of India. On an education junket to Rajasthan, an Indian state, as she listened to a folk musician, a traveling bard, play a melody, she felt as the music touched her soul at a deep vibrational level. After listening to the folk musician, she decided to follow some children climbing to a rooftop to gain a better view of the town. As she was scaling the wall, she grabbed onto a tile, which gave way. She fell to the ground and the tile fell on her thumb, severing it from the rest of her hand. Jan recalls that, without alarming her parents, she wrote home, "I left a part of myself in Rajasthan."

Over the years, Jan returned to India to study, but also to deepen her spiritual life. She needed to hear that melody again! No longer active in the church of her youth, she felt a deep, primal, perhaps even primordial, or past life, connection, to the music and spirituality of India. Deep down, in ways that transcend reason, she felt the tug of the melody she heard as a college student.

Twenty-five years later, she returned to India for doctoral work on the spirituality and liturgy of Indian Sikh sacred musical communities. When by chance, or was it providence, she encountered the hymn that had inspired her as a college student in a Sikh morning worship liturgy, she felt like she had come home, perhaps to a place that transcends space and time. She had found the part of herself that had been left behind, the spirit that speaks to your soul. Synchronously, or providentially, the melody that touched her was a melody describing the adventures of an injured prince, similar to her own experience of having a severed thumb. Jan's commitment to the Sikh tradition gradually evolved through singing the hymns of the Adi Granth, the Living Word, the light of God, and eventuated in her being initiated among a community of new "converts" at a Sikh holy place in Punjab.

The deep, infinite, and intimate vibrations of Light and Love speak to and through Jan -who "received the name Gurleen, absorbed in God, Kaur at initiation and goes by this name amongst the Sikh community"—in the "praise songs" of the Adi Granth out into the universe where all things are joined in the deep melody of the Divine. This deep melody resonates in every religious tradition. Deeply committed to her own Sikh spirituality, Jan appreciates the progressive Christianity of a Mennonite church in Lancaster. Wherever there is joy and wisdom, God is present.

While no one perspective can define a spiritual path, for Jan, the heart of the Sikh tradition involves commitment to the scriptures, being married to their wisdom. External symbols are less important than the inner experience of faith, in Jan's case, the Adi Granth is "a living scripture that transformed me from the inside out. I have made a commitment to be guided by something greater than myself, the Living Guru, the Living Bible."

Jan sees one of the Sikh spiritual tradition's gifts to the world as mindfulness, "how you break the cycle of falsehood and how can we to live the truth in the holiness of the present moment." This reflects what in "Sikh theology is Hukam, Divine order." Jan believes that truth is found in opening to a Divine Ground, a power shaping all things, far greater than us, such that "what is *is* exactly as it is supposed to be and living in the wholeness of the present moment." Jan continues, "The Universal Presence, is moving through us. We all are being acted on by Divine Reality. Everything you need is on the inside." Jan asserts that Sikh spirituality also reminds us that we need to look beyond the chaos of the external world, "the truth is on the inside," the Holiness within. As a Sikh hymn says, "I am so glad I found God in my own home. I will serve forever." This is a source of true and deep happiness as one Sikh hymn proclaims,

Sing God's scriptures.
Listen to God's scriptures.
Keep them close to your heart.
And you will find happiness.
(5th Stanza from the Japji Sahib)

Perhaps those song leaders and hymn singers of our Baptist and Brethren in Christ parents were on the right track after all!

WHAT CHRISTIANS CAN LEARN FROM SIKHS

Sikhs remind Christians of the power of the Name. According to Sikh theology, "God created Himself and assumed Name...Nam sustains and controls all beings. Nam supports the universe and all its regions."[42] In many ways, the Sikh understanding of the Divine Creative Name mirrors the Hebraic notion of Divine Word (Dabhar) that creates the universe, as revealed in Genesis 1:3, "And God said, 'Let there be light.'" In the New Testament, John describes the Logos similarly, "In the beginning was the Word and the Word was with God and the Word was God...All things came into being through the Word...the light of all people." (See John 1:1-4)

Often, Westerners misuse the name of God, making it subservient to our personal and political agendas. We assume that God is on our side and blesses our behaviors, and loosely identify events in the world with God's will. Persons swear, using God's name to curse others and express anger or dislike. Misusing God's name, whether in loose language or political discourse, is playing with religious fire. Sikhs remind us that although God has many names, we need to treat God's name with reverence, recognizing its holiness and power. To invoke Jesus' name is to transform oneself and the world, and to seek a blessing for our activities. We need to take God's name with us, reverently, lovingly, and repeat it throughout the day to keep our hearts centered on what is most important. Let God's name be the searchlight by which we navigate the chaos and darkness of our world.

---

42. *Sikh Religion*, 258.

CHRISTIANITY'S GIFT TO SIKHISM

Christians can appreciate much in the robust spirituality of Sikhism as it seeks to join earth and heaven and reminds us that God is as present as fully when putting a child to sleep as in the evening prayers of the monastery. Christianity focuses on the interplay of absolute and relative, and eternal and temporal, whether in daily life, religious practice, imaging God, or understanding scripture. Christian faith can invite Sikhs to explore the interplay of time and eternity, and the absolute and the flexible, in scripture. The perfection of scripture, including the Adi Granth, may be found in its adaptability rather than in its permanence, and in its concrete humanity and not in its timeless perfection. Although scripture reflects God's wisdom, God's wisdom is always timely, grounded in the real world. The form and symbolism of Divine Wisdom may vary according to our life circumstances and the global situation. Asking hard questions of scripture, and reflecting on its historical origins, is an act of faith. A Living Word may also be a changing word, embodying God's Vision and requiring reinterpretation in ways appropriate to our life situation. God may choose to adapt God's revelations to real time, thus liberating them from timelessness to speak to our current situation.

A SIKH SPIRITUAL PRACTICE

The Sufi (Muslim) mystic Rumi asserted that there are hundred ways to kneel and kiss the ground. There are surely hundreds of prayer and meditation practices, not to mention names for God. Sikh's proclaim the importance of Nam, the divine word that creates the universe and ourselves. *Waheguru,* or "Wonderful God" or "Thou Art Wonderful" is the primary word reflecting God's nature in the world. Chanting *Waheguru* aligns us with the Creative Power and Wisdom of the Universe and accelerates our path to spiritual illumination. Keeping the Name of God, or names of God, on our mind enables us to stay focused on the Divine in our domestic activities, joining sacred and secular in praise of God.

As a child growing up in a small-town Baptist church, I learned the hymn, "Take the Name of Jesus with You." The hymn reflects the importance of filtering our experience through God's providential, empowering, and sustaining love for us.

144

Take the Name of Jesus with you,
Child of sorrow and of woe,
It will joy and comfort give you;
Take it then, where'er you go.

Refrain:
Precious Name, oh, how sweet!
Hope of earth and joy of Heav'n;
Precious Name, oh, how sweet!
Hope of earth and joy of Heav'n.

Take the Name of Jesus ever,
As a shield from every snare;
If temptations round you gather,
Breathe that holy Name in prayer.[43]

You may choose to invoke a name of God, whether from the Christian, Sikh, or another faith tradition, both in your quiet meditations and as a spiritual reminder throughout the day. You may choose to focus on one of the many names of God, "El Shaddai," "Yahweh," "Elohim," "Chokmah" (pronounced "Hokmah"), "Logos," "Sophia," "Spirit," "Jesus," "Light," "Love" or the name of God from another faith, such as "Aum," "Shanti," or "Waheguru," remembering with Carl Jung, that "Bidden or not, God is present."

---

43. Lydia Baxter, "Take the Name of Jesus With You." (1871)

CHAPTER TWELVE

Confucianism/Ruism

David Tracy titles one of his most important books, *Blessed Rage for Order.* This title, in many ways, captures the essence of Confucianism, or Ruism, and its quest for personal and social order in a world where chaos and self-interest often reign. Philosophers and theologians have wrestled with the questions, "Are human beings inherently solitary or social beings? Is the essence of humanity good, evil, or neutral? Is this world the primary focus of the human adventure, or should we look toward past or future existence in terms of our current situation and future hope?" How we answer these questions determines our understandings of what it means to be fully human and ethically responsible and shapes the goals of human life.

Alfred North Whitehead sought to resolve the tension between individualism and culture by noting that although religion initially emerges from solitary experiences such as Moses' encounter with the burning bush, Jesus' temptations in the wilderness, and Gautama meditating under the Bo Tree, human life and religious faith are profoundly social in nature. Each creature's moment by moment process of self-creation involves our private choices, the impact of the environmental and social context on our decision-making, and the effect of our choices on those around us. The whole universe, the philosopher avers, conspires to create each moment of experience. God's vision for each moment of our lives

147

joins the immediacy of private self-creation with the best possibility for shaping future experiences of ourselves and others, grounded in our personal history and social context.

In the United States, the tension between individual and society, and freedom and responsibility, rages, even though the world has never been more dynamically interdependent. People shout, "it's my right" and "it's nobody's business" whether this involves gun ownership, private property, corporate decision-making, vaccination, or abortion. Others respond with calls to social responsibility in terms of lifestyle and global climate change, restrictions on gun ownership, promotion of human rights, and mask-wearing and vaccinations. They believe that our rights end, or are significantly shaped, by their impact on our contemporaries and future generations.

Chinese spirituality wrestled with a similar interplay of the personal and the cultural in the contrasting visions of Confucianism and Daoism. In a time of social upheaval, the seventh and sixth centuries BCE, the sages Confucius, known as Kung Fu-tzu, and Lao Tzu, the respective parents of Confucianism and Daoism (Taoism), proposed different, yet interconnected visions, of human wholeness and social responsibility. Like the dynamics of yin and yang, celebrated in Chinese cosmology and ethics, Daoism represented spontaneous, individualistic, open-spirited religion, while Confucianism, advocated for orderly, social, and ritual-oriented religion. Unlike the binary truth-error, saved-unsaved, approach of many conservative Christians, the spirit of Chinese religion emphasized inclusion and harmony of opposites. Accordingly, while the current Chinese government seems light years in spirit from the teachings of Confucius, Chinese wisdom once suggested that "Every Chinese person wears a Confucian cap, a Daoist robe, and Buddhist sandals." A variation of this observation noted, Chinese are Confucian at work, Daoist at leisure, and Buddhist at death.[44] In today's pluralistic world, we would do well to embrace a variation of this practical theology, recognizing the complementary nature of different spiritual paths, as well as their contrasting beliefs and practices. There is much to be gained by cosmopolitan faiths that seek the truth everywhere and are willing to be "inter-spiritual" and "hybrid," using what is helpful and inspirational in other faiths to complement their own spiritual practices and belief systems.

---

44. Stephen Prothero, *God is Not One: The Eight Rival Religions that Run the World* (San Francisco: Harper One, 2010), 103.

There is a question as to whether the term "Confucian" is an appropriate term to describe the way of life articulated by Master Kung and his followers. According to Confucian scholar Bin Song, currently Assistant Professor of Philosophy and Religion at Washington College in Chestertown, Maryland, "Confucianism is a misnomer. It was created by early Christian missionaries for the purpose of comparison and, especially, of conversion. Although Christian missionaries created many names to describe other world religions, the term 'Confucianism' is especially unfortunate since it says nothing at all that is essential about the tradition that the name purports to describe."[45] A better term, according to Big Song is "Ruism." According to Bin Song:

If we now combined these two meanings of Ru, "being soft" and "to moisten," we can recognize that the standard meaning of Ru, as it is received in the Ruist tradition, is "non-violent transformation." To be a Ru is thus to be commissioned as a non-violent warrior and fighter who employs every resource of human civilization toward the realization of dynamic harmony in the world. A Ru is someone who tries to transform the world into an all-encompassing symbiotic ecosphere by employing his or her own personal moral cultivation. As a consequence, please do not forget that Confucius is not a Confucian; he is a Ru.[46]

The mission of Confucius, Master Kung (551-479 BCE), can be described affirmatively as a creative synthesis of the personages of Moses the law giver, Socrates the teacher and spiritual agnostic, Plato the believer in the spiritual benefits of good governance, and Jesus whose humble beginnings gave birth to a world-transforming movement. Like Jesus, Confucius' birth was described as humble and miraculous at the same time. His mother, it is said, after praying to have a son, gave birth to Confucius, the out-of-wedlock child of her liaison with a Chinese noble. Other traditions speak of divine intervention that led to his birth, but also note that his father died when Confucius was only three years old, leaving the family in dire straits.

At age fifteen, Confucius committed himself to a life of learning, and soon became an expert in China's great holy books. During a time of national chaos, Confucius looked back to the early days of the Zhou dynasty as the "best of times," the golden era when harmony and order reigned from the palace to the marketplace.

45. Bin Song, "Is Confucius a Confucian?" Is Confucius a Confucian? - Confucius Academy (wpcomstaging.com)
46. Bing Song, "A Confucian Cathechism: Is Confucius and Confucian?" A Catechism of Confucianism: Is Confucius a Confucian? | HuffPost Communities

Confucius spent his professional life in public service, rising to the position of chief advisor to the provincial leader, Duke Ting, in 496 BCE. As a teacher-politician, he was committed to national renewal through self-cultivation and personal transformation, beginning with the nation's leaders and extending to the working class. He left high office, feeling deeply discouraged for having failed to effect transformation at a national level. After that, Confucius focused on teaching a loyal band of disciples who would become the apostles of his message of moral leadership, horizontal spirituality, and right relationships. Although he did not teach a theological vision of the Holy, Confucius felt that he had been sent on a divine mission to share the holiness he saw in the daily horizontal relationships of life. Providence is at work in the affairs of human life–family, community, government—and his mission was to help people become fulfilled humans living in a just and supportive society. When his life was threatened by a rival, Confucius assured his followers that "Heaven has endowed me with a moral destiny (or mission), what can Huan Tuei do to me?"[47] In describing himself, Confucius admitted: "I am a man who forgets to eat when he is enthusiastic about something, who forgets his worries when he is happy, and is not aware that old age is coming on."[48] Although Confucius never described himself as a saint—true saints never call themselves "holy," true prophets don't describe themselves as a "divine spokespersons," and true mystics don't speak of themselves as "enlightened" - he did assert that he was tireless in seeking, and then teaching, the truth that will lead to harmonious and healthy relationships and nations.

Like Socrates, who confessed his fallibilities and considered his greatest virtue to be his recognition of his personal limitations, Confucius believed that the way to wisdom was found in self-awareness, including the recognition that knowing what you don't know, is as important as what you do know. As the sage asserted, "When you know a thing, recognize that you know it; and when you do not, to know that you don't know—that is knowledge."[49] In contrast to the political prevarication we see in today's United States and throughout the world, Confucius believed that honesty about our accomplishments and our limitations was the path to national and personal health. In speaking of himself, Confucius noted:

47. Lin Yu Tang, *The Wisdom of Socrates* (New York: The Modern Library, 1938), 71.
48. Ibid., 25.
49. Huston Smith, *The World's Religions* (New York: HarperCollins, 1986), 159.

There are four things in the Way of the profound person, none of which I have been able to do. To serve my father as I would expect my son to serve me. To serve my ruler as I would expect my ministers to serve me. To serve my elder brother as I would expect my younger brothers to serve me. To be the first to treat friends as I would expect them to treat me.[50]

Toward the end of his life, Confucius recognized that the ideals he sought to teach exceeded the reach of most political leaders. In a spirit of frustration like that of the Hebraic prophets, Confucius lamented: "No intelligent monarch arises; there is not one in the kingdom who will make me his master. My time has come to die."[51]

A lover of music and ritual, Confucius believed that music nurtured the inner life, while ritual gave order to outer behavior. Like Plato and Pythagoras, Confucius believed that music plays an essential role in statecraft. When rulers align themselves with the harmonies of music, they become harmonious in their leadership. When citizens live attuned to great books and inspiring music, nations reflect the moral arc, described by Unitarian pastor Theodore Parker, that runs through history, bringing justice, peace, and prosperity to the people and to foreign relationships.

SPIRITUALITY AS HEALTHY PEOPLE IN HEALTHY COMMUNITIES ON A HEALTHY PLANET

In one of the congregations that I served in the early 2000s, a favorite hymn was "Standing on Holy Ground" the first words of which are "We are standing on holy ground and I know there are angels all around." Whenever I think of that hymn, I turn to Jacob's dream of a ladder of angels. With nothing but a stone for a pillow, the rascal Jacob falls asleep and dreams of angels on a ladder, ascending from earth to heaven. What always has struck me about this story is that the angels rise from the earth. They are not heaven-sent but emerge right where we are on earth. Confucius would have appreciated that story. He saw everyday life and governmental policy as revealing holiness. We don't have to go anywhere to live a holy life. We can do so right where we are. As Jesus proclaims in the Gospel of Thomas, "Cleave the wood and I am there. Turn over the stone and you will find me." (Logia 77) The goal of life is not to get to heaven but to experience heaven,

---

50. Ibid., 157.
51. Prothero, *God is Not One*, 114.

to have joy and fulfillment, and be fully human, in this lifetime, among family, friends, co-workers, and in political policy.

Some scholars have questioned whether Confucianism or Ruism is a religion, and Confucius is an authentic spiritual leader. While Confucius' ethics and public policy were not grounded in a mystical call like Moses' from the burning bush or his reception of the Torah on Mt. Sinai, he saw law and government, earthly rule, as reflecting heavenly wisdom. The goal of life is to join the microcosm with the macrocosm, and individuals and their community, with the laws embedded in Universal Order. Divine Wisdom and Holy Harmony are reflected in just and respectful relationships among humans, whether in the family or the nation. Unlike some heaven-bound Christians, who assert that "This world is not my home, I'm just a passing through," Confucius believed that the sacred was secular, and that the secular was sacred. Like the Hebraic prophets, who saw accurate and honest weights and measures as holy and of concern to God, Confucius believed that our conduct with our neighbor and the characters of rulers were of divine interest. Whatever shapes human experience participates in the sacred. The Holy relates as much to this life as to the next.

On his death bed, Henry David Thoreau was asked if he had an intuition of the afterlife, to which the Transcendental philosopher replied, "One world at a time." Similarly, when he was asked about how to serve the spirits of the dead, Confucius replied, "You are not even able to serve people. How can you serve the spirits?" Asked about death, the sage responded, "You do not even understand life. How can you understand death?"[52] Five centuries after Confucius, Jesus broke the barrier between sacred and secular when he told the parable of the judgment of the nations:

Then the righteous will answer him, "Lord, when was it that we saw you hungry and gave you food, or thirsty and gave you something to drink? And when was it that we saw you a stranger and welcomed you, or naked and gave you clothing? And when was it that we saw you sick or in prison and visited you?" And the king will answer them, "Truly I tell you, just as you did it to one of the least of these who are members of my family, you did it to me." (Matthew 25:37-40)

---

52. Smith, 185.

You love the Creator by loving the creatures. When you love the creatures, you embody the Tao of Heaven. Or, as I often quipped during the time of pandemic in response to the "Honk, if you love Jesus" bumper sticker, "If you love Jesus, wear a mask. Any fool can honk."

At the heart of the earth-centered spirituality of Confucius are the following affirmations, joining sacred and secular in harmonious unity:

- *Earthly-minded Spirituality.* Confucius has been described as the ultimate humanist. He would appreciate the sentiments of the organ donor bumper sticker, "Don't take your organs to heaven. They belong on earth." Spirituality is ultimately this-worldly in nature. Like Moses and the Hebraic patriarchs, Confucius believed that this world is where wholeness and salvation occurs. If we take care of this world, and the time in which we live, heaven will take care of itself. While Confucius did not scorn the Divine, or Heaven, or the practice of honoring ancestors through sacrifice, his focus was the here-now world of politics, family life, and relationships. Healthy communities and leaders promote human fulfillment. Sacred and secular permeate one another and are in fact one reality. We promote the work of Heaven by living fully today in positive family and political relationships. Spirituality is embodied, not ethereal.

- *The Reality of Relationships.* We are profoundly relational beings. Peoples' lives emerge from their relationships, and the quality of their relationships shapes the wider community. According to Confucius:

  If there is righteousness in the heart, there will be beauty in character.
  If there is beauty in character, there will be harmony in the home.
  If there is harmony in the home, there will be order in the nation.
  If there is order in the nation, there will be peace in the world.[53]

  The primary relationships in community are parent and child, husband and wife, elder sibling and junior sibling, elder friend and junior friend, and ruler and subjects. While these relationships can devolve into domination, paternalism, and formalism, Confucius intended for these relationships to be reciprocal and mutual in nature. A dishonest and unjust

---

53. Smith, 174.

sovereign destroys a nation and is unworthy of allegiance. Sovereignty is intended to be relational, albeit hierarchical. Husbands, elder siblings and friends, parents and children, and rulers and subjects, need one another, and are intended to encourage flourishing appropriate to their place in society. While these relationships can become static and authoritarian, a progressive approach to Confucianism encourages unity in diversity, respect in difference, and equality in affirmation. The ultimate issue is that all relationships are intended to be reverential, respectful, and reciprocal.

- *Cultivating Virtue.* Character is everything in statecraft and personal and family relationships. For Confucius, a person's word is their bond. Nations cannot be just without just leaders. To create a flourishing society, the leader must be committed to learning, honesty, open-spiritedness, respect, and integrity in speech and action. Trust emerges when a leader sets the highest example, embodying in their conduct an example for the citizenry. In the United States and other nations, the negative impact of egocentric, prevaricating, and self-interested political leaders has led to hate crimes against minorities, mistrust of science, incivility in discourse, attempts to undermine democracy, and violence to achieve political aims. The Confucian sage-ruler, like Plato's philosopher-king, sees power as a means to improving society, and places world and national loyalty ahead of self-interest. At the heart of Confucian ethics is what has been described as the Silver Rule, "What you do not want done to yourself, you do not do to others," whether in national leadership, business, family life, and friendship. Less activist than the Golden "Do unto others" Rule, the Silver Rule is intended to create space for personal responsibility and self-development.

- *Commitment to Character and Honesty.* The early Christian theologian Irenaeus proclaimed that the glory of God is a fully alive human. Confucius would concur. Fully human persons join their inner life and outer behaviors. Whether alone, in a crowd, or a leading a nation, the fully human person cultivates integrity. Every aspect of their life is integrated around the center of social responsibility and care for others with the same commitment as they care for themselves. While Confucius and his followers affirmed the essential goodness, or at least, neutrality, of human nature, they believed that human nature needs to be cultivated. Our vocation is to be the horticulturists of our own nature and the natures of those around us, providing the necessary resources as well as healthy boundaries to promote the fullest expression of humanity. As Confucius admits, this is a lifelong task. Saints, if there are such, emerge due to their self-awareness, study, following the example of great ancestors, and carefully chosen, or mindful, behaviors. Good character is the result of constant pruning and choosing what is best for others and oneself. Eliminating the superfluous and unhealthy and choosing the harmonious, orderly, and socially beneficial actions, time after time, until integrity of character becomes "second nature," whether alone or in public.

- *Politics as a Spiritual Practice.* These days, politics and politicians have a bad name. In the United States, many citizens believe that the government that governs best, governs least. Politicians are viewed as dishonest and self-interested and, this perception, often encouraged by demagogues, threatens the structures of democracy. In contrast, Confucius, Moses, Plato, and the Hebraic prophets recognize the positive value of government, despite the constant threats of injustice, misuse of power, and self-interest. Good government creates the possibility of good people. Good leaders not only promote justice and civic harmony; they also provide examples for subjects to emulate in their own self-cultivation.

Politics is spiritual in nature because it has the potential to create the environment for full humanity. A friendly community, grounded in integrity, justice, and respect inspires and provides the fertile ground for personal growth. For Confucius, as for Moses and Plato, law is intended to be a guidebook and inspiration for social and personal wellbeing. While law may appear coercive at times, its intent is to promote fully human flourishing. Rules and rituals bring out our true nature, encourage spiritual growth, and are congruent with the inner law of our being. The Heaven above and the moral law within mirror one another. When political rule truly promotes community, we realize our divine destiny as persons in community here on earth.

A RU (CONFUCIAN) CONVERSATION:
PRACTICAL ENLIGHTENMENT

Bin Song is currently Assistant Professor of Philosophy and Religion at Washington College in Chestertown, Maryland. Raised in a Ru (Confucian) family in China, Bin Song emigrated to the United States at thirty and received his Ph.D. at Boston University. He describes himself as "a traditional Ru (Confucian) scholar who tries to make the world better through reviving the tradition in a global and contemporary context. This may imply responding to global philosophical discussions using traditional Ru sources or tackling shared problems of local and global human societies drawing upon Ru and global philosophies."[54]

The spiritual quest often begins with unplanned mystical experiences, and Bin Song's spiritual journey is no exception. While translating the Buddhist Platform Sutra, Bin Song went outside for a study break. As Bin Song's interviewer notes for a blog post: "There, he had an overwhelming emotional experience of wholeness that seemed, as he described it, to be ecstatic. Afterwards, he wanted to articulate what the experience meant and how to maintain its otherwise transient quality. This plunged him deeper into philosophy and religion to understand what had happened."[55] Reflections on his experience led him on a spiritual journey that took him to France where he received a Ph.D. in Philosophy. His spiritual quest then took him to the United States, where he received a doctorate in Religion at Boston University.

Bin Song's vision of Ruism (Confucianism) joins philosophy, religion, and the mysticism of everyday life. Ruism is grounded in daily life, in joining Tian (heaven) and earth in a dynamic harmony. The goal of life is to live in harmony with oneself, others, and the universe in such a way that our personal harmony, lived out in daily life, contributes to the dynamic relational harmony of the community and the cosmos.

Key to Bin Song's understanding of Ruism is the quest to experience the world as a dynamic harmony, embracing every aspect of life, through meditation in action or, what I have described as contemplative activism.[56]

54. Jeremy Bendik-Keymer, "On Flight: Bin Song," *Philosophy as a Way of Life, On Flight: Bin Song* (part I) | Blog of the APA (apaonline.org) On Flight: Bin Song (part I) | Blog of the APA (apaonline.org).
55. Ibid.
56. Bruce Epperly, *Prophetic Healing: Howard Thurman's Vision of Contemplative Activism* (Richmond, IN: Friends United Press, 2020) and *Mystics in Action: Twelve Saints for Today* (Maryknoll, NY: Orbis Press, 2020).

Ruist meditation is a form of practical enlightenment in which "there is no preference of quietude over action," Big Song avers. Enlightenment can occur in the here and now, at work, caring for children, or on the floor of the Senate, and not solely on a monastic retreat. The goal of meditation, of alignment with the dynamic harmony of the universe reflected in one's personal life, is to become a fully civilized human being, experiencing self-fulfillment in all of one's relationships. Non-violent in nature, Ru meditation and ethics seeks to bring forth the best in one's own nature and the nature of those around us. Wu-wei, or non-action, involves going with one's own personal gifts in the context of one's vocation in the social order. In many ways, Ru spirituality is congruent with the wisdom of early Christian theologian Iranaeus, who proclaimed that "the glory of God is a fully alive human."

This personal liveliness, reflecting the dynamic harmony of the universe, shapes every aspect of one's life, including one's professional life, citizenship, marriage, parenting, and friendships. In contrast to critiques of Confucianism as hierarchical, Bin Song sees the ordering of society as involving integrity, reciprocity, mutuality, and respect, that promotes egalitarian and growing relationships.

In conversing with Bin Song, I realized that Ruism (Confucianism) has an important gift for American politics. We need a spirituality of politics grounded in the quest to become fully civilized persons, characterized by honesty, sincerity, and compassion which embraces society in all its diversity. The fully civilized citizen and politician will look beyond their own self-interest to promote the well-being of the community, nation, and, by implication, the planet. They will be known for their honesty and respect for others. Ruism asserts that politics can be—and should be—and moral enterprise, with the goal of promoting authentic well-being in every sector of society.

WHAT CHRISTIANS CAN LEARN FROM RUISM/CONFUCIANISM

While conservative Christians are too embedded in tradition in terms of doctrine, scripture, sexuality, and gender roles, often progressive Christians appear rudderless by comparison, tacking with the winds of change and jettisoning valuable traditions when these traditions don't measure up to our more enlightened world views. Confucius affirmed the importance of knowing our past and honoring the experiences of our elders in the faith. Youth has its insights and injects new possibilities into institutional and theological structures. Yet, youth with its visions and dreams needs the "tragic beauty" of age to provide guideposts for growth. Tradition is not the same thing as traditionalism. There can be ritual without inflexibility.

Confucianism/Ruism reminds us of the importance of studying patterns of history and honoring the insights of the past even when they aren't always as "woke" as our current insights. We need to remember to judge past traditions, theologians, and spiritual guides with grace, knowing that other generations may judge our own parochialisms with the severity equal that with which we judge others. Confucianism/Ruism reminds us that although God is constantly doing a new thing, God also treasures the inspirations of the past. We need to ask ourselves, "What 'imperfect' traditions are still valuable? What can we learn from our ancestors in the faith? Where might the ancestors help us chart our way in responding to the current challenges of economics, environment, pluralism, politics, and pandemic?" We need to give thanks, honor, and embrace the best of the past as we lean toward the spiritual and moral arcs of the future.

CHRISTIANITY'S GIFT TO CONFUCIANISM/RUISM

Honoring tradition is essential to spiritual growth. It can also be stifling to the spiritual adventure. Ironically, Confucianism's greatest strengths—its honoring of tradition and recognition of the importance of ritual and relational norms - is also its greatest weakness. Tradition, ritual, and relational etiquette can degenerate, as it did in some forms of Confucianism/Ruism, to lifeless formalism, idolatry of the status quo and past achievement, and paternalistic relationships. Confucius himself recognized the importance of context in relationships and public policy. The sage responds to the concrete situation, guided by past traditions and rituals, but not imprisoned by ritualism or formalism. The spirit of Confucianism can embrace novel ideas and rituals, updating them to respond to the demands of a changing world, such as, the equality of women and fluidity in social standing.

Christianity and Judaism proclaim that although God is ever faithful, God's mercies are new every morning. God is constantly doing a new thing and calling us to be part of God's emerging vision of ethics, politics, and relationships. The pure conservative, as Whitehead asserts, goes against the grain of the universe. Process and openness Christianity invites Confucianism to open its windows to novelty as well as order, to embrace change while honoring traditions, and to encourage innovation while maintaining patterns of ritual. Process and openness Christianity asserts that we can hold in balance past, present, and future achievements and possibilities as a reflection of God's own commitment to propelling the moral and spiritual arcs of history toward the far horizons of Shalom.

A CONFUCIAN/RUIST SPIRITUAL PRACTICE

Confucius made a commitment to learning. He believed that the fully human person is cosmopolitan in nature. The fully human person is constantly growing, as Jesus did, in wisdom and stature. The fully human person, as process-relational theologian Bernard Loomer asserts, is committed to becoming a person of stature, who embraces contrasts, diversity, and pluralism without losing their personal center.

For Confucius, like the sages of the rabbinical tradition, study is a form of prayer and worship. We are intended to be large-spirited and broad-minded persons who recognize that their limitations and parochialism are an invitation to growth, self-criticism, and study. Our studies should be lifelong in nature, constantly pushing our current ethical, intellectual, and spiritual limits. However, study is more than just book learning. Study also involves, as Confucius noted, a commitment to learn about other peoples' cultures and experiences and to grow in empathy and compassion. Study involves a commitment to the arts, in particular music, which harmonizes the soul and the community. Today, following Confucius might lead us to the symphony and art gallery, to the Holocaust, African American and Native American museums in Washington DC, to tours of national parks and aquariums, as well as to play a musical instrument or learn a new language.

Cosmopolitan persons are cosmic in orientation. They are globalists, pluralists, and artists of the spirit, dedicated to pushing the frontiers of their spiritual and intellectual growth toward the farthest horizons of the human adventure.

CHAPTER THIRTEEN

Daoism

Life can be thought of as polar in nature. The nature of things can be described as a dynamic interplay of order and novelty, night and day, dark and light, death and life, youth and age, and tradition and innovation. The same applies to culture, religion, and politics. There are those who prize ancient rituals, familiar patterns of behavior, and unassailable traditions. Any change, whether in terms of demographics, scriptural interpretation, liturgical rituals, or gender roles, is a threat, putting at risk our familiar way of life and religious certainties. Stuck in the past, they believe that life was better in the 1950s when America was a "Christian" nation and people knew their place in society and the roles of women and men and children and parents were clear-cut.

In contrast, there are those who privilege transformation. From their perspective, the old order is, by definition, regressive, corrupt, and paternalistic. The politics, literary canon, and religious leadership of old white males must give way to youth and diversity. New voices must be heard, and older voices muted. The old-time religion may have been good enough for our parents, but it fails the contemporary test. No longer seen as unquestionable, religious authorities are viewed as finite and fallible, and scriptures are subject to interpretation and innovation. The fundamentalist "the Bible says it, I believe it, and that settles it" gives way to the hermeneutic of suspicion and critique, and its challenging "Who says so?" The past is unredeemable—corrupt, sexist, racist, irrelevant—and must be discarded to move forward. There are problems with both approaches. In one, the gifts of the past are lost. In the other, the ambiguities and limitations of our faith fail to be taken into consideration.

Alfred North Whitehead asserted that the pure conservative goes against the nature of the universe, and that the process is the reality. However, Whitehead also recognized the importance of predictable structures in religion and in culture. Whether in religion, culture, politics, and family life, well-being depends on a creative and flexible interplay of order and novelty, and tradition and innovation. We need the wisdom of tradition and the insight of holy books as well as the dynamism and concreteness of new voices and visions. Without memories and rituals, we are caught in the prison house of the isolated now. Predictability is essential to healthy relationships, not to mention in agriculture and for parenting. Yet, without novel experiences, the forward movement of life is stifled and life degenerates. Relationships need the zest of surprise. Healthy communities need critique and change. Similarly, God is ever faithful, and yet God's mercies are new every morning!

In the adventure of Chinese religion, Daoism and Confucianism/Ruism represent the dynamic spiritual and ethical yin and yang. These contrasting traditions are so intimately connected that many Chinese governmental officials were followers of Confucius during the week, upholding the value of tradition and the importance of seeking excellence in social relationships, and Daoists on the weekend, enjoying the values of spontaneity and "going with the flow."

The Great Master Confucius taught the importance of spiritual and ethical order and the unique responsibilities built into every relationship. While not himself legalistic, Confucius believed that the good life comes from ethical nurture and personal development. Character is developed by repetition. We become good persons by consistently doing good things, appropriate to our station and situation. In the ideal society, everyone knows what is expected of them and their neighbor not in a rigid fashion, although Confucianism can degenerate into rigidity and formalism, but in terms of ethical and spiritual guideposts that promote a great society and great persons.

For the Daoist, inspired by Lao Tzu and Chuang Tzu, the good life is spontaneous. It is a matter of following nature. The ideal person returns to the "uncarved block" eschewing formality and living in the dynamic now. The Confucian plans. The Daoist goes with the flow. The Confucian prizes self-improvement. The Daoist rejoices in childlike playfulness. For the Daoist, culture corrupts, alienating us from our true nature. The good life is found in subtraction, not addition, in fewer rituals and requirements, rather than prescribed behaviors.

The origins of Daoism (Taoism) are shrouded in mystery. The emergence of Daoism is identified with Lao Tzu (Laozi), "the venerable one," "the old gentleman," who is believed to have been a sixth century BCE contemporary of Confucius. An archivist at the national library, Lao Tzu grew tired of the contrasting realities of rigidity and chaos in Chinese society. He abandoned his post and left society, headed to the Western boundaries, mounted on a water buffalo. On the verge of leaving the Empire, he was asked by a border official to share his philosophy of life. He accommodated the official by writing the *Tao Te Ching,* "the way of power," a short text of eighty-one poetic passages. Chuang Tzu (Zhuang Zhou) is the other great philosopher-spiritual guide of Daoism. Living in the fourth century BCE, Chuang Tzu was known for his parables, encouraging seekers to turn away from the complexity and hypocrisy of politics and culture to be in harmony with the flowing energy of Tao.

Today, most Westerners experience the wisdom of Daoism through Qigong, Tai Chi, Kung Fu, and acupuncture as well as Japanese Aikido, all of which seek to promote balance, and harmony with the energy of the universe, Chi, which flows through the universe and our lives. Harmony with Chi enhances spiritual centeredness and physical wellbeing. During my college years, I often consulted the Daoist-Confucian I Ching, a spiritual divination tool, to gain insight for making decisions related to relationships and vocation. Later in life, I learned and became a Teacher-Master of Reiki Healing Touch, a Japanese healing practice grounded in the philosophy of Chi.

GOING WITH THE FLOW OF DAOISM

Process and open and relational theologians and physicists tell us that we live in a dynamic, relational, and energetic universe. Our universe is alive and throbbing with energy. We are the children of stardust and wonder. Energy courses through us, process-relational theologians assert, in terms of possibility, creativity, and production of beauty. Relationships and relativity characterize the reality of stars, planets, ecosystems, cells, quanta, and human communities.

Over 2500 years ago, Daoist sages identified the nature of reality in a similar fashion. Chi, or dynamic energy, is the deepest reality, which flows through and gives life to all things. We are children of Chi. Our wellbeing depends on our openness to this vital energy. Opening to energy brings wisdom and health. Leaky or blocked energy leads to stagnation and disease. This applies to communities as well as to persons. The energy of the universe, the ever-flowing chi, is sufficient for our well-being. Personal and communal health depends on a process of simplifying and eliminating everything that blocks the "glow flow" of chi energy.

In the following sections, I will give a brief description of the energetic reality of Daoist spirituality:

- *The Tao.* The great mystery of the universe is the universe itself. Theologian Paul Tillich spoke of the "ontological shock of non-being," grounded in unanswerable questions, such as: Why there is something rather than nothing? Why is the universe the way it is? Why must we die? Alfred North Whitehead speaks of God as the ultimate irrationality, that is, the great unexplainable factor upon which all rationality and explanation depend. Daoist cosmology speaks similarly: "The Tao that can be told is not the true Tao." The Tao is the "Mystery of Mysteries. The Gateway to All Marvels." (Saying 1)[57] Though mysterious, the Tao gives life to all things. It is the energy of creation and destruction, yin and yang, positive and negative, and life and death. Flowing through all things, it bursts forth in the wondrous variety of creation. In the spirit of Western apophatic theology, the Tao is beyond words and names. If you think you know it, if you can get a handle on it and you can define it, it is not the Tao, but one of the many manifestations of the primal and everlasting

57. There are a variety of translations of the Tao Te Ching. I have followed John Minford, Tao Te Ching (New York: Viking, 2018).

Energy of the Universe. As the Daoist sage observes, "Who Knows/Does not speak/Who speaks/Does not know." (Saying 56)

Transcendent, and beyond all; the Tao is also immanent and within all. Nothing can exist apart from its energy. Although the Tao is beyond personality, it gives birth to personality and a pantheon of gods and spiritual beings, revered by later Daoists, who extended their metaphysical vision far beyond the simplicity of Lao Tzu.

The Universe has neither a beginning nor end, but is the evolving, dynamic, rising, dying, various, united, manifestation of this unnamable and ubiquitous Cosmic Energy.

- *The Spirit of Simplicity.* The Dao is like flowing water, beneath all things and barely noticed, yet transforming the contours of the riverbank and wearing away solid rocks. The sage experiences the fullness of life by letting go of the weight of civilization that bears down on us. Daoists go to work, raise families, and seek excellence in their professions. The good life they seek is found by living according to nature as much as possible. By becoming aware of the unique manifestation of Universal Energy flowing through us, we become fulfilled by becoming ourselves, following our inner energy, and not adapting to the rigidity of formalism, conformity, and regimentation. Daoists live in the world but are not of it. They aspire toward excellence, but realize that they can fulfill their duties while remaining unattached to the results, and spiritually free from others' expectations. This is the meaning of *wu wei,* the non-action and non-attachment that allows the Tao to flow unobstructed through our lives.

In many ways, Jesus joined a passion for God's Realm of Shalom with the spontaneity of spiritual freedom. The realm of God is like a child, who is dependent on God and living in the moment. Consider the lilies, they neither toil nor spin, and yet, Jesus says, they are arrayed with greater beauty than Solomon and Caesar. Seek God's realm first and hang loose on others' expectations. Jesus spoke of himself as the "vine" whose energy of love is constantly flowing through the branches. When the branches are connected to the vine, they flourish and bear fruit. Disconnected from the energetic vine, they wither and die. To ensure the health of the vine, the spiritual vinedresser prunes everything that blocks God's life-giving energy.

In many ways, the first ten chapters of Mark's Gospel join Confucian/Ruist goal-orientation, seeking to embody God's realm, with Daoist spontaneity. Always on a journey, Jesus stops in his tracks and changes course whenever he sees a need. Jesus looks to the far horizons of Shalom, but lives moment to moment, going with the flow of a world in need. As Mark's Gospel recounts repeatedly, Jesus "immediately," that is, spontaneously gets up to respond to God's moment by moment, often unrehearsed and unplanned, call.

For the Daoist, greatness comes from humility. The best leader gently guides, without intrusion. Statecraft, at its best, evokes possibility. The "soft power" does not dominate, coerce, or demand. When the job is finished, the citizenry rejoices in the work they have done, not the work they have been told to do by their leaders. The New Testament image of Jesus letting go of power (kenosis) is seen as the model of healthy relationships.

The Daoist, like Transcendentalist poet and essayist Henry David Thoreau, experiences God in the sauntering. Daoists wonder as they wander, letting the wondrous variety of life flow through them, giving thanks for the amazing reality of each day and the life-giving energy of the Dao.

The Daoist seeks excellence in the art of living, but excellence comes from letting go. "The Taoist Acts/Without attachment/Achieves/Without dwelling/On achievement/And so never loses." (Saying 2) Going with the flow of Life, the Taoist ideal notes that:

The more they have,
The more they share,
The more is theirs.

The Tao of Heaven
Brings benefit,

Never Harm.
The Taoist accomplishes
But never contends.
(Saying 81)

- *Ever-flowing Spiritual Energy.* Just as most Westerner's primary encounter with Hinduism is through yoga and meditation, most Westerners experience the spirit of Daoism through complementary medicine, energy work, and the martial arts. Tai Chi, Qigong, Acupuncture, Aikido, Reiki Healing Touch, and Kung Fu all have their primordial origins in Daoist cosmology and its emphasis on Life-giving Energy. Daoism's vision of a dynamic, ever-flowing energetic universe, in which the quality of energetic flow is the source of health and illness, has inspired millions to explore various Daoist-based practices. Although the Reiki Healing Touch I have practiced since the mid-1980s has its specific origins in the insights of Japanese spiritual guide Mikao Usui, the "Ki" of Reiki, universal energy, is a child of Daoist "Chi." In Reiki, either by touch or distant intentionality, one enhances, balances, and harmonizes personal and communal energy. In harmony with the Dao, with Chi, by engaging in physical and spiritual practices, we can experience fullness of life, longevity, and vitality.

The energy of Chi inspires the healing potential of every person. Daoist energy practices can be used in concert with diet, healthy lifestyle, and Western medicine to promote the well-being of body, mind, and spirit.

A DIALOGUE WITH DAOIST IN ME

I first encountered Daoism as a high school senior in 1970. I had just finished reading Carlos Castenada's *Teachings of Don Juan: A Yaqui Way of Knowledge* and was in search of a path with a heart. My friend Glenn Reeves shared a copy of the *Tao Te Ching* and Lao Tzu's ancient text captivated my spirit. Perhaps it was the image of the flowing river, similar in movement to the ripples of the creek in Alum Rock Park in San Jose where I pilgrimed to still my soul and bathe my senses in the splashes and gurgles. Perhaps the text resonated with my inclination to keep my footprint as simple and small as possible as a result of growing up in an emotionally tumultuous family. But, then and now, the words of the ancient sage still speak to my spirit and have shaped my personal and professional life. In the creative synthesis of my spiritual life, Daoism inspires my embrace of new spiritual movements and Hinduism as complements to my Christian faith.

For me, Daoism is the path of quiet creativity and silent healing. Letting the flow of the universe animate and flow through me, expanding my sense of self and blurring the boundaries between self and other. We are all in the same flow. Life flows through us, energizing and calming, and sometimes capsizing our inflexible habits and belief systems. Life flows through us and when I let the river propel me, a sense of effortlessness characterizes my daily tasks. Pausing and noticing and then going with the flow of ideas, intuitions, and emotions, I experience a higher creativity and wisdom flowing through my own creativity and wisdom. The roadblocks and writer's blocks are carried away by the stream of life.

In many ways, Jesus had a Daoist spirit. He had a vision and vocation, but—especially evident in Mark's Gospel—Jesus responded to the immediacy of the moment. His agenda always took second place to the need he saw along his path. Jesus stopped in mid-journey and mid-sentence to the call of the moment, to the flow of life revealed in random, but truly synchronous encounters. I followed that same Daoist spirit as a parent and professional, a seminary administrator and senior pastor, in relationship with my staff, colleagues, and child and grandchildren. I had a clear vision of my work and parenting goals, but never an inflexible agenda. Like the Daoist sage, I responded to problems, as Emily Dickinson counsels, "slant," that is, elliptically and indirectly. I looked for the giftedness of others and then inspired them to bring forth their gifts in their current life situation. In the spirit of the Tao, I saw my primary role in terms of creating a healthy and safe playing field in which my son, grandchildren, and colleagues could join maximal freedom and creativity for their own enrichment and the wellbeing of the whole. Now as a grandparent, I seek lovingly to nurture the "uncarved block," the inner gifts of my grandchildren through listening to them, observing their joys, giving them space to grow, and providing flexible and loving structures, grounded in putting their gifts and joy above my adult agenda for them.

Constantly opening to the flow of my life situation, whether in family or professional life, I still seek to get my ego out of the way, recognize that there are many "right" answers, and embrace change in those with whom I interacted. Going with the flow of Life requires strong boundaries, but these personal and professional boundaries involve self-awareness, rather than external coercion. Embracing the Tao, I seek inner and outer integrity consistent with flexible and porous boundaries. In many ways, the Tao is the still, small voice of God, congruent with every change, inspiring and enlivening and not coercing, presenting a plethora of possibilities appropriate to each moment and encounter.

As I begin retirement, after over forty years of pastoring, teaching, and administration, I am learning to let the Tao of the moment and life season guide my way. Life is flowing and I must welcome change. I need to flow with a new identity and new possibilities. I need to let go of past responsibilities, including a congregation I loved deeply, to embrace new adventures and allow my former congregation to flow freely toward the future. I go with the current of each day, guided by a vision, but open to novelty, changing course, and letting go of my plans to respond to an unexpected possibility or the need of another person. In retirement, I have found that very little in my daily life is urgent, even as I recognize the urgency of responding to our planetary and national crises. I can honestly describe myself as a Daoist Christian, balancing my commitment to the directionality of the moral and spiritual arcs of history with an openness to taking Life as it is, living in the unprogrammed and open-ended moment.

Following the Tao, I've learned the gift of simplicity. Spiritual, as well as material, decluttering is essential to the journey ahead. Letting go of everything, being content with the moment, and opening to the gifts of retirement and aging. Not holding on to the past, even the positive past and even the joys of youth, opens my spirit to the unique gifts and griefs of the aging process. Not fighting the "necessary losses" and "unfixable" aspects of aging, I find joy and contentment in the Holy Here and Now, and affirm, with UN General Secretary Dag Hammarskjold:

> *For all that has been—thanks!*
> *For all that shall be—yes!*

WHAT CHRISTIANS CAN LEARN FROM DAOISM

One of the best-selling books in Christian history is Rick Warren's *Purpose Driven Life,* in which Warren provides spiritual practices to enable persons to align themselves with God's purpose for their lives. For Warren, God has planned out all the significant events and personal characteristics of our lives in advance. Warren believes that God has a clear plan for all of us, and we find fulfillment in following God's clearly articulated agenda for our lives. Although we have freedom, Warren asserts that our freedom is ultimately determined by divine providence. Just follow the directions and you will find success and salvation. Warren's intent is to provide positive spiritual guidance and many people have benefitted from his book. Yet, for many people, Warren's Calvinistic vision of purposefulness has only inspired more driven and task-oriented behavior, inspired by a driven and controlling God. Always on the go, looking for opportunities to grow, constantly updating their phone calendars, purpose driven people leave little room for spontaneity, creating the spiritual version of the nanny state, or divine helicopter parenting, in which any deviation from one's God-driven life plan is an annoyance and failure.

Christian spirituality tends to be both providential and purposeful. We are called to be God's hands and feet and agents of God's realm. Nevertheless, too much purpose and planning lead to attachment and anxiety. Winning and succeeding become everything or, as football coach Vince Lombardi asserted, the only thing. To fail God's agenda is to risk your eternal happiness or bring misfortune in this lifetime. In contrast, process and open and relational theology and Daoism see fulfillment as the interplay of order and novelty. Daoists have purposes, but they recognize that life can change in a millisecond. New occasions inspire new possibilities. Authentic life, to quote John Lennon, happens while you are making other plans. For the Daoist, and for the open and relational Christian and process theologian, providence is open-ended, not coercive or determining. Providence inspires possibility and novelty, not inflexibility and legalism.

Purpose driven Christians need to go with the divine flow as it emerges. Purposeful Christians need to "chillax," that is chill in relaxation, trusting the Energetic Dao and the Grace of God. Even God has a Daoist spirit and is willing to change course as circumstances. What is best for us and for the world is constantly changing, within the movements of the spiritual and moral arcs of history and personal life. God is moving within the lively and spontaneous energy of life. God has a vision, but never a coercive agenda for our lives or for the world. In fact, God enjoys novelty and surprise. Going with the flow, rather than always trying to control the flow, brings us greater freedom, peace of mind, and calm. Perhaps the Sabbath is God's version of the purposeless and unplanned life characterized by the interplay of resting, playing, and making space, all for the pure joy of it. The Jewish mystical concept of *Tzimzum,* God's making space for creation, is God's commitment to *wu wei,* the non-doing that makes creaturely creativity possible, doing things that involve neither toiling nor spinning, but giving glory to God simply by being: gazing at a grasshopper all afternoon with Mary Oliver; sauntering in the woods with Thoreau; splashing; skipping, finger painting and singing; lying on your back beholding the heavens above; or bathing your soul with the warmth of the sun. Let go and let God. Pause and let the waters of life carry you downstream, delighting in the pure wonder of all being.

CHRISTIANITY'S GIFT TO DAOISM

Once we get beyond Western Christianity's emphasis on drive and purpose, we can experience a healthier Christian spirituality that joins intentionality with spontaneity, and order with innovation. The dynamics of grace embrace the freely given, never-earned love of God. We don't need to "do" anything to experience grace. Salvation, healing, joy, wholeness, everlasting life are present realities available to us just for the asking, or by opening to God's Holy Here and Now. Grace begets grace, and a spacious trust in God. Grace gives the Tao a direction toward justice and healing.

From the perspective of process and open and relational theology, grace is the energy of love which lovingly flows through us, filling and healing us, and inspiring and transforming us, so that the flow of grace is directed toward our neighbors and their needs. Grace is spontaneous and free, and intentional and active. The *wu wei* of grace is that, in not doing anything to merit it, we can joyfully share it as God's companions in healing the world.

A DAOIST SPIRITUAL PRACTICE

I invite you to explore, and learn from, two Daoist practices. First, simply *do* something countercultural: don't do something, just do nothing. Practice *wu wei,* happily doing nothing, and letting life gracefully happen. You may discover how difficult it is to let go of your agenda. I know that it is difficult for me. There's always a good idea or insight to follow up on for a project, book, or sermon. I do my best "doing nothing" when I take my sunrise walks. Often, I just become, as the North African monk says, "all sense." I let the whole universe flow into my senses—the breeze, my footstep on the beach or pavement, the sound of waves, the diving seagulls, the scudding clouds, or bright sunrise. I let thoughts flow through my mind, without holding on to any. I rejoice in experiencing the moment.

A second practice involves exploring the Daoist concept of Chi, first-hand. Enroll in an introductory Qigong or Tai Chi course. Schedule an acupuncture or Reiki treatment simply for the joy of it. Simply relax and feel the benefit of going with the flow of the universe, feeling divine healing energy flowing in and through you. You may decide you want to learn Reiki healing touch as part of your self-care and support of others' wellbeing

CHAPTER FOURTEEN

Shinto

Celtic Christians, and their indigenous ancestors, referred to places where heaven and earth meet as "thin places." You can feel the presence of holiness at Stonehenge, Avebury, Avalon (the Tor of Glastonbury), on the Isle of Iona and in the Findhorn spiritual community. You can also experience the divine presence in Sedona, Mecca, at the Bo Tree where Buddha experienced enlightenment, on the Ganges River, and in Jerusalem. Abraham and Sarah erected an altar at the Oak of Mamre. The biblical tradition is replete with "thin places." Jacob has a dream of a ladder of angels, awakens, exclaims "God was in this place, and I did not know it," and calls the place "Beth-El," the "house of God." To Christians, the Garden of Gethsemane and the Cross on Calvary also mediate God's saving presence to humankind. Throughout history, certain places have been set apart as unique dwelling places of the Holy, or places where divinity meets humanity, providing inspiration, illumination, spiritual guidance, and law.

In recent years, process theologians and environmentalists have recognized the holiness of creation apart from human interests. In the spirit of James Lovelock's vision of Gaia, earth is viewed as a dynamic, interdependent, and self-regulating organism, having a life and intentionality of its own. Experience is everywhere. Value is universal. All things are touched by God: streams, rocks, trees, human beings, and the whole earth, Gaia, itself. Some refer to this as animism, nature alive with spirit. Process and open and relational theologians use the words "panpsy-chism" and "pan-experientialism" to describe the universality of experience and value. While there are obvious levels of experiential complexity, every creature, from quarks to angels, experiences the touch of God, enlivening and inspiring, energizing and guiding. All creation can, as the Psalm 148 and 150 proclaim, praise God, and, whatever can praise, is worthy of our reverence.

Religions have also spoken of certain persons and people as being "chosen" by God. Abraham, Isaac, and Jacob are told that they will be the parent of a great nation. Moses leads the Hebrew people out of captivity with the promise of a land of their own. The Hebrews perceive themselves as a chosen people, set apart by God's unmerited grace, and later destined to be a light unto the nations. Prophets are called forth to speak for God. Muhammed receives the divine commission to "proclaim" God's truth. Jesus is perceived by traditional Christians as the unique Son of God, fully human and fully divine, spiritually and metaphysically set apart from humankind. More progressive Christians see Jesus as uniquely related to God, revealing the fullness of divinity in human experience, but not metaphysi-cally different from us. Jesus' full humanity and divinity reflect his complete open-ness to and, revelation of God's call. Jesus' full humanity is the model and inspira-tion of our own Christ-like possibilities.

The indigenous religion of Japan, Shinto, "the way of the Gods," or *kami no michi*, "the way of *kami*," is as old as its homeland. Shinto asserts that nature in its entirety is animated by spirit and that the nation of Japan and its people are a unique and highly charged manifestation of kami, or spirit. At various times of its history, the Emperor was viewed as divine, a descendent of the high divinity Amaterasu, and thus a representation of the spirit of the nation. Shinto as the state religion, with its affirmation of the superiority of the descendants of *kami*, was abolished following Japan's defeat in World War II. Although Shinto has no founder, no revelational scripture, no missionary impulse, nor required doctrine, its followers delight in a living universe where the divine is found everywhere, including in their own experience.

THE LIVING SPIRIT OF SHINTO

Kami no michi, the spiritual path of kami, is found everywhere in nature, in our homes, and in religious shrines. The naturalistic theism, or spirituality of Shinto, joining sacred and secular, and heaven and earth, can be described through the following ideas:

- *The Spirit in All Things.* Shinto spirituality proclaims a God-filled world. There are *kami*-spirits everywhere, most particularly in trees and woodlands. The spiritual energy of the universe, *chi,* ranges from the heavens to earth. There are a variety of divinities, most importantly, Amaterasu, the sun deity, who gives life to all things. There is a myriad of demigods, including negative spirits, in the pantheon of *kami.* What is most important to us is that spirit or *kami* is with us right where we are in our daily pastimes, with hopes and dreams, social responsibilities, and worship. We don't have to go anywhere to experience holiness; it is already present in the Holy Here and Now. There are spirits in trees, brooks, mountains, and animals. There are also spirits, *kami,* in human-kind. We are the children of spirit, a reflection of spirit, and those who purify themselves may evolve into *kami.* Our ancestors may have evolved to become holy spirits, whose vocation is to help us navigate the challenges of life from birth to death. Spirit is everywhere, giving energy and life to all creation. We may become "good ancestors" ourselves, uniting heaven and earth in our care for our descendants.

- *Hybrid Spirituality.* Not doctrinal in nature, Shinto is comfortable embracing the best of other traditions, in particular Buddhism. Shinto has added Buddhist deities, most particularly the Bodhisattva Amaterasu, to its pantheon of kami divinities. This fluidity of boundaries manifests itself, for example, in Japanese households where Shinto and Buddhist domestic shrines stand side by side. In Japan, it is commonplace for families to have Shinto rituals for infants and Buddhist rituals for the dying and deceased. In many ways, Shinto is a forerunner of today's movements in hybrid inter-spirituality.

- *Purifying Spirit.* Spirit is everywhere and our calling as humans is to embody and embrace the spirit in our lives. We embrace our inner spirit through acts of purification, most especially through *misogi,* a rite similar to baptism, in which a person covers themself with cold water and often does physical exercises as a way of transforming mind, body, spirit, and relationships, creating a congruence with *kami.* In purifying our spirit, we enhance our evolution from "earth" to "heaven," taking the first steps to becoming *kami* ourselves. By purifying our spirits, we become more open and attractive to the benevolent *kami* spirits.

Shinto sees ethics in binary terms: "straight" versus "curved," positive versus negative, pure versus unclean, and harmonious opposed to chaotic. Ethics involves embracing order, balance, and harmony in our personal lives and citizenship. In contrast, evil behavior involves disorder, imbalance, and disharmony, whether caused by ordinary people or political leaders who foment violence, dishonesty, and division. While Shinto has no commandments like those found in Jewish or Muslim law, the Eightfold Path, the Sermon on the Mount, or in Confucian/Ruist propriety, the Daoist spirit of Shinto sees congruence between the harmonies of nature and human life. Aligned with the spirits, we will bring beauty and order to the world.

As in Confucian spirituality, Shinto proclaims the significance of relationships, both with our contemporaries and with our ancestors. Since we are first and foremost social beings, our personal and communal purification are interdependent, and benefit ourselves and support the health of our families and society.

- *Holy Places.* There are "thin places," as the Celts assert, everywhere. Yet, some places, Shinto believes, particularly attract the divine. Shinto is known for the simplicity and beauty of their shrines as homes for *kami*-spirits. Shrines are spiritual antennas attracting, by their holiness, kami to populate them, and to provide for our wellbeing. Like the spirit-filled groves of the Greeks, Celts, and indigenous peoples, groves of trees are especially spirit-filled places. Populated by *kami,* forests are places of calm and recuperation, of opening to the holiness of the world and oneself.

- *Spirit's Destiny.* Shinto is profoundly this worldly. Shinto proclaims the spiritual energy of the Holy Here and Now. Our lives are here, meaning is here, and love is here in community and in nature. Heaven will take care of itself if we seek balance, order, harmony, and purity in this lifetime. Still, in a spirit-filled world, the many dimensions of life interpenetrate one another. Shinto encourages faithfulness to our ancestors, whose vocation is to support human flourishing, especially in times of transition.

Although we live in the here and now, our calling is to become "good ancestors" in this life, caring for future generations, as a prelude to our future ancestral adventures. As reflections of *kami,* our destiny is to become fully *kami* ourselves through our commitment to purification and harmony. Death is not the termination of our spiritual journey but the continuation of an evolving spiritual adventure in which we will promote the well-being of our children, grandchildren, and future generations. The afterlife is not focused on "flying away" from this world to heaven but involves continuing positive care for this world. In this regard, Shinto, Confucianism, and the Yoruba religions share a common affirmation that the veil between the living and the dead is transparent, and that our post-mortem destinies involve continuing care for our loved ones and the planet.

LIVING THE SHINTO SPIRIT

One of the greatest challenges in my quest to interview persons from a variety of religious traditions was finding a practitioner of Shinto in the United States. As always, my classmate and friend Jay McDaniel came through with the suggestion that Rev. Barnaby Feder, Senior Pastor at the Champlain Valley Unitarian Universalist Society of Middlebury, Vermont, would be a good conversation partner. While Barnaby is not a practitioner of Shinto, the Shinto tradition has shaped his spirituality and, in his own words influenced "my relationship with Unitarian Universalism and primed me for a deeper appreciation of Native American spirituality as a basis for thinking about Earth-grounded Beloved Community."

Barnaby and I discovered that we had much in common. Both of us were raised in the San Francisco Bay Area and lived through the summer of love in the late 1960s. Both of us are writers: Barnaby was a staff reporter for the *New York Times* prior to attending seminary in midlife. Both of us are influenced by process theology. In

Barnaby's case, Catherine Keller, my classmate at Claremont Graduate School, was also his process theology professor at Drew Divinity School.

Barnaby's first serious encounter with Shinto came in 2010 when he received a scholarship to study at the renowned Tsubaki Grand Shrine in Suzuka, Japan. Barnaby lived at the Tsubaki Grand Shrine for two weeks, immersing himself in the spirit of Shinto. In recalling his experience at the Shrine, Barnaby notes: "I am a lifelong UU who has never felt fully at home in either the Christian or secular humanist wings of our denomination. Shinto has raised for me the possibility that I might progress spiritually by worrying less about defining what I believe and more about how I feel with constant commitment to certain practices. Misogi [a form of water purification, conducted under a waterfall at the Tsubaki Shrine] was the most dramatic ritual I encountered. But it was everyday practices like joining the priests to sweep the ground of leaves and the morning service with its drumming and its prayer chants, or *norito,* that became a part of the rhythm of my life at Tsubaki and a more frequent source for reflection."[58]

Barnaby finds Shinto's open-ended vision of deity liberating. "Shinto," he avers, "proclaims a multiplicity of deities, liberating us from the constraints of traditional theism." Shinto affirms the ubiquity of deity. "Moreover, Shinto's connection with Japan and its culture helped me to be spiritually grounded in the place where I live," Barnaby notes. In that regard, Shinto has helped Barnaby embrace the embodied, earth-based spirituality of the Native American tribes.

During his stay at Tzubaki Grand Shrine, Barnaby came to appreciate the daily discipline of sweeping the paths around the shrine. When he asked an elderly monk to explain the importance of sweeping the path, the monk replied, "The solution to any problem I was dealing with came while I was sweeping the path." In sweeping the path, like Buddhist walking meditation or the Benedictine Christian cloister walk, we live in the present moment and allow new insights to emerge without resistance or stress. For Barnaby, the heart of Shinto is the simple affirmation: "harmony reigns when creation is aligned with kami nature."[59]

Simple acts align us with the divine enlivening all creation and remind us of the profound interconnectedness of life. Although Shinto does not seek to evangelize

---

58. Barnaby Feder, "Exploring the Way of Kami." Exploring the Way of the Kami | International Unitarian Universalism | UUA.org (October 7, 2010)
59. Ibid.

and is profoundly rooted in, and creative of, Japanese culture, Shinto has an important gift to the world: a sense of the spirituality of all things and the holiness of the earth. Barnaby and I closed our conversation with the mutual affirmation that the planet, now more than ever, needs the earth-based spirit of Shinto, operating in concert with other earth-based spiritualities to heal the world.

WHAT CHRISTIANITY CAN LEARN FROM SHINTO

Shinto affirms the universality of value and experience. *Kami* is present in all things heavenly and earthly. The world is God-filled. Nature is the sanctuary of *kami*. Accordingly, Shinto encourages an environmental ethic, grounded in the value of each living thing. Sacred and secular are one reality. Our vocation is here on earth, and not in heaven. From Shinto, Christians can learn greater emphasis on the Holy Here and Now, living out God's vision "on earth as it is in heaven," We can let heaven take care of itself, trusting God's future for us, while we train our eyes toward the healing of the planet and its creatures.

CHRISTIANITY'S GIFT TO SHINTO

Christianity can encourage Shinto to expand its vision beyond its homeland. While the topography of Japan and the Japanese people can proclaim the uniqueness of their land, spirituality, and culture, especially in terms of its God-filled reality, Christianity can share with Shinto the spirit of universality, affirming that the *kami*-spirit is global, rather than national in scope. In the spirit of Rabbi Bradley Artson's understanding of being "chosen," process and openness theologians affirm that all places and all people are chosen, and are holy, to reflect God's presence. Spirit is alive not only in Japan but also in every time and place. Spirit gives life to every person and inspires revelation in every nation and generation. There are "thin places" everywhere, energizing everyone. While there are qualitative differences in the current manifestations of the spirit, revelation is global in nature: no nation, or people, is superior. All are vested with divine spirit, each in its unique way.

A SHINTO SPIRITUAL PRACTICE

Shinto proclaims the universality of spirit. The *kami*-spirit is present in all things and in you. In this practice, I invite you to open your senses to the holiness of yourself, and of everyone you encounter. Embrace the spirit within you. Embrace the spirit in everyone you meet. Look for spirit in the world around you—trees, birds, wolves, pangolins, right whales, chimpanzees, beaches, ponds, wind, and sea. Make a commitment to speak for our voiceless planet. Make a commitment to choose life for the non-human world.

CHAPTER FIFTEEN

Earth-Based and Pagan Spirituality

Throughout history, persons, ethnicities, and communities that differ from the social, political, religious, ethnic, or sexual "norm" are described by terms of the self-proclaimed guardians of the norms in pejorative language. The word "Christian" first emerges as a description by outsiders, not necessarily positive, for followers of Jesus. (Acts 11:26, Acts 26:28) Later, "Christian" morphed into a positive self-description of the movement initiated by the Healer of Galilee, the Risen Savior, Jesus. The word "queer," now used positively in the GLBTQ community, was first used to describe people who were perceived to be strange, bent, and not quite right. This same linguistic transformation has emerged in the use of the words, "pagan" and "witch." The Latin word for "pagan," was invoked to describe "people of the country," that is, persons who were "rustic," and far less sophisticated than city dwellers, not unlike the term "redneck" in contemporary USA vocabulary. When Christianity became dominant, "pagan" referred to followers of the old ways, polytheists, and those whose spirituality involved fertility rituals and seasonal celebrations. Later, "pagan" was used to describe non-believers and heathens in need of the salvation that only Christ can give. The same movement from pejorative to positive applies to witchcraft. As a religion primarily involving women and earth-based rituals, witchcraft was considered demonic and dangerous by supposedly orthodox Christians. Cackling witches envisioned as flying on broomsticks, casting spells, and giving allegiance to the dark forces were to be exterminated, or used to frighten young children into good behavior. In the 1600s, those accused of being witches in New England, notably in Salem, Massachusetts, were tried, found guilty, and burned at the stake for practicing alternative spiritualities, including the healing arts. These women, walking to the beat of a different drummer, threatened male dominance in the strict and humorless culture of the pilgrims. Accordingly, they deserved ostracism, persecution, and punishment.

As recounted in the First or Old Testament, the occupation of Canaan by the children of Israel involved conflict with persons who could later be described as pagans: those practicing indigenous, earth-based, seasonal, and fertility religions, usually associated with worshipping female as well as male deities. They were considered immoral and polytheistic idolators by the conquering forces, whose God was seen as male, and transcendent to earth and its seasons. This same sense of spiritual superiority, leading to genocide and forced conversion, was at the heart of the European Christian conquest of the Americas.

Today, the words "Paganism" and "Witchcraft" have been embraced as positive terms and as an antidote to the rampant materialism and ecological destruction characteristic of Western Christian civilizations. Positive images of witchcraft have even made it to the mainstream media with "Bewitched," "Sabrina," and recently "The Good Witch," airing on the very middle- American Hallmark Channel! While there are many varieties of Paganism, Pagan spirituality serves as an alternative to the ethically rigid, dualistic, earth destroying, and sky-God worshipping religion of many conservative Christians. Although Pagan movement identifies sacred spaces and spiritual leaders, it has no required doctrines or institutional authorities. Flexible, eclectic, and experiential in spirit, Paganism embraces witchcraft, wicca, Druidic spirituality, and shamanism, and often intersects with Yoruba, Santeria, and First/Native American spiritualities.

Seen as demonic and evil by conservative Christians, Paganism provides an alternative earth-based, creation-loving spirituality that many progressive Christians affirm and integrate in their own spiritual journeys. Indeed, in my own work as a Christian minister, I sponsored solstice and equinox services, integrating earth-based spiritualities with the Christian liturgical year. I believe that the God of Jesus embraces both Earth and Sky, and joins, rather than separates humankind from the non-human world. In contrast to conservative Christianity's separation of humankind and nature, process-relational and openness theology believes that the omnipresent, or amipresent, God creates a wondrous universe in which embodiment is positive, the seasons reflect God's faithfulness, and "all nature sings and around me rings the music of the spheres." The *imago dei,* the image of God, is not restricted to humankind: all things bear God's imprint and are spiritually continuous with humankind.

PATHWAYS OF PAGANISM

Today's Pagans are the children of our planet's first spiritual seekers. Earth-affirming, Paganism is flexible in spirit, and claiming no institutional hierarchy, holy scripture, or established doctrine. Paganism can be integrated with a variety of Earth-affirming and creation-oriented spiritualities. Its insights are compatible with those of Celtic Christianity, Matthew Fox's creation spirituality, feminist and womanist spirituality and theology, African and Caribbean spirituality, and process-relational and earth-affirming aspects of openness spirituality and theology. One of my goals in my eight-year ministry on Cape Cod was to reach out to earth-affirming spiritual seekers. Our congregation sought to make this connection by holding beach services to mark the summer and winter solstice, fall and spring equinox, as well as May Day and the Halloween harvest festival. We made connections at our Advent candlelight service with the ancient hopes of solstice light overcoming darkness on the shortest day of the year. In the seasonal beach prayer services, I sought to show the connection between the Christian liturgical calendar and the eight seasonal Pagan festivals as a way of affirming the onward progress of history, marked by interplay of the forward movement of the moral and spiritual arcs of justice, and the yearly turning of the seasons. As a process theologian, I find much to affirm in the flexible and dynamic principles of Paganism, most especially its vision of an enchanted, interdependent universe in which human agency can shape the future.

- *The Divine Feminine and the Immanent God.* Paganism emphasizes divine immanence. God is within the world process. Not enthroned on high or beyond history, God is deeply embedded within the cycles of nature and the seasons of life. While most pagans believe that the Divine cannot be encompassed by human concepts, many Pagans, most especially witches and wiccans, perceive the divine as ultimately feminine in nature. As my friend and colleague Cyndi Simpson recalls, her spiritual breakthrough came when she realized that God was a woman, and not the bearded old man, ruling from the sky, revered by many traditional believers.

One of the leading "thealogians" (a feminine alternative to theologian) and spiritual leaders in the Paganism and the Reclaiming-Witchcraft movement, Starhawk affirms that "the Goddess, the Gods, are embodied, that we are each a manifestation of the living being of the earth, that nature, culture, and life in all their diversity is sacred."[60] For Starhawk and for many witches and wiccans, the Mother Goddess is the source of life, while the male Horned God constantly dies and is reborn in the changing seasons of life. The Divine Feminine, Starhawk believes, is the womb of creation, giving birth to all things, and enlivening the masculine spirit of the universe. According to Starhawk, the Goddess, who is beyond male and female, has "infinite aspects and thousands of names— She is the reality behind many metaphors. She is the reality, the manifest deity, omnipresent in all of life, in each of us. She is not separate from the world—She is the world and all the things in it."[61] Radically different from God the Father and King, the Goddess "does not rule the world; She *is* the world. Manifest in each of us, She can be known internally by every individual, in all her magnificent diversity."[62] God is not only with us, God is in us. For Pagans, the Sky God above history and beyond embodiment has been superseded by the Divine Feminine, the Womb of Vitality and Wisdom, who is within all the seasons, cycles of life, and all creatures of life. In many ways, the Goddess is like the Tao, the ever-flowing stream of energy, moving through and giving life to all things. Beckoning us to be her companions, the Goddess reminds us that returning to the flow gives us energy and power to change the world for the good.

• *The Holiness of the Earth and Embodiment.* Goddess is present throughout the world as its deepest energetic reality. Divine immanence gives birth to the sacredness of creation: the world is the embodiment of Divinity. All things are revelations of God. All things contain sparks of energy and

60. Starhawk, *The Spiral Dance: Twentieth Anniversary Edition* (New York: Harper One, 1999), 22.
61. Ibid., 32.
62. Ibid., 33.

can communicate with one another. Existence is sacred in its origins. We cannot obliterate the Divine Energy within us, regardless of how far we deviate from our deepest nature. Nor can we humans separate ourselves from the energy that runs through us and through all creation.

The vision of a sacred universe leads Pagan spiritual guides Joyce and River Higginbotham to assert that at the heart of Paganism is "the belief that every part of the universe is blessed in its nature, and that there is nothing wrong with the universe or you."[63] We live in an animated universe, chock full of divinity. Revealing Divine Energy are the seasons of nature and cycles of life. All is good. All is holy. All is to be revered. The original wholeness remains even when we turn away from what is best for us. There are thin places everywhere, not only in places like Iona, Stonehenge, Sedona, and Avalon, but in us and all things.

One December morning, a few days before the Winter Solstice, as I took my beach walk, I spied a coin placed on a post at the beach parking lot. On the coin were the words, "Where will you spend eternity?" The coin obviously was intended to remind passersby that our primary goal in life is to go to heaven and that in accepting Jesus as Savior, we will be saved. While Pagans–and progressive and process-relational and openness Christians - see a connection between this life and the afterlife, however we imagine the afterlife, the goal of life is to live this Holy Moment, this World of Beauty, with its changing seasons and cycles from birth to death. Immersion in this world is the heart of the spiritual journey. As we embrace a life grounded in the changing seasons, in delighting in the wonder of creation, and in sharing our gifts with others, we will discover that eternity will take care of itself. The Holy Here and Now stretches into eternity when we realize that every place and moment is a "thin place," where body, mind, and spirit are united, and time and eternity meet.

- *Connection and Community.* According to the Higginbothams, "the belief that every part of the universe is profoundly interconnected shapes how Pagans view the Divine, the sorts of possible relationships with the Divine and the universe, and the Pagan approach to prayer and magic."[64]

63. Joyce and River Higginbotham, *Paganism: An Introduction to Earth Centered Religions* (Woodbury, MA: Llewellyn Publications, 2020), 2.
64. Ibid., 2.

The universe flows through us, and we flow through the universe. Everything is connected and in that deep connection, each of us plays a role in shaping the universe around us. Communication is inherent in a lively interdependent and intelligent universe. In a living universe, we can communicate not only with the Divine and our fellow humans but also with non-human animals, and natural objects like trees and plants. Prayer and magic, often described as *magick,* are possible because of this dynamic and intricate connection in which thoughts, intentions, visualization, and feelings shape the contours of the world around us and allow our lives to be catalysts for change in the world. Pagans live out the reality of the Southern African vision of *ubuntu,* "I am because of you, you are because of me, and we are because of one another." When I change myself, living by my deepest spiritual intentions, I share in changing the world, healing the earth, and uniting all creation.

- *Rituals of Transformation.* The goal of Pagan ritual is to change ourselves and the world. Rituals are grounded in our intentions, our vision of what can emerge when we focus on what is best for ourselves and others. Transformation is grounded in the reality of a living universe, in which all parts are interconnected, and communicate and cooperate with one another. When we set an intention, we raise energy and power, to embody our goals in the world of time and space. The magic, or *magick,* so feared and maligned by conservative Christians, does not manipulate the universe or control others, but enables us to align ourselves with the flow of the universe, working with the inherent and natural powers of things, to achieve which is best for ourselves and others. *Magick* is a way we express our agency as co-creators with Divinity in shaping in a positive direction the energy of the universe.

According to British occultist Alistair Crowley, "*Magick* is the Art and Science of Causing change to occur in conformity with will." Further, "*magick* is the actions of many consciousnesses working together within an aware interconnected universe to bring about one or more desired results."[65] From this perspective, magic is natural, cooperative, and can be used by anyone. "*Magick* is performed by putting yourself in a receptive

---

65. Ibid., 164.

state, forming your concern or intention clearly, projecting this intention into the universe, and then letting it go do its work."[66] *Magick* is not supernatural nor does it violate the laws of the universe. Our intentions, or visions, raise the energies of life when they are in accordance with the deeper laws of the universe, and are fulfilled in relationship to the intentions of others. *Magick* is grounded in our choice to be change agents in an interconnected universe in which energy follows thought, vision, and intentionality. Accordingly, aligning oneself with the deeper intentionally of the universe is similar in spirit to the workings of prayer in an interdependent universe in which God works within and with us to achieve the highest good, and invites us to be partners in creating a beautiful and just world for ourselves for and all creation. Contrary to the vilification of conservative Christians, pagan *magick,* like prayer in a process and open-spirited universe, is an act of intentionally, aimed at healing and wholeness, and congruent with the aims of Divinity. *Magick,* like open and relational prayer, moves us from self-interest to world loyalty.

A WITCH'S TALE

One of my former students and now ministerial colleague, Rev. Cyndi Simpson, described herself as a "Unitarian Universalist Witch," when we first met in 2005. Although we have become close friends and progressive colleagues—I jokingly call her "my favorite witch!" - I had never inquired *about* her call to embrace witchcraft as a spiritual practice until recently. Cyndi told me that she was drawn to witchcraft for the first time when she ventured into a metaphysical bookstore in, of all places, Lubbock, Texas. As she describes it, "when I picked up Riane Eisler's *The Chalice and the Blade,* I wasn't a Pagan. When I set it down, I was." Eisler's book provided a life-changing connection between the feminism and ecological consciousness that was at the heart of Cyndi's quest. Cyndi asserts that "feminism brought me to Paganism." Paganism focuses on the Goddess, challenging the often violent and binary Sky God religion, with its controlling and often oppressive male patriarchy, and dualism of heaven and earth, and spirit and body. As Cyndi avers, "Paganism introduced me to the Divine Feminine. I realized that God was a woman." She felt a sense of rightness and harmony with the feminine vision of divinity and

---

66. Ibid., 165.

realized that "this is what I need." Cyndi recognized that the pagan movement, of which witchcraft is a manifestation, was congruent with the Seven Principles of Unitarian Universalism, most particularly, the Seventh Principle, "respect for the interdependent web of existence of which we are a part."

In describing the contours of Paganism, Cyndi notes that "you can put anything on top of it that you want to. Earth-based spirituality is natural to us. We all, deep down, can all relate to the seasons and cycles of life." Pagans, Cyndi continues, "don't worship the Earth. We have reverence for the non-human world and affirm our unity and connection with it. We learn from the seasons and cycles of the natural world—literally and metaphorically." Cyndi gave an example of the importance of earth-based spirituality. "The Pagan holiday Imbolc, celebrated on February 1st and known in the Christian liturgical calendar as Candlemas, speaks to the ending of winter. The days are much longer, but in many places, it is still cold. Snowdrops and crocuses might be peeking out of the ground. The spiritual tasks of Imbolc are to rededicate ourselves sacramentally as Witches to the most important roles and tasks in our lives, especially the ones we might be focusing on for the next year. I might rededicate myself to my religious leadership, my friendship for others, my care for the environment, my sisterhood, and my continuing self-awareness, among others. A second focus of Imbolc is cleansing and re-dedicating spiritual tools and altars. Both of these spiritual practices are inspired by the growing light and clarity of Imbolc and the bare beginnings of the new spring."

Cyndi is part of the Reclaiming Tradition of Witchcraft and its affirmation of the positive values of witchcraft: its connection with nature, recognition of the wholeness of life, and the promotion of the importance of the Divine Feminine. "I like to use the word 'Witch' because it is about being a wise and powerful woman." Cyndi notes that the word "warlock" to describe males involved in witchcraft is derivative. Men can be Witches, too! In the course of our conversation, I noted that "I might be a Witch, based on your definition," to which Cyndi responded with the open-spirited mirth I have come to know in our friendship, "Of course you are, Bruce!"

Historically, the rituals of witchcraft have been misunderstood, especially by male religious leaders, who see them as demonic attempts to bend others to their evil intentions. Such descriptions are a distortion of the true nature of witchcraft, Cyndi contends. "We don't believe in the devil or worship the devil. Our rituals are about transformation. They are about setting an intention, the raising of power aimed at positive outcomes." Setting an intention is similar in practice and function to the Christian understanding of prayer in its joining of energy and power for the good, "the best and highest for me and others." Cyndi recalls participating in a gathering of witches on Spring Equinox 2003, the eve of the beginning of the War in Iraq. The group gathered, set the intention of "peace," seeking to work energetically together to support planetary harmony. Like the image of the moral and spiritual arc of the universe, I have invoked throughout this text, the Pagan path seeks wholeness for persons, communities, and the planet. It seeks to affirm our rootedness in the Earth. Cyndi concluded our conversation with the strong affirmation, "We are all pagans. We just don't know it. It is our birthright!"

WHAT CHRISTIANS CAN LEARN FROM PAGANISM

While process and openness theologies are earth-affirming, Paganism's greatest gift to persons of faith is its affirmation of the holiness of creation and embodiment. Our spiritual calling is to embrace the earth and delight in its beauty. While we may affirm the existence of the afterlife and its spiritual and ethical continuity with this lifetime, our vocation is to be concerned with one world at a time, as Thoreau noted on his deathbed. The physical world is the holy of holies. Divinity delights and lives in the world of flesh and blood. Nature and the non-human world are inherently valuable. Embodiment is not a fall from grace. Sexuality is sacred and is a joyful expression of our love for one another, and not a threat to our spiritual journeys. We can love God in the world of the flesh just as we can love God in times of prayer and meditation. Both monastic silence and making love reflect the Divine intent for us. The sacred nature of sexuality, embodiment, and the non-human world make ethical claims on us. While Paganism does not focus on shame or guilt, or narrow understandings of morality, our calling, paganism believes, is to bring beauty to our relationships, to treasure the planet, and to promote equality and respect. The earth is our mother, revealing wise creativity and care, at every level. Accordingly, Pagans place reverence for life, and environmental care, at the heart of any authentic spiritual journey. Spirit and flesh are joined as reflections of the sacred. Our healing and enlightenment go through the body, and not around it, and not through bodily denial or mortification of the flesh.

CHRISTIANITY'S GIFT TO PAGANISM

Progressive and process-relational and openness Christians affirm much of the Pagan world view. At the heart of the process and open and relational world view is the immanence of God, the holiness of the non-human world, delight in the world of the flesh, and the universality of experience, all of which are affirmed in the Pagan spirituality.

Progressive, process-relational, and openness Christianity are also profoundly prophetic in spirit. Spirituality takes shape in political and social transformation. Our beliefs ground us in the earth and inspire us to protect the earth and its peoples. With Hebraic prophets, process-relational and openness theology sees politics as holy, insofar as it can be a force for social transformation, equality, repairing injustice, and protecting the planet and future generations. While certain Pagan spiritual leaders such as Starhawk, and Cyndi Simpson, have come to affirm the importance of political action, especially in response to climate change, women's equality, and human rights, Christianity at its best joins the personal and political to support the growth of God's realm "on earth as it is in heaven." Heaven is not an ethereal realm, but the realm of Shalom in the here and now as God envisions it. Shalom is our goal. Wholeness is our quest whether in our personal lives or in political action. Delighting in embodiment and the joys of the earth's seasons, we claim our place as God's companions in the healing of this good Earth. Process theology and openness theology can support pagan spirituality's quest for a politics of that strives to heal the earth and its peoples.

A PAGAN SPIRITUAL PRACTICE

At the heart of my personal spirituality is the Celtic encircling prayer, the *caim,* in which participants draw a circle around themselves, creating a sacred and protective place around them wherever they might be. No doubt the Celtic encircling employed by many Christians had its origins in dialogue with the indigenous druidic spiritualities of today's British Isles. The Celtic *caim* is a portable shrine reminding us that wherever we are, God is with us, guiding and protecting us, and giving us God's peace. It affirms, in the words of St. Bonaventure, that God is a circle whose center is everywhere and whose circumference is nowhere. I join my practice of Celtic Christian encircling with a version of the Prayer of St. Patrick:

I arise today
Through the strength of heaven;
Light of the sun,
Splendor of fire,
Speed of lightning,
Swiftness of the wind,
Depth of the sea,
Stability of the earth,
Firmness of the rock.
I arise today
Through God's strength to pilot me;
God's might to uphold me,
God's wisdom to guide me,
God's eye to look before me,
God's ear to hear me,
God's word to speak for me,
God's hand to guard me,
God's way to lie before me,
God's shield to protect me,
God's hosts to save me
Afar and anear,
Alone or in a multitude.
Christ shield me today
Against wounding
Christ with me, Christ before me, Christ behind me,
Christ in me, Christ beneath me, Christ above me,
Christ on my right, Christ on my left,
Christ when I lie down, Christ when I sit down,
Christ in the heart of everyone who thinks of me,
Christ in the mouth of everyone who speaks of me,
Christ in the eye that sees me,
Christ in the ear that hears me.

The Pagan practice of casting a circle follows a similar pattern. The goal of casting a circle, like the Celtic *caim*, is to create a sacred space in which we live, move, and have our being. In casting a circle, practitioners of witchcraft invoke the spirits of the Earth, the divinity in all four directions, to lend their guidance, power, and protection to our lives and the planet. Within the circle, we deepen our spiritual our lives, ground our spiritual intentions, and build holy community. A circle can surround an individual or a group, not unlike the opening prayers at a Christian worship service. According to pagan/witchcraft spiritual guide Starhawk, "We define a new space and a new time whenever we cast a circle to begin a ritual. The circle exists on the boundaries of ordinary space and time; 'between the worlds' of seen and unseen…a space in which alternative realities meet, in which past and future are open to us."[67] Casting a circle is an "enacted meditation…a living mandala, in which we are centered."[68]

In the spirit of Paganism and Celtic Christianity, you may choose to cast a spiritual circle, or a spiral that embraces and transforms your life and those around you, not bending them to your will, but to God's vision in the context of their own free and creative decisions, what is best for all involved. You might begin with a prayer, such as St. Patrick's Breastplate or an Invocation of the Elements and Energies of Life. Then, you might, as my friend Cyndi suggests, set an intention in words, images, or actions to raise the energies of life and love to accomplish something of value for yourself and for the world.

This morning, for example, as prepared to write these words, I made an intention that "the words I write be true, flow easily, and bless everyone that reads them; and that my writing be faithful to God." It is my prayer that, as you read these words, you will be blessed with abundant life, light, and love. And, in the spirit of my Pagan friends, I conclude this exercise and chapter with the words, "Blessed be."

67. Starhawk, *Spiral Dance*, 83.
68. Ibid., 83.

CHAPTER SIXTEEN

Native and First American

The parent of Western philosophy, Plato, noted that the love of wisdom begins with wonder. Nearly twenty-five hundred years later, Jewish theologian Abraham Joshua Heschel described "radical amazement" as the heart of religious experience. Heschel believed that if you aren't amazed, astounded, and awestruck at the great mysteries of life, you can't claim to be religious. Amazement and enchantment at the tragic beauty of life that gave birth to past spiritual adventures, in both the East and the West, inspires mystics and seekers today.

Historians of religion note three stages in humankind's relationship to the world. In this first stage, people perceive that the universe is filled with spirits beneath, within, and behind every tree, flying overhead, populating land and sea, and uniquely present in mountains, chimney rocks, and sacred islands. The realm of burning bushes and ladders of angels, talking beasts, and messages written in the heavens is the world of indigenous peoples, Celtic adventures, and Biblical pilgrims, in which there are "thin places," sacred spaces, transparent to divinity, everywhere.

When civilization and urbanization, belief in the sky gods, the external and distant creators, triumphed. With the emergence of science and technology, and the coming of age of modernity, people believed that the world was divided into sacred and secular, mind and body, spiritual and physical. Finally came the eclipse of spirituality entirely, at least in intellectual and scientific circles.

The disenchanted world of Newtonian scientists, entrepreneurs, and industrialists was soulless and existed entirely as material for human artifice and manipulation. Smokestacks, coal mines, sweat shops, pipelines, and the defiant cry "drill, baby, drill" characterized the disenchanted universe in which even humans morphed into human resources, consumers, and commodities.

Today, with earth's survival in the balance, many persons are returning to the enchanted reality of Celtic adventurers, First American visionaries, heaven-gazing philosophers, and crones and midwives. In this reimagining of sacred, science is joined with spirituality, medicine is joined with meditation, and physics inspires prayer. Delight in starry, starry nights and viewing images from the Mars rover or the Hubble Telescope provoke mystical experiences. In this re-enchanted world, spiritual seekers are reclaiming the world of mystics, pagans, druids, monastics, and shaman. We are reclaiming a world in which, out of nowhere, we discover a wardrobe leading to Narnia, are summoned to an adventure with Gandalf, stumble upon Platform 9 ¾, or find ourselves tutored by Yoda or Obi Wan Kenobi. We are discovering with the enchanted Jacob that "God is in this place—and now we know it!" and this knowledge will shape our religion, economics, and politics in a marriage of earth care, reverence for creation, and green technologies. We are reclaiming the wisdom of indigenous peoples and nature mystics, including the first settlers of the Americas as well as Europe.

Indeed, the very discovery of the American continent was born out of experiences of wonder, enchantment, and adventure. Some 16,000 years ago, intrepid adventurers crossed the Bering Sea to the Americas. Venturing forth across an unknown and unexplored terrain, these explorers fanned out from Alaska to Chile, hunting game, planting crops, and building cities. Like their companions in Asia, Africa, Australia, and Europe, their experiences of the Great Mystery evoked stories and rituals to make sense of the astounding, and sometimes threatening, world around them. These first American pilgrims told stories of gods and goddesses, heroic adventures, and spirit animals. They formulated spiritual practices meant to bring themselves into harmony with the cosmos, align themselves with the seasons, and ensure prosperity and well-being for persons and tribes. Around campfires and in lodges, they told stories to explain creation, the origins of humankind, and the reality of evil and suffering, similar in spirit to the poetic and mystical stories of the Hebrews, Indians, and Chinese. The indigenous peoples of the Americas had their own Abrahams and Sarahs, and Jobs and Esthers. They had their own Yahwehs, Thors, and Zeuses. The six hundred tribes of North America were not primitive or savages as European Christian exceptionalist and expansionists viewed them. They were theologians, philosophers, spirit guides, priests, and healers seeking to make sense of the Great Mystery and discern ways to be in harmony with the deeper laws that guide the seasons of growth and decay, and life and death. They lived and died, gave birth and raised children, built communities, created nations and democracies, and fought enemies, all in an enchanted reality in which spirits greet us everywhere, and gods walk among humans as guides and tricksters.

In their interactions with white settlers who eventually became their conquerors, these indigenous tribal peoples maintained their vision of an enchanted reality. The First Americans remained committed to seeing the earth as sacred, and not as a commodity to be bought, possessed, or stolen. These original inhabitants of North America were decimated by disease, defeat, and destruction at the hands of white interlopers, who justified their conquest as a reflection of divine providence in imitation of the Hebraic occupation of the promised land. Moreover, their heartless and aggressive deity required conversion to escape damnation. Faced with these stresses, the First American way of life flickered, and yet survived, often underground or in syntheses with Christianity. Today, despite physical and cultural genocide, the way of the earth treasured by the First Americans bursts forth, a pathway to wholeness and survival, and an inspiration to a re-enchanted way of seeing and being for a planet in danger.

There are as many native spiritualities as there are Native tribes and nations, each with their own perspective grounded in the contours of air, sky, sea, and land, and in their unique occupations of hunting and gathering, agriculture, and commerce, as well as distinctive environments of plains, mountains, forests, deserts, and seashores. There is no authoritative scripture for all First Americans: indeed, much is oral tradition shared from sage to sage and parent to child. Nor is there a clear institutional hierarchy, although there are many wise spiritual leaders. There is no one voice to speak for the diverse tribal and for nation spiritualities. Accordingly, with a sense of my own limitations, I have focused on the messages of five First American spiritual leaders to give us a glimpse, albeit incomplete, of First

American spirituality: Wallowa Nez Perce Chief Joseph (1840-1904), Lakota Sioux Black Elk (1863-1959), Suquamish Chief Seattle (1786-1866), Ogala Sioux Chief Luther Standing Bear (1868-1939), and Santee Sioux Charles Alexander Eastman, named Ohiyesa (1858-1939). Each of these spiritual guides was grounded in the spirituality of the earth and sky, and interacted, for the most part more in conflict than in collegiality, with the expansionism of white settlers and their oppressive political leaders. Each was viewed as primitive and savage by the occupying settlers, despite their wisdom and spiritual acuity.

THE GEOGRAPHY OF FIRST AMERICAN SPIRITUALITY

Broadly speaking and with recognition of the diversity of tribes and nations, First, or Native, American spirituality invites us to embrace an enchanted, or re-enchanted universe, in which the Great Mystery speaks to us in rocks, trees, chimney rocks, whispering winds, owls, and coyotes. Each season of life is holy. Rituals awaken us to our destiny as spirit persons ourselves. The geography of First American spirituality invites us to experience the holy through the interplay of vision and practice.

- *A Living Universe.* Native American spirituality is grounded in the vision of an enchanted universe, a living, interdependent world, in which all creation reveals divinity. The wisdom of enchantment inspires us to see the world in a sacred way, in which everything reveals the movements of the Great Spirit, not unlike the Psalmist who asserted that everything that breathes praises God. (Psalm 148 and 150) In describing the rituals of his people, Lakota Sioux spiritual guide Black Elk asserts: "We should understand well that all things are works of the Great Spirit. We should know that He is within all things: the trees, the rivers, the grasses, the mountains, and all four-legged animals, and the winged peoples; and even more important, we should understand that He is above all these things and peoples. When we do understand this deeply in our hearts, then we will fear, and know, and love the Great Spirit, and then we will be and act and live as He intends.[69]

---

69. Brown, Joseph Epes Bown, *The Sacred Pipe: Black Elk's Account of the Seven Rites of the Oglala Sioux* (Norman, OK: University of Oklahoma Press, 1989), xx.

Another Oglala Sioux visionary, Walking Buffalo, noted "we saw the Great Spirit's work almost everything, in sun, moon, trees, and mountains. Sometimes we approached him through these things."[70] What appeared to be idolatry to the Christian missionaries, blinded by their dualistic world views and visions of divine transcendence and insentient to other frames of reference, and the investing of certain creatures and venues with holiness was, in fact, the honoring of the Great Spirit, who is alive in every creature. Having forgotten the sacred places of their own tradition—Beth-El, the burning bush, Sinai—Christian missionaries could no longer see the holiness of "thin places" everywhere. In contrast, for the first American spirit guides, all things are sacred, including the daily tasks of childcare, cooking, and work. Everything one encounters is sacred. Chimney rocks, or hoodoos, turn our spirits toward the divine. The flight of an eagle, or the dive of an osprey awakens us to the divine movements in our own lives. Reading with a grandchild, cooking supper, diapering a baby, giving a COVID vaccine, putting on a face mask, playing catch, making love with your beloved, are all sacred. According to Ohiyesa (Eastman), "we see miracles on every hand—the miracle of life in seed and egg, the miracle of death in lightning flash and swelling deep…We believe that spirit pervades all creation and that every creature possesses a soul in some degree, though not necessarily a soul conscious of itself. The tree, the waterfall, the grizzly bear, each is an embodied Force, and as such an object of reverence."[71]

Sacred and secular are one. Ohiyesa (Eastman) affirms that "prayer—the daily recognition of the Unseen and the Eternal—is our one inevitable duty…our whole life is prayer because every act of our lives is, in a very real sense, a religious act."[72]

Learning comes as much from observing nature as reading books. Chief Luther Standing Bear observes, "Knowledge was inherent in all things. The world is a library and its books are stones, leaves, brooks, and the birds, and animals that shared, alike with us, the storms and blessings of the earth," all of which evokes the perception of beauty.[73] The profound

---

70. Oldmeadow, *Black Elk: Lakota Visionary* (Bloomington, IN: World Wisdom, 2018, 11.
71. Kent Nerburn, editor, *The Wisdom of the Native Americans* (Novato, CA: New World Library, 1999), 85, 88.
72. Ibid., 90, 91.
73. Ibid., 16.

interdependence, characteristic of a living universe, has ethical and political implications. As Wallowa Nez Perce Chief Joseph asserts, "All men
were made by the Great Spirit Chief. The earth is the mother of all people,
and all people should have equal rights on it."[74] The sacredness of nature
demands care for the earth that supersedes possession and profit. In the
words a speech attributed to Chief Seattle, during treaty negotiations with
the governor of the Washington territory, nature is holy as the home of
the living and of the dead: "Our dead never forget the beautiful world that
gave them being. They still love its verdant valleys, its murmuring rivers,
its magnificent mountains…and ever yearn in tender, fond affection over
the lonely hearted living, and often return from the Great Beyond to visit,
guide, console, and comfort them."[75] The great chief continues, trying to
enlighten the apparently insentient white political leadership, "even the
rocks which appear to be dumb and dead as they swelter in the sun along
a silent shore, thrill with memories of stirring events connected with the
lives of my people…our bare feet are conscious of sympathetic touch."[76]

In an enchanted universe, pipelines must give way to sacred spaces, and
profit to the honoring of past ancestors and future generations. There is
no secular reality except in the eyes of those who see God far off, exiled in
divine transcendence, and humankind mired in sin, unworthy of divine
love. Joining sacred and secular, seeing holiness in all things, re-enchants
and heals the planet, and is the only thing that can save us.

- *Holy Visions.* "Where there is no vision, the people perish," so proclaims
  Proverbs 29:18. Dare we go further and say, "that without a vision quest,
  humankind is lost. That when we go forth seeking a vision, divinity will
  provide a way to wholeness and vocation for us and our people." The
  twentieth century classic on First American spirituality, *Black Elk Speaks,*
  describes the power of a holy vision. Like young Samuel, described in
  the Bible, Black Elk initially experienced God coming to him unexpect-
  edly, overwhelming him with vision and vocation. Black Elk describes
  his breakthrough vision: "I was seeing in a sacred manner the shape of all
  things in the spirit, and the shape of all things as they must live together

74. Ibid., 186.
75. Ibid., 196.
76. Ibid, 198.

like one being. And I saw that the sacred hoop of my people was one of many hoops that made one circle, wide as daylight and as starlight, and in the center grew one mighty flowering tree to shelter all the children of one mother and one father. And I saw that it was holy."[77]

Although Black Elk's visions initially came unbidden, Black Elk himself, later in life, prepared to discern God's presence by "crying for a vision." This practice involves prayerful preparation through purifying ceremonies and times of retreat from everyday life. Vision quests, not unlike Thoreau's wilderness sauntering and Jesus' retreat in the wilderness, enable us to awaken to God's voice once the many voices of society have been stilled. Inspired by their visions, Black Elk, the prophets, and Jesus discover that their vocation is relational, intended to embody God's own vision of a transformed and healthy social order, "on earth as it is in heaven."

- *The Power of Visionary Ritual.* While religion begins, as Whitehead asserts, in solitude, it must be enacted and embodied in ritual and ethics to transform the visionaries and their people. Bidden or unbidden, visions transform our lives. In an enchanted universe, everyone is a potential visionary. Everyone is touched by God, and when the Great Spirit cleanses the doors of perception, we see holiness in the moment and gain wisdom for the future.

As a child and youth, Black Elk received a vision but was hesitant to share it to the larger community. Like the young prophet Jeremiah, he doubted that he had the stature to be a spiritual leader. Yet, the Great Spirit challenged him. As the Lakota spiritual guide relates: The non-human world—the world of crows and coyotes—called out to him, "It is time! It is time."[78] Still, Black Elk waited until an aged medicine man challenged him, "You must do your duty and perform this vision for your people on earth."[79] The vision must be incarnated. It must take form among the people. Black Elk asserts that "a man who has a vision is not able to use the power of it until after he has performed the vision on earth for people to see." When Black Elk performed his vision, the people felt new hope

---

77. John G. Niehardt, *Black Elk Speaks* (Lincoln, NE: University of Nebraska Press, 1961, 43.
78. Ibid., 164.
79. Ibid., 165.

and the visionary's own anxiety disappeared, and he claimed his role as a healer and medicine man. New energies flowed through Black Elk to bring healing to the anxious and diseased: "I cured with the power that came through me. Of course, it was not I who cured. It was the power from the outer world, and the visions and ceremonies had only made me like a hole through which power could come to the two leggeds. If I thought I was doing it myself, the hole would close up and no power would flow through me."[80]

Native American visionary Wovoka (1856-1932) initiated the Ghost Dance religion, grounded in his vision of the ancestors and the other world. Wovoka affirmed the coming of a new world order that would cleanse the earth and bring peace to the First American people if the people participated in a sacred circle dance. Enacting this vision in dance would, it was believed, bring the living and the dead together in a healed world. Called by some "the dance of Christ," embodying Wovoka's vision in dance would be a prelude to the Day of Judgment, and the restoration of beauty and peace to the planet. Convinced that Wovoka's great vision was coming true, Black Elk became a Ghost Dancer. The emergence of First American spirituality frightened the white settlers and military, and their fears took shape in the massacre at Wounded Knee, an atrocity which dashed the hopes for peace of Wovoka, Black Elk, and First Americans throughout North America. We still look toward the realization of Wovoka's prophetic vision: the lion with the lamb, the abandonment of war, and the kinship of humankind and all creation![81]

In more recent years, First Americans in the Southwest have, like Wovoka, integrated indigenous elements with Christian imagery, in the Native American Church, with its use of peyote, a hallucinogenic, as a sacrament fostering mystical experiences and spiritual transformation. Quanah Parker, one of the parents of Peyote religion, spoke of the relationship of Christianity and native religion in challenging words: "The white man goes into his church house and talks *about* Jesus, but the Indian goes into his tepee and talks *to* Jesus."[82] As a forerunner of

---

80. Ibid., 208-209.
81. For more on Ghost Dance Religion, see Joel Martin, *The Land Looks After Us: A History of Native American Religion* (New York: Oxford University Press, 2001), 84-97.
82. Ibid., 105.

today's inter-spirituality, the Native American Church was established to promote "the Christian religion with the practice of the Peyote sacrament."[83] In sacramental experiences with peyote, one participant noted that "we expect to see the face of Jesus and the face of our dead relatives. We are worshipping God and Jesus, the same God that the white people worship."[84]

A FIRST AMERICAN VISION

I have known Mark Charles since 2006, when I first met him at a Calvin Institute of Christian Worship conference, where he serves as a consultant. Mark is a Native American activist, public speaker, consultant, and author as well as a journalist, blogger, and Reformed pastor. Mark ran as an independent candidate for president in the 2020 United States presidential election. His book *Unsettling Truths: The Ongoing Dehumanizing Legacy of the Doctrine of Discovery,* is an honest and prophetic critique of theologically based genocide perpetrated by European Christianity.[85]

Mark was raised as an "evangelical Christian in the Christian Reformed Church. His grandparents had gone to Christian reformed boarding school. In their time, being a Christian meant abandoning Native culture and becoming white." Mark notes that he also grew up "thinking his culture didn't matter and that God wasn't concerned with the spirituality of his ancestors."

Mark's vocation as a Christian Reformed pastor has enabled him to call his fellow Christians to repentance, healing, and recognition of the gifts of indigenous peoples, including his own Navajo nation. The son of a Navajo father and a Dutch-American mother, Mark grew up in Gallup, New Mexico. Raised in the Christian Reformed Church, he was unaware of the gifts of the Navajo spiritual tradition until the Denver, Colorado, congregation to which he was called as pastor wanted to explore what it meant to be Native and Christian. They were on a quest for contextualized worship, that is, decolonized worship that expresses faith in the music, images, and symbols of indigenous peoples' cultures and not merely the

---

83. Ibid., 107.
84. Ibid., 112.
85. Mark Charles and Soong Chan-Rah, *Unsettling Truths: The Ongoing Dehumanizing Legacy of the Doctrine of Discovery* (Downers Grove, IL: Intervarsity Press, 2019).

hymns, musical style, and language of Western culture superimposed on the experiences and cultures of indigenous peoples.

Mark discovered the importance of understanding Christianity in the context of the religious and cultural symbols and practices of Navajo nation and its spirituality when his Denver congregation sent him to Hawaii to attend the World Christian Gathering of Indigenous Peoples. Initially, the various forms of indigenous worship—Maori, Hawaiian, Plains Indian, and other indigenous peoples—was unsettling. It was unlike anything he had previously experienced in worship. Yet, his unfamiliarity became a window to new possibilities for worshipping the Creator.[86] As a result of his new experiences and spiritual reflection, Mark became committed to "decolonizing his faith and discovering how Navajo culture can help us experience our Creator."

Awakened to Navajo spirituality, Mark actively cultivated relationships with other indigenous Christians, seeking to decolonize Christian faith by embracing their indigenous spirituality. Today, Mark worships God as a Navajo Christian, using the gifts of Navajo culture in living out his relationship with Jesus.

One area that Mark has explored is the contrast between Western and Navajo understandings of time. For Western people, time is linear and being on time, whether at worship or class is paramount. In contrast, the circular time sense of the Navajo people involves focusing on the task at hand, until it is completed for example, letting worship evolve organically rather than being tied to the parameters of an hourlong service. Schedules are secondary to discerning a sense of completeness in worship and daily life.

Neither linear nor circular time is superior. Each has its virtues and healthy spirituality, I believe, joins vision and agenda, flexibility and scheduling, and planning and spontaneity.

At the heart of Mark's spirituality is the Navajo spiritual practice of welcoming the sunrise. When he lived on the reservation, Mark greeted each day at sunrise, opening his senses to the holiness of the human and non-human world. Mark notes that the spirit of welcoming the sunrise goes against much of Western culture. "Western culture is all about control, even in the church. One of the worst

---

86. Mark tells about his journey in a talk I attended at the Calvin Institute for Christian Worship.

things for persons of Western culture is to be out of control. Welcoming the sunrise reminds us that we are not in control. We can discover a sense of peace dealing with what we can control in life." When Mark and his family moved to Washington DC, he initially had difficulty finding a spot to view the sunrise. "There was no place you could go," Mark notes, "where you could touch the ground." Now, a few days each week, Mark greets the sunrise at a quiet spot along the Potomac River.[87] An activist and contemplative, Mark's political involvement comes both from letting go, and recognizing what is out of his control, as well as "changing what I cannot accept."[88]

WHAT CHRISTIANS CAN LEARN FROM FIRST AMERICANS

While process theology has been, from the start, earth-affirming in its recognition that we live in an experiential universe, much of Christianity has been dualistic and binary in nature in its separation of humankind and nature, and God and the world. First Americans see the Great Spirit as immanent in the universe. The earth, and the universe, is the body of God, permeated with the divine spirit. The Jewish and Christian vision of humankind as created in the "image of God" need not, as some Christians assert, separate us from nature experientially or ethically. The spiritual separation of humankind from nature has led to the destruction of nature solely for short-term human benefit and for giving unique privileges to human fetuses while devaluing Right Whales and Chimpanzees, despite their more complicated levels of experience and relatedness. Dualistic views of humanity and nature have led to the destruction of non-human life: woodlands, ponds and streams, and mountainsides without consideration to their inherent value.

First American spirituality awakens today's Christians to an earth-centered/ creation centered ethic, in which each creature declares the glory of God, and a world of praise in which each creature honors God in its unique way. First American spirituality challenges Christians to give God glory, by loving the creatures as well as the Creator. The lively, experiential universe, described by process theologians as "pan-experientialism" or "panpsychism," widens the scope of Christian spiritual and ethical formation to embrace all creation. First American

---

87. Mark often shares his films and photos of the sunrise on social media – www.facebook.com/MarkCharlesWirelesshogan.
88. A saying attributed to political activist Angela Davis.

spirituality reminds us that we arc the guardians, the gardeners and nurturers, of the non-human world and future generations.

CHRISTIANITY'S GIFT TO FIRST AMERICAN SPIRITUALITY

Given the history of Christian and European genocide, Christianity's gift to First American spiritual traditions is the gift of confession and restoration. It is a path we must take to recognize and atone for our own sins in relationship to the indigenous peoples of North America. Progressive Christians need to be leaders in apologizing to and asking forgiveness from our First American kin. We need to admit that the theology of our ancestors, the theology of occupation and domination, is both dangerous and theologically bankrupt. We can no longer affirm certain biblical stories, including God's call for Abraham to sacrifice Isaac, the destruction of Sodom and Gomorrah, the displacement of the Canaanites, and the slaughter at Jericho, without significant critique. We need to read these stories from the point of view of those who were victimized, not just from the perspective of the victors. We need to ask for forgiveness for our ancestors' behaviors. Moreover, progressive and openness Christians need to be pioneers in restorative justice, whether in relationship to First Americans or to the descendants of slaves. The nature of this restorative justice may involve words of apology as well as ensuring economic and political justice for communities of indigenous peoples and the African American community. Georgetown University, where I spent nearly two decades as a university chaplain and professor, has chosen to respond to its tragic history of Jesuit slave ownership by giving preferential admissions status and scholarships to the descendants of slaves sold by the university. Our calling as Christians is to go from hopes and prayers to action, to transformative and justice-seeking activism to heal the pain and nurture hope for the future for all God's children.

A FIRST AMERICAN SPIRITUAL PRACTICE

God comes to us through our five senses as well as the inward journeys of meditative prayer and contemplation. First American spirituality proclaims with Psalm 148 and 150 that everything that breathes praises God. More than that, all creation praises God. We live in a sacred reality, but often the doors of perception need to be cleansed so we can experience life as it is—infinite and spirit-filled. In this spiritual practice, we will live out the Navaho Blessing Way prayer:

> *With beauty before me I walk*
> *With beauty behind me I walk*
> *With beauty above me I walk*
> *With beauty around me I walk.*
> *I walk with beauty before me. I walk with beauty behind me.*
> *I walk with beauty below me. I walk with beauty above me.*
> *I walk with beauty around me. My words will be beautiful.*
>
> *In beauty all day long may I walk.*
> *Through the returning seasons, may I walk.*
> *On the trail marked with pollen may I walk.*
> *With dew about my feet, may I walk.*
> *With beauty before me may I walk.*
> *With beauty behind me may I walk.*
> *With beauty below me may I walk.*
> *With beauty above me may I walk.*
> *With beauty all around me may I walk.*

If you are physically able, take a walk with your senses open to the world. Pause and notice beauty, open to wonder, give thanks for every creature and life-form you see. Listen. See. Smell. Touch. Taste. Delight in the Spirit moving through you and through all things, giving life to you and to all creation. Give thanks for life, sense, thought, and beauty. Embrace Spirit in whatever way the divine way come you. With beauty all around us, we walk.

Upon returning home, recognizing that we are all part of a dynamic, living organism, as First Americans discovered, and as more recently postulated by James Lovelock's "Gaia Hypothesis," in what ways can you add to the beauty of the living earth? In what ways can you be a "good ancestor" to unborn generations?

CHAPTER SEVENTEEN

Yoruba and Its Spiritual Children

Religions are always in the making. Spiritualities are always morphing in the interplay of divine inspiration, human response and interpretation, and social and cultural setting. When the world changes, so should our religions. New images of the universe provoke new visions of God. Travel, whether elective or by the compulsion of others, transforms our religious viewpoints. Tradition is updated to respond to new encounters and changed social situations. Contrary to the views of some conservatives, diversity and change in religious traditions are not a fall from a primordial grace, but a reflection of a lively and empathetic God. A living, relational God responds to the needs of changing environments and religious communities, and to the experiences and innovations of spiritual leaders seeking to be faithful to divine revelation in their time and place.

Only a dead elephant is unmoving. Only a dead religion is unchanging. Every religion has its contours and emphases, but these are always in flux. Orthodoxy is always shaped in dialogue with orthopraxis, right and appropriate behavior, and doxology, praise for God's wondrous love and creativity. Faithfulness is embodied in dynamic praise and gratitude. When someone says, "I'm an orthodox Christian," I often respond with "Which orthodoxy are your talking about?" For there have been many Christianities and many orthodoxies. Inspired by the life and teachings of their Teacher and Savior, Jesus' first followers made it up as they were going along, as the movement morphed from a Jewish sect to a global religion At this point, the scriptures had not been fully articulated and institutional hierarchies did not yet exist. Fourth and fifth century Christianity was characterized by the development of the creeds and by rooting out heresies: the roads not taken such as the ideas of Pelagius, the Gnostic movements, and the inspired theologian Montanus. Today, these so-called heresies can be seen as augmenting the classical doctrinal formulae in many ways. As time passed, the Roman Catholic hierarchical and sacramental religion became dominant in the West. The Eastern church developed its own institutional and spiritual practices. In the 1500s, Christianity became imbued with the prophetic spirit of the Protestant Reformation, and soon thereafter the contest between Calvinist predestination and Arminian and Wesleyan freedom emerged. In our time, we have the contrasting messages of revival evangelicalism, doctrinaire fundamentalism, open-ended liberalism, and activist social gospel, not to mention liberation, feminist, womanist, indigenous, global, and creation-centered theologies. Living elephants and living faiths are constantly on the move, adapting and innovating to respond to changing circumstances.

This is surely the case of the Yoruba religious movement. It has no fixed and final scriptures or hierarchical authorities, and no clearly defined date of origination. Despite Christian and Muslim persecution, Yoruba flourishes in Africa and now is a major spiritual movement in the Americas. Yoruba provides one of the most graphic examples of inter-spirituality in its adaptation, utilization, and transforming of Christian symbolism and ritual, most particularly that of Roman Catholicism and its saints, Eucharist, and priesthood. Yoruba practitioners came to the Americas against their will, victims of the tragic and dehumanizing slave trade, often perpetuated by a dubious mixture of Christian evangelism and European colonization. In the Americas, Yoruba continued to respond to the spiritual and survival needs of persons of African descent, providing meaning, inspiration, and purpose, in a hostile, dehumanizing social order. A religion of the oppressed, Yoruba and its American kin provided spirituality, vision, ritual, and metaphysics to enable its practitioners to survive and even flourish in an antagonistic society. Today, Yoruba is known by the names of Santeria or Lucumí in Cuba, Candomblé in Brazil and Portuguese speaking communities, and Voudon (Voodoo, Vodun) in Haiti, to name the most well-known Western manifestations of Yoruba. Yoruba and its kin has been seen as primitive, superstitious, and even demonic by colonialist Christianity, and in recent times has been caricatured as threatening and diabolical in B-movies. However, Yoruba and its spiritual children present a complex metaphysical vision, inspirational spiritual messengers, and transformative spiritual practices involving divination and self-discovery. Many "sophisticated" practitioners of Christianity may look down on the myths and legends of Yoruba, which they condescendingly describe as primitive. However, the Yoruba myths bear resemblance to the divine-human relationships portrayed in the scriptures of other religions, including Judaism, Islam, and Christianity. Parallels to the Christian understanding of angels and incarnation can also be noted, as well as the ecstasy of revelational and Pentecostal experiences.

Over a period of more than three thousand years, Yoruba evolved as humans began to ponder their place in the universe and conclude that humans cannot survive without the support of higher spiritual beings, both intimate and transcendent. While we cannot pinpoint a beginning date for Yoruba, in contrast to Judaism, Christianity, Islam, Buddhism, and Confucianism, many believe that Yoruba as we know it today is based on the teachings of Orunmila, who lived sometime between the ages of Plato and Jesus. According to Yoruba or Ifa spiritual teachings, Orunmila was a Yoruba man "who came to the city of Ile Ife to teach a system of ethics, religious belief, and mystic vision. Toward the end of his life Orunmila is reported to have introduced a system of divination known as *dafa*...when *dafa* is cast, it represents direct communication with the Spirit of Orunmila."[89] During his lifetime, Orunmila may have traveled throughout Africa, including Egypt, sharing and learning the wisdom of the Yoruba oral scriptures.

In many ways, Orunmila parallels Jesus Christ. Yoruba cosmology sees Orunmila as pre-existent, present with Supreme Creator God Olódùmarè, also known as Olórun, at the beginning of creation and, also, able to intervene through guidance and protection across the centuries. Yoruba emerged from Africa to become a global religion, adapting to new environments, especially in the Americas. It provided a pathway to self-discovery, survival, and vocation for those displaced because of the painful and oppressive African diaspora.

---

89. Awo Fa'lokun Fatunmbi *Iwa-Pele* (Create Space, 2011), 36.

THE LIVELY UNIVERSE OF YORUBA

Initially, I found the Yoruba tradition a challenge to understand. Not only is there a pantheon of intermediate and created deities, with all their various duties, of which there are many African and American variants, but ancestors who serve as post-mortem guides and protectors are central to the Yoruba world view. However, I have discovered that when I don't initially grasp my neighbor's spiritual insights, I need to put myself in their place, to see the world from their eyes and to look for connections with other religious traditions, including my own. I need to study with an awakened heart as well as illuminated mind. Recognizing the biases and limitations of my own cultural and religious perspective. I need to realize that what Westerners often describe from their "superior" vantage point as myths in indigenous religions are also found in Judaism and Christianity, or in the spiritual traditions of Greeks, Romans, and Scandinavians. While not claiming to be a Yoruba scholar, I hope to capture the heart of Yoruba spirituality and show that the Yoruba understandings of intermediate deities, ancestors, and divination, can be found in historic Christian and Western affirmations of divine transcendence and creation, angels, saints, predestination, providence, prophesy, and divine inspiration. Moreover, when we judge as "inferior" or "mythical," in a derogatory sense, the apparent humanity and emotional outbursts of divine pantheons of Greece, Roman, Scandinavia, and Africa, we need to remember the ethically and theologically challenging stories of our own faith: God walking in the Garden and Eden and later destroying the world by flood, God asking Abraham to kill his son Isaac, and God's threat to kill Israelites in the wilderness. Other passages difficult for us today are the God-provoked genocide of the indigenous peoples of Canaan, the massacre at Jericho, and God's requirement of a blood sacrifice to save humankind from its sinfulness. When Christians critique the animal sacrifices among certain Yoruba communities, we must also think of similar animal sacrifices in the Hebraic tradition and God's command that Abraham sacrifice his son Isaac.

With greater appreciation for the similarities of our religious tradition to others, especially of Yoruba and its Western manifestations, we can approach Yoruba as a spiritual movement from which we can learn, and whose practices may illuminate our own spiritual journeys. As I explore Yoruba spirituality, I have found the following guideposts helpful for understanding their dynamic faith.

- *Divinity Everywhere.* Practitioners of Yoruba truly live in a god-filled universe. There are a variety of divine expressions, both infinite and intimate. The High God Olódùmarè/Ọlọrun is the Infinite Energy of the Universe, beyond name and form, unapproachable and unknowable yet the womb of creation. Like the Big Bang, the energy of the distant deity flows through everything. Without Olódùmarè, nothing would exist. "Nature is viewed as the manifestation of Olódùmarè, through infinite degrees of material or spiritual substance." Yoruba spirituality sees Olódùmarè as "the primal essence of all things. It's not the tree, the rock, the statue that African ancestors revere and worship, but the deep energy that brought about its being."[90] Similar to the relationship between God and Sophia/Chokmah (Proverbs 8) and God and the Logos (John 1), there are within the Godhead, eternal manifestations that directly shape the universe. These manifestations were with Olódùmarè at creation, as spiritual seeds within the divine womb, and these divine manifestations give birth to the universe in its entirety, including the intermediate deities, known as the Orishas. Through the wisdom of Olódùmarè, each person receives their destiny, prior to birth. The divine intermediators, the orishas, created and emanating from the Godhead, guide our destinies in each lifetime. The orishas have direct relations with human beings, providing guidance, counsel, and protection, as do angels in the Abrahamic religions. In the Americas, the orishas were connected to Roman Catholic saints, personifying them in daily life. Although African Yoruba speaks of hundreds of orisha, there are only twenty or so that are singled out for worship in the Americas.

The connection to the Roman Catholic understanding of angels added gravitas to Yoruba spirituality in the New World. It also was a way for oppressed people to disguise their indigenous faith from their oppressors. Reflected in the forces of nature, each orisha, like the Greek, Roman, and Scandinavian Pantheon, has unique responsibilities and personalities. They also have unique tastes in color palette, food preferences, and relate more convivially to specific natural phenomena. The various orishas have a reciprocal relationship with humankind, providing guidance and energy. In return for their help, humans provide food and

---

90. Baba Ifa Karade, *The Handbook of Yoruba Religious Concepts* (Newburyport, MA: Weiser Books, 2020), 29-30.

animal sacrifices to orishas give them power and enable them to be more effective in human life. In the United States, many have objected to animal sacrifices as cruel and primitive, forgetting that sacrifice was once an essential aspect of divine-human relationships in the Hebraic tradition and to some Christians, Jesus' sacrificial death, necessary for God to ransom sinful humanity, is the ultimate sacrifice bridging the gulf between God and humankind. As one commentator notes, "You can kill a turkey in your front yard, put it on the table, say a prayer, and serve it for Thanksgiving, but if we pray over the turkey, kill it, then eat, we violate the law."[91]

The final divine emanation is the realm of the ancestors. There is a thin veil between the living and the ancestral world. Ancestors energize and guide, and bless and protect, family lines. Honored by their human descendants through sacrifice and adoration, they grow in power and deepen the connection between this world and the next. Good ancestors may become divine in the next world. They may also reincarnate to help family members navigate the challenges of this lifetime. The affirmation of ancestral spirits enabled the followers of Yoruba spirituality in the Americas to accept and synthesize their ancestral reverence with prayers to the saints. Just as traditional Roman Catholics pray to St. Francis and Mary the Mother of Jesus, and ask deceased relatives to look after them, followers of Santeria and other Yoruba spiritualities petition the ancestors to help them find success in this lifetime, and live in harmony with their destiny. Not all deceased persons are considered ancestors. "The ancestors are people who have distinguished themselves on the moral plane. They are therefore accorded great respect and held up as models for the living to emulate...They aren't worshipped in the way West Africans worship God...They're, however, revered, honored, and respected, not as gods but as spirits and predecessors...who are next to the Creator."[92] Theologian Monica Coleman notes that orisha are "ancestors who did not return to earth because of their *iwa* (human character and consciousness) was so closely aligned with Olódùmarè."[93]

91. Miguel De La Torre, *Santeria: The Beliefs and Rituals of a Growing in America* (Grand Rapids: William Eerdmans Publishing Company, 2004), 209.
92. Baba Ifa Karade, *The Handbook of Yoruba Religious Concepts*, 82.
93. Monica Coleman, *Making a Way Out of No Way: A Womanist Theology* (Minneapolis: Fortress Press, 2008), 109.

- *Human Destiny.* Yoruba spirituality describes a lively, spirit-filled, interdependent, and purposeful universe in which human beings have a role in perfecting the world. Each human is destined for wholeness. Each person is an ancestor in the making. Prior to its first incarnation, each soul communicates with Olódùmarè, and comes to an agreement about its personal destiny. The human adventure takes place over many lifetimes, lived with our families, as we seek to embody our destiny. Created for wholeness, without the stain of original sin, our lives are a learning pilgrimage in which we integrate personal destiny with family and community responsibility. Following each lifetime, we go through a period of post-mortem reflection, which involves a meeting with the Divine to evaluate what we need to learn in our next incarnation. In images similar to those described by the philosopher Plato, after our post-mortem self-examination and destiny deliberations, we forget the contours of destiny when we take birth again in this world. While we may not be aware of our destiny, the broad scope of our encounters and family ties are intended to help us harmonize with our personal spiritual destiny. Each rebirth is within our family linage and promises the possibility of wholeness for ourselves and our families. The eventual goal of the human adventure is to become a good ancestor, helping our families as spiritual beings, and possibly being reborn in our family linage as good ancestors to further the evolution of our relatives.

Destiny is not determinism. Although the contours of our lives are chosen prenatally, not all the events of our lives preordained. Freedom is real, although conditioned by our destiny. Our choices can align themselves with our spiritual destiny or run amuck. Hell is a temporary possibility for misguided souls. Wayward ancestors can negatively intrude into our lives from the spirit realm. Nevertheless, within our choices, there is an unconscious movement toward harmony with our destiny and those around us. The goal of human life is to become aware of our destinies and live them out in our relationships and responsibilities, thus preparing the way to become good and saintly ancestors ourselves. As good ancestors, we live on, guiding others in their own process of spiritual evolution.

- *Divining the Divine.* Religious movements have their origins in transcendent or paranormal encounters with the Divine. God can be approached in many ways: through meditation and contemplation, dance and ecstasy, sacrament and ritual, prayer and prophesy, and activism and social change. God can also take possession of a soul, speaking on behalf of the Divine to humankind. While Yoruba spirituality and its American counterparts recognize the value of contemplation, sacrament, and activism, a unique aspect of Yoruba spirituality, especially in the Americas, is divination, the discerning of our destiny in companionship with both earthly and divine spiritual guides. In the process of divination, a person visits a specially trained priest, or spiritual guide, whose responsibility is to connect them with the orishas or spirits, or the ancestors, to discern their destiny in this lifetime, and harmonize themselves with their spiritual destiny. The diviner serves as a mediator between humankind and the spiritual realm. Diviners are conduits through which the spirits remind us of our destiny and vocation in this lifetime. Sometimes the Spirit takes possession of the diviner, "channeling" its wisdom and revelation to the recipient. The major source of personal, relational, and social pain in this lifetime is our disconnection from our destiny, which can be remedied by our commitment to follow the counsel of the spirits. In the process of divination, there is a ritual preparation, involving prayer and the casting of shells or nuts, whose unique pattern provides spiritual information and guidance from the Yoruba scriptures, which are living and vital revelations of the divine. In hearing and thus following the wisdom revealed, we receive guidance to align ourselves with our destiny and, thus, experience personal wholeness, spiritual evolution, and fulfill our vocation in our family and community.

Christians who look down on such divination as primitive or as demonic need to be reminded that Acts 1 describes the early church casting lots to choose the apostle who would succeed the disgraced Judas. In the Hebraic scriptures, the warrior and ruler Saul seeks and receives military guidance from the Witch of Endor who appears to summon and channel the spirit of Samuel. (I Samuel 28:3-2) Moreover, many Westerners have gained wisdom from the use of the I Ching, a Chinese tool of divination, dating to the time of Confucius. According to Monica Coleman, divination, or "spirit possession, leads to such phenomena as speaking in tongues, the transmission of messages from the dead, and other mystical gifts. Spirit possession occurs when an ancestor's spirit strongly influences the living person in order to communicate to and through this person, displacing his or her normal sense of consciousness."[94]

Divination awakens persons to the deeper movements of the spirit, unconsciously guiding them. Through the wisdom of prayer, synchronicity, the casting of sacred objects, and scripture, they can make a connection with the deeper currents of life and discover our life's vocation.

A YORUBAN ADVENTURE

The spiritual journey is always in process. Spirituality is about finding a home and moving forward toward new possibilities. It's about looking beyond the faith in which we were raised to discover God's presence in the experiences of our ancestors as well as our contemporaries. Faith looks toward the far horizon even as it gives thanks for the wisdom of those who have come before us.

Process theologian, Christian minister, and Yoruba/Ifa priestess, Monica Coleman has seamlessly joined her Christian faith with her roots in African Yoruba/Ifa spirituality. An ordained elder in the African Methodist Episcopal Church, who experienced the call to Christian ministry at age 19, Monica Coleman experienced a similar call to spiritual leadership in the Yoruba tradition. Professor Coleman is a priestess of Obatala and Osun in traditional Yoruba religion. Formerly, on the faculty at the Claremont School of Theology, Coleman is now Professor of Africana Studies at the University of Delaware.

Coleman first encountered Yoruba spirituality while taking a course at Harvard University. Her initial response was "this is cool, this makes sense." A few years later, while studying at Vanderbilt Divinity School, she encountered another Yoruba community and felt at home with its spirituality. Still, Monica did not delve deeply into Yoruba spirituality until she moved to California to teach theology at Claremont School of Theology. There she found a lively community and was told that "she was already practicing Yoruba rituals, including honoring her ancestors, without knowing it." Throughout her life, she had, in the spirit of Yoruba, prayed

---

94. Ibid., 118.

to her grandmother, when she needed guidance. The discovery of the congruence of her spiritual practices with Yoruba spirituality led Coleman on a journey that eventuated in her initiation as a priestess.

Today, Coleman is a leading process theologian and the author of one of the most inspirational texts in process theology, *Making a Way Out of No Way: A Womanist Theology*. Based on her dissertation, *Making a Way Out of No Way,* surprises certain readers, Coleman avers, by its affirmation of both Christian and Yoruba spirituality as complementary paths whose practices enrich one another. The integration of Christian and Yoruba spirituality seems natural to Coleman. Even as a youth, she didn't confine spirituality to Christianity but had a universalist spirit. Her parents raised her to honor her African roots and that came to include African spirituality. As a youth, Coleman believed that "there was more than one way to meet God." Like myself, she recognized that we don't have to choose either/or but can creatively embrace the fullness of many religious traditions.

Coleman sees the heart of Yoruba involving honoring your ancestors, praying for divine guidance, using the power for good inherent in the universe, honoring ancestors, and divination as guidance for our spiritual journeys. Our calling is to be persons of integrity and goodness, bringing health and wholeness to our relationships and the world.

Today, Monica asserts that "the Holy Spirit was the ancestor spirit of Jesus." Accordingly, it is clear to her that "you can do both. You can practice both Christian and Yoruba spirituality. Revelation is universal and God was at work before and after Jesus." Indeed, "God comes to us in many ways"—through prayers addressed to Jesus and our ancestors as well as mystical experiences of God and divination of deep truths in Ifa scriptures. "God lives in everything. Jesus is not more God than us, just a deeper expression of what we can become. Jesus is the model for our own spiritual journeys." As Coleman's and my theological mentor John Cobb, affirms "Christ is the way that excludes no ways." In the spirit of both Yoruba and Christianity, Coleman counsels that, in the challenges of life, and she has had many, the Divine makes a way where there was no way.

WHAT CHRISTIANS CAN LEARN FROM YORUBA

At the heart of Yoruba spirituality is the affirmation that we are connected with previous generations of our family. Our ancestors are not dead, but continue to shape our lives, providing protection and guidance. We are beneficiaries of their wisdom and resilience as well as of their DNA. We need a sense of our spiritual and relational past to make sense of the present and hope for the future.

Over the years, I have gained appreciation of my parents and their struggles and achievements. I recognize the impact of deceased mentors, teachers, and spiritual friends, and call upon their guidance in gratitude. One of the reasons for the popularity of Ancestry.com is our need for spiritual as well as biological roots, to locate ourselves in a larger universe and to realize that we stand on the shoulders of others. Henry Louis Gates' "Finding Your Roots" on PBS is a testimony to the gift of discovering your family tree, and to the resilience, struggles, and triumphs of previous generations. The wisdom of our ancestors can inspire us to face the challenges of our own lives.

Yoruba spirituality invites us to recognize our dependence on and interdependence with our ancestors. It invites us to give thanks for the past and seek wisdom for the future. Their love lives on in our lives and genes. They are not dead or lost, but still creatively shape our lives. Recognizing the gifts of our ancestors inspires a long-term vision of life, helps us deal with temporary setbacks, and gives us courage to face challenges. We are not alone. The love in heaven flows back to earth, enriching us with wisdom, insight, and humility.

CHRISTIANITY'S GIFT TO YORUBA

Yoruba proclaims the transcendental power of the Great Mystery Olódùmarè, who brings forth the universe, and then, after sending forth divine creative energy, withdraws from involvement in the affairs of persons and planets. Worshippers look to intermediaries, eternal manifestations of Olódùmarè/Ọlọrun, orishas, ancestors, and nature spirits, for guidance and protection. Olódùmarè/Ọlọrun is, to use the language of the German mystic Meister Eckhart, the Ground of Being, the God beyond God, beyond description or even personality as we understand it.

The *apophatic* way, described as divinity without images or language, characterizes the mysticism of Yoruba as well as that Christianity, Islam, and Hinduism.

Process and openness theologies speak of God as not only as eternal and unchanging but also as relational and changing. God is the heart of the universe, the fellow sufferer who understands, the ultimate empath. While Yoruba followers need not embrace the creative-responsive, intimate, and changing God of process, open and relational, and progressive theology, the *kataphatic* vision of God balances the known and unknowable God, enabling followers to experience themselves as known, loved, blessed, and intimately guided by the Creative Wisdom of the Universe. Joining infinite and intimate, the creative-relational love of God inspires both global vision and intimate, historical involvement, and reminds us that wherever we are, God is with us as our companion, inviting us to be companions in healing the world.

A YORUBAN SPIRITUAL PRACTICE

Virtually every morning on my prayer and exercise walk, I spend a few moments connecting with my closest spiritual friend, my *anamcara,* who passed away in 2014. I give thanks for our friendship and then ask for her guidance in my writing and speaking. You might say she is the spirit of creativity for me. From my teaching and writing related to mysticism, I have come to recognize the significance of saints and models as spiritual examples and sources of wisdom. I also regularly give thanks for my deceased parents, brother, mentors, and close friends. I can't claim that my spiritual friend directly communicates to me from the other world Indeed, I may be invoking the characteristics and talents that she called forth in this lifetime, but since beginning this practice, writing has become more joyful and easy for me.

Remembering that we stand on the shoulders of others, that the wisdom of *ubuntu,* "I am because of you" and "we are because of one another," opens us to new possibilities for spiritual growth and guidance, whether directly from saints and ancestors, from our deepest wisdom, or from what Carl Jung described as the collective unconscious that joins us with universal wisdom across the ages.

In this practice, we join the gifts of ancestors and our goal of becoming a good ancestor, positively shaping the lives of our family, future generations, and people we will never meet. Begin with silence, connecting your Spirit with God's Spirit in that deep awareness where we experience "the sighs too deep for words." (Romans 8:26) After you feel calm and centered, review the persons who have positively shaped your life: parents, mentors, teachers, friends, and so forth, giving thanks for their impact on your life and asking for a blessing. What gift might you seek from a beloved friend or professor, a parent or deceased spouse? How might you embody in your unique way their values? You can even extend this to your animal companions. Next, reflect on those whom you think of as saints and holy persons. Give thanks for their impact on your life, and then ask for a similar gift. In my own reflections, I chose St. Francis, Dag Hammarskjold, Howard Thurman, Columba, Patrick, Julian of Norwich, and Hildegard of Bingen. What gift can these saints give you to deepen your faith? What inspiration can they provide to help you find your way in life's complexities?

Lest you be worry about short-circuiting Divinity in this practice, remember the New Testament description of the "thin place" that joins this world and our ancestors in faith: "Therefore, since we are surrounded by so great a cloud of witnesses, let us also lay aside every weight and the sin that clings so closely, and let us run with perseverance the race that is set before us, looking to Jesus the pioneer and perfecter of our faith." (Hebrews 12:1-2) The Apostles Creed speaks of the "communion of saints" as the spiritual union of the living and dead, continuing their lives in God's presence. When I reach out to saints and ancestors, I assume that they are in contact with God and are providing me with God-blessed guidance. You may choose, as I did, to begin with Divine Wisdom so that whatever guidance you receive be grounded in holiness, love, and compassion.

The second half of this spiritual practice involves your commitment to become a "good ancestor," planting the seeds that future generations will inherit. You are a saint and ancestor in the making if you choose to be. You will influence future generations whether you are aware of it or not. Mature spirituality roots us in an interdependent stream of becoming. Out of the gifts we have received from our ancestors, we commit ourselves to being good ancestors for future generations. For me, this means passing on the wisdom I have received in my relationship with my grandchildren, teaching young people in church, seminary, and collage, mentoring people through transitions, and being a good father to my adult son and spiritual guide and support to my grandsons. It also means that I recognize the impact of my actions on future generations in terms of advocating for just social structures and working for a healthy environment.

In this exercise, prayerfully reflect on your life—your experiences, gifts, talents, passions—and then ask God's guidance, or your ancestors' guidance, as to ways you can bring joy, healing, hope, and wellbeing to future generations. Let your life be devoted to being God's partner in healing the world you will not live to see and furthering the moral and spiritual arcs of history toward Shalom.

CHAPTER EIGHTEEN

The New Age and
New Spiritual Movements

Today, many people describe themselves as spiritual but not religious. They have a sense of the holy and are seeking something more than materialism and consumerism. But they don't identify their spiritual quest with any specific religious tradition. In fact, they are skeptical about organized and institutional religions. Their faith can be described as a mosaic or like a kaleidoscope, or, in the words of Diana Butler Bass, a *bricolage,* something constructed from a variety of spiritual materials. The growing and eclectic movements, often described as New Age or New Spiritual movements, reflect hybrid spirituality or inter-spirituality in its most graphic form. Many of today's seekers live out Ralph Waldo Emerson's observation, "A foolish consistency is the hobgoblin of little minds, adored by little statesmen and philosophers and divines. With consistency a great soul has simply nothing to do."

A dear friend represents the dynamic and flexible spirit of the new religious movements. Raised by old school Marxists, who were suspicious of anything that could be called spiritual, I encountered Susan in my junior at San Jose State at an anti-war protest.[95] We became good friends in college, and I have followed her

---

95. I have chosen to use a pseudonym at her request.

spiritual journey for close to fifty years. Still a political progressive and suspicious of organized religion—I may be the only active Christian among her friends—her spiritual journey has taken her through Buddhism, Yoga, Jewish mysticism, and the *Course on Miracles*. Susan is serious about her spirituality. Her daily practices involve devotional reading from the various religious traditions, followed by a few minutes of meditation she learned on Zen retreat, before doing yoga asanas or postures. She finds guidance in the writings of the Dalai Lama, Richard Rohr, and Eckhart. Susan recently reported that she is attending a Religious Science Church and is immersing herself in the writings of Martin Luther King and Critical Race Theory. Religious purists would have a field day with the menu selections on her "spiritual smorgasbord." But, to my friend, eclecticism, whose story is echoed in the lives of many active church members, even if its inconsistent, is not a problem. She has little time for dogmatism and religious boundaries. Although she doesn't describe herself as a theologian, clearly her faith is profoundly pragmatic and experiential. She is interested in what provides her with meaning and inspiration to get through day-to day-life and flourish in her relationships. What seems to inspire her faith is the affirmation that by changing our attitudes, by changing our minds, and by positive thinking, we can transform our lives and move from scarcity to abundance personally, relationally, and economically.

Jimmy Buffett counseled "changes in latitudes, changes in attitudes." And the Key West singer-songwriter is right. When we elevate our spiritual focus, our attitudes and lifestyles change. The answer, from the perspective of New Spiritual movements is the reverse, "changes in attitudes, changes in latitudes." When you change your mind, which is the most powerful instrument you have, your place in the universe changes.

As with Shinto and Yoruba, we cannot pinpoint an absolute beginning to the New Age and New Spiritual movements. In many ways, some form of spiritual science is found in what religion scholars have described as the "perennial philosophy." Many scholars associate the birth of the new age movement, the dawning of the age of Aquarius, with the emergence of Transcendentalism, New Thought, Mind Cure, and Theosophy in the nineteenth century. Joining German and English Romanticism, Westernized Hinduism and Buddhism, the positive teachings of Jesus, and the emerging recognition of the power of mind to transform reality, these movements proclaim the immortality of the soul, the wonder of embodiment and nature, self-healing, and positive thinking as tools for human evolution. These movements assert that, deep down, reality is spiritual. The physical world witnesses to the wondrous creativity of Divine Mind. Members of these movements believe that when we are in synch with the Divine Mind, we can do almost anything. Quoting scripture, nineteenth and early twentieth century spiritual adventurers proclaimed, "As a man thinketh in his heart, so is he." (Proverbs 23:7 KJV) You can "think and grow rich." (Napoleon Hill) You can connect with Universal Mind, experience healing of mind and body, recognizing that evil and pain, indeed embodiment itself, are projections of false thinking, so reflects Mary Baker Eddy, parent of Christian Science. These nineteenth century spiritual movements, precursors to twenty-first century New Age and New Spiritual movements, affirm: when we align ourselves with the Divine Mind or Spirit, our positive thinking leads to positive outcomes of body, mind, spirit, relationships, and economic status.

Today, updated versions of these perspectives are championed by spiritual teachers of the New Age and New spiritual movements, known by their books and workshops, and not their denominational ties: Deepak Chopra, Louis Hay, Eckhart Tolle, Marianne Williamson, Carolyn Myss, Barbara Brennan, Rhonda Byrne, to name a few of the most well-known luminaries.

AFFIRMATIONS FOR A NEW SPIRIT AND NEW AGE

According to New Age/New Spiritual movement teachers, in each moment of our lives, we can create our own realities. Visualization, affirmations, and meditation change our minds and change the world. The new age, or new spiritual, movements can be broadly described through the following foci.[96]

- *The Unity of All Life.* While there are many varieties of New Age and New Spiritual movements, virtually all of them affirm that all life is interdependent and grounded in one ultimate reality of which all things are manifestations. Attitudinal Healing teacher Jerry Jampolsky asserts that "Love is the only reality there is. Anything we perceive that doesn't mirror love is a misperception."[97] Susan Trout, with whom I studied Attitudinal

---

96. These foci are grounded in the work of Bruce Epperly, *Crystal and Cross: Christians and New Age in Creative Dialogue* (Mystic, CT: Twenty-third Publications, 1996) and Ted Peters, *Cosmic Self: A Penetrating Look at Today's New Age Movements* (New York: HarperSanFrancisco, 1991).
97. Jerry Jampolsky, *Love is Letting Go of Fear* (Milbrae, CA: Celestial Arts, 1971), 65.

Healing in Washington D.C., claims that "there is a Divine Source, an Eternal, a Higher Power, a God. Each of us is part of this Source, like a droplet of ocean water, while not being the ocean, is part of the ocean."[98] Whereas "orthodox" Christians believe that disobedience or willfulness, making choices against God's way, is the primary human failing or sin, New Age and New Spiritual movements see *separation* as the primary spiritual problem. As Susan Trout continues, "the basic problem in our lives is that we have forgotten our Oneness with the Divine Source. The solution is remembering our true identity."[99] Similar to Christian Science, most new age groups affirm that we are part of the Divine Mind, Christ, or God. The separation we perceive is an illusion, a distortion, a falsehood that is the source of pain, sickness, and death.

- *The Higher Self.* Deep down, we are always connected with God, and that connection is eternal and inspirational. Beneath the constantly changing world of experiences, thoughts, and feelings is a higher self that is constantly in touch with Divine Wisdom. According to Susan Trout, "each individual is a spark from the universal light; this spark is our essence."[100] In 1838, Ralph Waldo Emerson asked in his Harvard Divinity School Address, a precursor to the New Thought and New Age understanding of the higher self: "is man sensible that he is an infinite soul; that the earth and heavens are passing into his mind, that he is drinking forever the soul of God?" To the newly minted ministers, he announced, "Yourself a newborn bard of the Holy Ghost—cast behind you all conformity and acquaint yourself firsthand with Divinity."[101] Our minds are, as physician Larry Dossey observes, reflections of the infinite non-local rather than local finite mind: "If minds cannot be bound in space and time, we must be prepared to admit...that we are endowed with the godlike characteristics of immortality, omniscience, and unity."[102] We need to cast off the shackles of scientific materialism and sin-based religion to claim our true spiritual destiny as infinite, interdependent, and eternal.

98. Susan Trout, *To See Differently* (Washington DC: Three Roses Press, 1990), 32.
99. Ibid., 33.
100. Ibid., 32, 73.
101. Ralph Waldo Emerson, "The Harvard Divinity School Address," in *Three Prophets of Religious Liberalism* (Boston: Beacon Press, 1964), 103, 108.
102. Larry Dossey, *Recovering the Soul: A Scientific and Spiritual Search* (New York: Bantam Books, 1989), 286.

- *The Power of the Mind.* Whereas "orthodox" Christianity and Islam speak of the omnipotent god, New Spiritual and New Age movements portray the mind, connected with the Universal Mind, as omnipotent, creating its own reality and significantly shaping the world by the quality of its thoughts. The power of faith and mental transformation is found in Christianity as well as the new spiritual and new age movements. The Gospel of Mark tells the story a woman with a flow of blood whose faith has made her whole, opening her up to God's healing energy that flowed from the Healer to her. (Mark 5:25-34) The apostle Paul counsels us not to let the world limit us, to squeeze us into its mold, but to be transformed by the renewing of our minds. (Romans 12:2) The power of the mind to change and even create reality is at the heart of the New Spiritual, New Age, and Science of Mind movements.

As a college student, I was enthralled by Richard Bach's *Jonathan Livingston Seagull,* which portrays a seagull's journey from limitation to infinity. Dedicated to the Jonathan Livingston Seagull who lives in all of us, Bach's novel challenges us to affirm the unlimited power of the mind. "We can be free! We can learn to fly." We can exclaim as Jonathan learned, "I am a perfect unlimited gull" and then soar to new dimensions.[103] Jonathan discovers that "each of us is in truth an idea of the Great Gull... your whole body from wingtip to wingtip...is nothing more than your thought itself, in a form you can see. Break the chains of your thought, and you break the chains of your body, too."[104]

Ernest Holmes, parent of the Science of Mind movement, describes the liberating power of the mind through life-transforming affirmations: 1) We are completely surrounded and permeated by the Universal Mind. We are finite expressions of the infinite; 2) The mind is always creative and manifests what we believe in our experiences; 3) The Universal Mind creates for you according to your thoughts; 4) You can choose to remain in poverty or sickness, health or prosperity.[105] Not to be undone, attitudinal healing teacher Jerry Jampolsky asserts, "If we change our thoughts, the world will change automatically."[106] Actress and new age

---

103. Richard Bach, *Jonathan Livingston Seagull* (New York: Macmillan, 1970), 27, 59.
104. Ibid., 77.
105. Ernest Holmes, *How to Change Your Life* (New York: Science of Mind Publications, 1987), 25-26.
106. Jerry Jampolsky, *Love is Letting Go of Fear,* 85.

luminary Shirley MacLaine goes even further, "the new age is all about self-responsibility. New Age thinking asks each person to take responsibility for everything that happens in life."[107] At the farthest edge of the new age spectrum, new age healer Louise Hay asserts that "we are each 100% responsible for everything and for all our experiences...[we] create our experiences, our reality, and everyone in it."[108] According to Hay, we have drawn all our experiences into our life: success and wealth, cancer and AIDS, peace and gun violence, physical wellbeing and rape, through the impact of our actions in this or a previous life. We truly create our own realities, for good or for ill. While the affirmation that we create our own reality and the concepts of the prosperity gospel can be empowering, they can also exacerbate feelings of guilt and shame. If prosperity is the result of positive thinking, then poverty must result from negativity, or ignorance of our true spiritual nature. If positive affirmations and faith can cure illness, then those who do not recover from illness must suffer from a lack of faith or be imprisoned by negative thinking! A spiritual system that focuses on solidarity and unity ends up creating individualistic separation by asserting that everyone is totally responsible for their own lives. The interdependence of life, revealed in our impact on one another, and the impact of the environment of us, is sacrificed for spiritually undergirded, rugged individualism, reminiscent of free market, unrestrained capitalism.

• *Channeling Spirits.* While all the great religions emerge from extraordinary experiences and encounters with the Divine, New Age and New Spiritual movements proclaim a democracy of spirit in which spiritual beings can communicate "from beyond" to select human beings. This process, known in the New Spiritual movements as "channeling," has been described as "the communication of information to or through a physically embodied human being from a source that is said to exist at some other dimensions of reality from the physical as we know it, and that is not from the normal mind of the channel."[109] Channeled messages generally reflect the substance of new age and new spiritual thinking: the universal and all-powerful mind, reincarnation, and our ability to

107. Shirley MacLaine, *Going Within* (New York: Bantam Books, 1989), 182.
108. Louise Hay, *You Can Heal Your Life* (Santa Monica: Hay House, 1984), 5. 56.
109. Jon Klimo, *Channeling* (Los Angeles: Jeremy Tarcher, 1987), 2.

shape reality by our thoughts. Channeled beings appear in peoples' lives in ways similar to the ways God or other spiritual beings appeared to the biblical prophets and to Yoruba/Santeria priests, sometimes as a result of spiritual seeking; other times, by the choice of the disembodied spirit to seek out and speak to, and through, a human being. As researcher Jon Klimo observes a similarity between twentieth and twenty-first century channeling and nineteenth century spiritualism and mediumship, "Otherwise ordinary people seem to let themselves be taken by, or in other ways, receive messages from another personality who uses them as a conduit, medium, or channel for communication."[110] A classic channeling encounter occurred to Helen Schucman, the source of the new age "scripture" *A Course in Miracles,* who began to have visionary and psychic experiences which both frightened and repulsed her. The voice challenged her, "This is a course in miracles. Please take notes." And so, like Muhammed, her experiences over seven years were transcribed, producing the 1200-page, three-volume, *A Course in Miracles.* When she asked why she had been called to be share this new age gospel, the voice, claiming to be Christ, told her, "You are an excellent choice…because you'll do it."[111] Christian fundamentalists, hellbent on limiting revelation to the Bible, see channeling as demonic, and contrary to the inerrant and closed canon of scripture. In contrast New Age and New Spiritual adherents see channeling as a spiritual message from a higher dimension, connecting with our higher selves for the well-being of seekers.

Process and open and relational theologians may challenge the lack of historical or social concern in channeled messages, and remind new agers that, since channeling occurs from a finite spirit to finite humans, it is limited in awareness and reflects personal perspectives of both spirits and the humans who receive or channel their messages. Process and openness theologians do not deny the possibility of channeling in a universe in which God is constantly shaping our experiences through intuitions, and encounters. In principle, revelation is universal and all-pervasive, despite the fallibility, social context, and perspectives of the recipients of revelation.

---

110. Ibid., 74.
111. Robert Skutch, *Journey without Distance* (Berkeley, CA: Celestial Arts, 1984), 61.

- *Reincarnation.* The world's spiritual traditions proclaim that our lives are not bound by flesh and blood. We will live on in the memory of others and of God, what Whitehead calls "objective immortality," and in our offspring, as we seek to be good ancestors, through our impact on society through our relationships and our creativity. Quite possibly, we may live on, subjectively, in further adventures beyond the grave. Martin Luther King once noted, "You must make your plans big enough to include God and large enough to include eternity."[112]

Most Christians see our afterlife in terms of a series of "heavenly" adventures in relationship with God, in which our personal identity is preserved. Conservative Christians, alternatively, see eternal punishment for sin and unbelief in this life with Satan as our jailer. Indeed, prior to beginning my editorial working this morning (January 17, 2022), I came upon an advertisement, noting a sermon by a well-known fundamentalist preacher, Robert Jeffress, "Why God Sends Good People to Hell?" By contrast, New Age and New Spiritual movements affirm a multiplicity of lifetimes, in which our current lives have emerged from past lifetimes, and our present lifetime shapes our future incarnations on this or another planet. Eventually everyone will find wholeness. It's only a matter of time, or lifetimes!

One of the great mysteries of life involves what is described as "accidents of birth." Much of who we will become is shaped by when, where, and to whom we are born. While we should encourage individual initiative and creativity, clearly the realities of economic and racial privilege can expand or limit our possibilities and sense of agency. From the vantage point of my comfortable Arts and Crafts chair, writing after an hour-long walk in the woods, followed by a healthy breakfast, I ponder: Why was I born white and middle class in the USA, the child of parents who prized education, and not in a war-torn country or among refugee peoples? Why was I born healthy, and not with a disability of mind or body? Why was I born into a stable "normally neurotic" family and not into a profoundly dysfunctional, impoverished, or violent family? The circumstances of my birth may be purely accidental; they may also be the result of Divine

---

112. Martin Luther King, *Strength to Love* (New York: Harper and Row, 1963), 76.

providence or the impact of a previous lifetime. For most new age and new spiritual participants, the "accidents of birth" can be explained as part of the process of reincarnation. Channeled entity "Seth" asserts that "problems not faced in this life will be faced in another…We choose the circumstances in which we would be born and the challenges which could bring about our development."[113] In similar fashion, new age philosopher Gary Zukav, popularized by Oprah Winfrey, affirms that each person has "the freedom to become a king or pauper, lover or loved, enslaved or freed man—whatever illusion will provide the understanding your soul is needing for fulfillment."[114] Every birth and every lifetime is intended by the soul for its own education, and to deal with issues not faced in previous lifetimes. In contrast to the negative connotations of reincarnation in Buddhism and Hinduism, New Age and New Spiritual movements see reincarnation as part of soul's journey, allowing us to grow and to experience new things. Channeled spiritual guide "Lazaris" avers, "Those who are suffering tragically did create their own realities, but so did the one who witnesses—directly or indirectly—the human injustice."[115] There is ultimately no unfairness in this lifetime. As Gary Zukav observes, "When we see a person sleeping in the gutter in the winter, we do not know what is being completed for that soul…It is not appropriate that we perceive it as unfair because it is not."[116] Zukav believes that despite appearances of pain, the soul feels no pain. "Everyone is happy despite what they are experiencing."[117] From this perspective, evil itself is an illusion. Zukav continues, "You have never done anything wrong…all your wrongs, your failings, your errors are, what is called appropriately, 'steps to God.'"[118] In the optimism characteristic of new age and new spirituality teachers, Stephen Levine challenges certain Buddhist and Hindu understandings of rebirth as painful, a continuation of the suffering grounded in our attachment to particular outcomes, "Karma is not punishment. It is an aspect of the merciful nature of the universe to offer teachings that we have somehow misunderstood in the past, to allow us to learn from experience what we have not paid close enough attention to previously."[119] The

113. Jane Roberts, *The Seth Material* (Englewood Cliffs: Prentice Hall, 1970), 4.
114. Gary Zukav, *The Seat of the Soul* (New York: Simon and Schuster, 1989), 154.
115. Ruth Weston, *Channelers: A New Age Directory* (New York: Perigree Press, 1988), 97.
116. Gary Zukav, *Seat of the Soul*, 43.
117. Ibid., 163.
118. Ibid., 205.
119. Stephen Levine, *Who Dies?* (Garden City, NY: Doubleday, 1984), 103.

soul is always at peace, observing its embodied adventures from lifetime to lifetime, growing in experience and wisdom. History is the backdrop for the soul's journey, and not the real thing.

The optimism of New Age and New Spiritual movements appears to neglect the importance of history, the reality of injustice, and the severity of pain and suffering. From my experience of providing spiritual care for persons traumatized by both the prosperity gospel and new age optimism, there is a tendency to shame and blame the victim, or assume guilt for things for which one bears no responsibility, such as a child's chronic illnesses or a failed business in a time of recession. Compassion is viewed as optional, and political transformation is often viewed as an unnecessary intrusion on another's spiritual journey. The assumption that the physically and sexually abused, politically oppressed, food-insecure, and unsheltered somehow deserve their fate diminishes our desire to help them. In contrast, Jesus the Healer, along with the prophets before him, joined the soul with the body, and economics with history. To Jesus, this lifetime was real, and was the place where God and humanity meet in the quest for wholeness and justice. Although many members of the New Age and New Spiritual movements are active in the environmental movement, recycle, and place Black Lives Matter signs on their lawns, their quest for justice is blunted by their equally firm belief that this life is momentary, ephemeral, and not entirely real, but simply an expression of the soul's journey. In this regard, the optimistic vision of reincarnation bears some resemblance to the heavenly-minded vision of conservative Christians of my childhood church, who sang that "this world is not my home. I'm just a passing through."

- *Spiritual Technologies.* New Age and New Spirituality movements are profoundly eclectic, pragmatic, and experiential. During my studies of the relationship between the new age movement and Christianity in the 1980s and early 1990s, I participated in New Age study groups where I learned practices as varied as: chanting, bioenergetics, homeopathic medicine, energy work, meditation, visualization, affirmations, astrological readings, and communication skills. The new age sees itself as a "science of mind" in which alignment with our higher self, the divine within, can transform our attitudes and circumstances. Ernest Holmes, parent of the Science of Mind movement, which has not only influenced new age spiritual practices but also Christian prosperity gospel movements, believes that when we change our minds, we change our world. Holmes' "mind treatments" involve affirmations such as: "There is one life, that life is God, that life is perfect, and that is my life now" and "I am one with the infinite rhythm that flows through me in love, harmony, and peace."[120] In addition to spoken affirmations, the power of the mind to change our reality can be achieved, new age thinkers believe, through visualization practices. According to Shakti Gawain, "Creative visualization is the technique of using your imagination to create what you want in your life." After a period of relaxation, the practitioner of creative visualization imagines a positive outcome occurring in their lives, for example, a healthy relationship, a new job, or spiritual growth, and then closes with the affirmation, "This or something better, now manifests for me, in a totally satisfying or harmonious way, for the highest good of all concerned."[121] Through spiritual practices, we connect to our higher selves, changing our lives and changing the world.

A NEW AGE PILGRIMAGE

In this section, I will once again relate my experiences as a Christian whose spiritual pilgrimage, in this case, was shaped by my encounters with the New Age and New Spiritual movements. While I have been critical of the New Age movement in this text, my involvement in new age practices has also deepened my sense of spirituality and healing.

I first explicitly encountered the New Age movement in 1980 while teaching a course on Death and Dying at Central Michigan University. In my first year of full-time university teaching, I came upon the work of Jerry Jampolsky, a psychiatrist whose focus was working with children diagnosed with life-threatening cancers. Jampolsky's work in Attitudinal Healing was influenced by the new age scripture, *A Course in Miracles*. Like Thich Nhat Hanh's mindful Buddhism found in *Peace is Every Step*, Jampolsky's *Love is Letting Go of Fear*, struck a spiritual chord. It

120. Ernest Holmes, *How to Change Your Life* (New York: Science of Mind Publications, 1987), 249-251.
121. Shakti Gawain, *Creative Visualization* (Mill Valley, CA: Whatever Press, 1978), 13, 22.

was the right book at the right time. Its affirmations helped me put my challenges as a new non-tenure track professor and young parent into perspective and gave me guidance for my own spiritual growth. Jampolsky's affirmations such as: "I Am Determined to See Things Differently," "I Am Not the Victim of the World I See," "Today I Will Judge Nothing That Occurs," and "This Instant is the Only Time There Is" helped me navigate my own spiritual and emotional challenges, and awakened me to a broader perspective on Christianity.[122] Attitudinal healing inspired me to explore the healings of Jesus from a spiritual and medical perspective rather than the rationalism of liberal Protestantism. I began to see Jesus' healings as events that occurred, not as supernatural aberrations. I came to embrace a naturalistic understanding of healing, inspired by my studies of process-relational theology, the Gospels, and Attitudinal Healing. When we moved to Washington D.C. in 1982, where I was called to serve as Protestant University Chaplain and a professor of theology, I became involved in the Washington Center for Attitudinal Healing, where I continued my study of affirmations, visualization practices, and inner healing with Susan Trout. My work at the Center for Attitudinal Healing opened me to Reiki healing touch and to the use of biblical affirmations, later found in books such as my *The Power of Affirmative Faith, Holy Adventure,* and my four books in the "101 Soul Seeds" series.

Like the impact of Transcendental Meditation, New Age spiritualities have deepened my experience of Christian faith. They helped the healings of Jesus come alive, inspired my work and practices of Christian healing, and opened me to deeper understandings of scripture. My participation in the New Age movement has enabled me to join my rationalistic bent with mysticism and openness to God's healing touch found in the ministry of Jesus and available to persons like me. Today, I am a grateful critic, embracing the positive message of the New Age and New Spiritual movements and open to the ongoing adventures of spiritual growth.

---

122. Jerry Jampolsky, *Love is Letting Go of Fear* (Milbrae, CA: Celestial Arts, 1979).

WHAT CHRISTIANS CAN LEARN FROM THE NEW AGE AND NEW SPIRITUAL MOVEMENTS

At the heart of the New Age and New Spiritual movements is the affirmation of the power of the mind to transform reality. While Christians can appropriately object to the ultra-individualism of "you create your own reality," as well as Christian forms of the "prosperity gospel," which are similar in spirit, it is important to affirm the role of attitude and positive thinking, grounded in relationships and reality, to change our lives and the world around us. From the perspective of a Holocaust survivor, Viktor Frankl affirms, "Everything can be taken from a man but one thing: the last of the human freedoms—to choose one's attitude in any given set of circumstances, to choose one's own way." The apostle Paul affirmed, "Finally, beloved, whatever is true, whatever is honorable, whatever is just, whatever is pure, whatever is pleasing, whatever is commendable, if there is any excellence and if there is anything worthy of praise, think about these things." (Philippians 4:8)

New spiritual movements invite Christians to think big. God is willing to give us more than we can ask or imagine. When we are open to God, our faith can make us whole. Our calling is to expand rather than contract our consciousness and sense of possibility: to dream great things, to visualize ourselves as compassionate, successful, and powerful, and then take a risk on God. Seen from the perspective of the new spiritual movements, the moral and spiritual arcs of history that run through our lives are complemented by the arc of abundant life. The arc of achievement comes when we tap into God's power moving in and through our lives, aiming us toward healing and wholeness. While the mind is not all-powerful, as some new agers assert, our attitudes can shape our cells as well as our spirits. They can minimize pain, inspire energy, and be the tipping point between health and illness, and life and death. When Jesus said to the woman with the flow of blood, "Your faith has made you well" (Mark 5:34), he was invoking two interdependent aspects of healing and wholeness: the woman's faith that energized her and gave her the courage to touch Jesus, and the dynamic energy flowing from the Healer in response to her faith. Faith taps into divine energy, the universality of God's grace, which blesses us so that we can bless others.

CHRISTIANITY'S GIFT TO
THE NEW SPIRITUAL MOVEMENTS

Although new age and new spiritual teachings focus on the unity of all life, they often promote a hyper-individualism, enshrined by the affirmation, "You create your own reality." Often individual effort and positive thinking alone are viewed as the source of success. Illness and failure are often viewed as the result of negativity. Persons with chronic and life-threatening illnesses are often treated as "downers," getting in the way of our own spiritual and economic advancement.

In contrast, process-relational and openness visions of Christianity view success and failure as corporate as well as individual. We are all part of the body of Christ—which is the planet as well as the church—and the successes and failures of individual parts emerge from, and shape, the well-being of the whole. Jesus proclaimed that promoting abundant life was central to his mission. (John 10:10) But, for Jesus, abundance joined the individual and community. We are blessed to be a blessing. Our well-being is the result of the graceful interdependence of life and our support of one another. Our well-being is the inspiration to support others in their personal journeys toward wholeness, through compassion, advocacy, and political action. Christianity affirms *ubuntu,* "I am because of you" and asserts that along with God's grace, "we—not I—create our own realities."

A NEW AGE/NEW SPIRITUALITY PRACTICE

One of the most helpful aspects of the New Spiritual and new age movements is its focus on affirmations as a way of healing and energizing the mind. There is much truth, when seen as relational and interactive, in the power of the mind to shape reality. The belief that positive thoughts and emotions draw positive experiences to us may inspire us to respond to the events of our lives with a sense of affirmative agency.

Affirmations can change our attitudes and actions. As the apostle Paul asserts, "… think on these things." From my studies of Attitudinal Healing, championed by Jerry Jampolsky and Susan Trout, I learned to integrate affirmations with meditation, prayer, and Reiki healing touch.

Most of my affirmations are biblically based. Here are some that I have found powerful in my own spiritual journey.

- I can do all things with Christ who strengthens me. (Philippians 4:13)
- My God will satisfy all my needs. (Philippians 4:19)
- Nothing can separate me from the love of God. (Romans 8:38-39)
- I am blessed to be a blessing. (Genesis 12:2-3)
- By God's grace I can accomplish more than I can ask or imagine. (Ephesians 3:20)
- I have all the time, talent, and treasure to serve God, love my neighbor, and experience abundant life.
- I am strong in God.
- I am a powerhouse of love, creativity, compassion, writing, and teaching.

Our positive affirmations and visualizations are tipping points toward success, healing, and agency in transforming the world.

CHAPTER NINETEEN

Spiritualities in the Making

I struggled with ending this book with nineteen chapters. As an author, I prefer that my completed books have a meaningful, or even, number of chapters. A book with nineteen chapters seems incomplete and begs for something more. And, yet, as I pondered "nineteen" rather than my desired "twenty," I realized that nineteen chapters is appropriate for describing a moving elephant or a moving religion. The stories of our world's wisdom traditions are incomplete. The impact of encounters among religions in an increasingly globalized and, ironically, polarized world, is unfinished and still in process. The future of the planet and the fate of spirituality is uncertain. There are still questions to be asked and chapters to be written in the story of the human adventure. How will increasing globalization shape the future of spirituality and our respective faith traditions? In what ways will technology—including artificial intelligence—transform the way we look at ourselves and our destiny as humans? Will we have the courage and wisdom to respond to global climate change? Will the religions of the world be a force for moving from self-interest and nationalism to world loyalty, or will they only exacerbate parochialism, nationalism, and unilateralism? Can they, despite their differences, find common ground in healing the planet?

I studied the interface of process-relational and openness theology with these sixteen spiritual movements, including Christianity, and learned in dialogue with seminar participants from Claremont School of Theology and South Congregational Church, United Church of Christ, Centerville, Massachusetts, other Cape Cod communities, and individuals from California, Colorado, and Minnesota. Having done so, I came to embrace the following affirmations, that characterize living spiritual movements:

- The mystical experiences of unique spiritual personages and their followers gave birth to and still shape religious movements. Spiritual traditions are grounded in and enlivened by mystical experiences, ancient and modern.

- While each wisdom tradition is unique, it shares characteristics with other faith traditions.

- Religious movements are constantly changing and growing in relationship to their environments, technology, and other wisdom traditions.

- We are part of a great adventure which embraces not only this lifetime but goes beyond.

- Spiritual forces, which may include angels and ancestors, shape and condition our lives, even if we are unaware of their impact.

- Spiritual growth involves the interplay of solitude and society, of individuality and community.

- The calling of today's living faiths involves coming to terms with the realities of globalism, climate change, and polarization.

- Divine Truth is larger than any tradition can fathom, making humility and hospitality important religious virtues.

- The Holy One gives birth to a variety of human, cultural, and religious expressions, appropriate to time, place, culture, and need.

- God is not finished with the human adventure, or with the adventures of spiritual traditions.

- Open to the Holy, persons can expect extraordinary experiences, greater wisdom and power, and go beyond self-imposed limits.

- The planetary future depends on practitioners of the great religious traditions finding common cause, including partnerships with agnostics, humanists, and atheists, to challenge the nations of the world and their leaders to prioritize social and economic justice, confronting racism and the other destructive "isms," and planetary healing.

While fundamentalists emphasize the need for "absolutes" to guide our path, and to orient our lives around certainties in a world of change, the quest for absolutes is always in process and takes us toward a constantly receding horizon. If the divine elephant is constantly moving, then there is no stopping point for scientific, intellectual, experiential, or spiritual growth. Even when we have mystical encounters with the Holy, we must recognize that our experiences and descriptions of these experiences are always finite, perspectival, and subject to further growth. *Plus ultra,* "there is more" is the inspiration for the spiritual adventure and religions in the making.

I conclude with words from Reinhold Niebuhr from his *Irony of American History.* These words inspire my hopes for spiritualities in the making, and for my own spiritual journey in which I embrace the Great Mystery of God and the wondrous diversity of spiritual inspiration and practice.

> *Nothing that is worth doing can be achieved in our lifetime;*
> *therefore we must be saved by hope.*
>
> *Nothing which is true or beautiful or good*
> *makes complete sense in any immediate context of history;*
> *therefore we must be saved by faith.*
>
> *Nothing we do, however virtuous, can be accomplished alone;*
> *therefore we must be saved by love.*
>
> *No virtuous act is quite as virtuous from the standpoint*
> *of our friend or foe as it is from our standpoint.*
> *Therefore, we must be saved by the final form of love,*
> *which is forgiveness.*

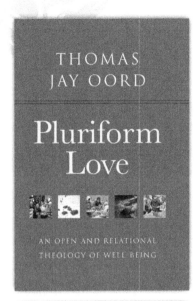
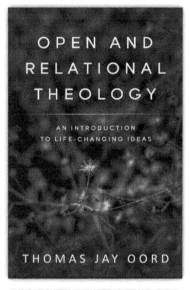
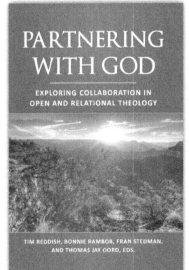
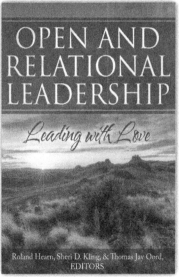

Made in the USA
Middletown, DE
10 September 2023

38303219R00139